MILK STREET

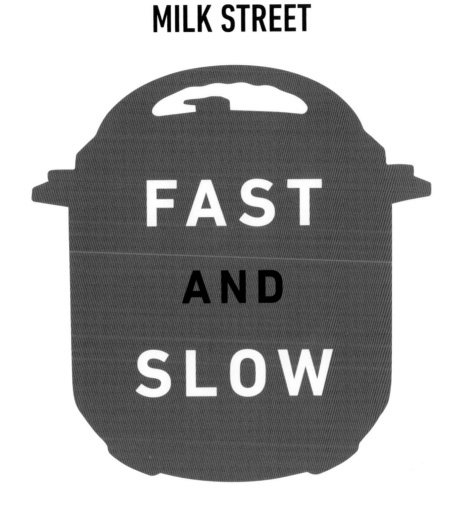

FAST
AND
SLOW

MILK STREET

FAST

AND

SLOW

Instant Pot® Cooking at the Speed You Need

CHRISTOPHER KIMBALL

Writing and editing by
J.M. Hirsch and Michelle Locke

Recipes by
Matthew Card, Diane Unger and the cooks at Milk Street

Art direction by
Jennifer Baldino Cox and Brianna Coleman

Photography by
Connie Miller of CB Creatives

Food Styling by
Christine Tobin

VORACIOUS

LITTLE, BROWN AND COMPANY
NEW YORK BOSTON LONDON

Voracious

Little, Brown and Company
Hachette Book Group
1290 Avenue of the Americas, New York, NY 10104
littlebrown.com

First Edition: April 2020

Voracious is an imprint of Little, Brown and Company, a division of Hachette Book Group, Inc. The Voracious name and logo are trademarks of Hachette Book Group, Inc.

The publisher is not responsible for websites (or their content) that are not owned by the publisher.

The Hachette Speakers Bureau provides a wide range of authors for speaking events. To find out more, go to hachettespeakersbureau.com or call (866) 376-6591.

Photography credits: Connie Miller of CB Creatives. Other photography by page: Ben Shaefer, pages 286 (bottom image), 288 (bottom image), 289 (bottom images); Channing Johnson, page 290.

Food styling by Christine Tobin.

Prop styling by Brianna Coleman.

ISBN 978-0-316-42307-6
LCCN 2019949476

10 9 8 7 6 5 4 3 2 1

IM

Print book interior design by Gary Tooth / Empire Design Studio

Printed in China

CONTENTS

INTRODUCTION

My favorite kitchen items are a stovetop terra cotta rice cooker from Japan, a nakiri knife with a gorgeous octagonal wood handle, and an inexpensive 8-inch carbon-steel skillet that I use for scrambled eggs.

So the notion of an Instant Pot does not come naturally. At various times, I have tried to like slow cookers (good for meal planning since the prep is done in the morning) and pressure cookers (love them in an off-and-on way, which means mine most of the time resides in the basement).

But as our kitchen started developing recipes for the Instant Pot, it became clear this wasn't just another device to consume counter real estate. The food was top notch. I expected stews and tough cuts of meat to be ideal, but we also started making pasta dishes (the puttanesca was wonderful and the pasta was, incredibly, al dente), lots of beans, vegetables, soups, etc.

And then, as I tested recipes at home, it also became clear that combining a pressure cooker with a slow cooker makes so much sense. Plus, you can sauté in the same pot in

which you pressure or slow cook, and the timer makes it easy to walk away without worry.

Most of all, however, I had to admit that this is serious cookware for serious cooking. This isn't a collection of second-class recipes shoehorned into a countertop appliance. It is Basque Leek and Potato Soup and Three-Cheese Pasta with Basil and Black Pepper. This is great food. So good, in fact, everyone in the kitchen kept taking home leftovers.

There are lots of tricks to using an Instant Pot—or any similar multicooker—including how to keep long-cooked foods tasting fresh, how to cook more delicate items, how to cook dried beans without soaking, and how to stagger your cooking so each ingredient is cooked only as long as suits it. But one of the great things about the Instant Pot is that you don't need a lot of culinary tricks. It does most of the work (and thinking) for you.

Sure, I love to come home, look in the refrigerator, grab a wok or skillet and improvise dinner. I like the sounds and aromas. I like to hear the food cook. But I also like to throw ingredients in a pot after just a bit of prep and come back within the hour and dinner is served. There is room in my kitchen for both approaches.

One last thought. We've applied the Milk Street approach here—fresh flavor combinations and a few new techniques from our travels. We hope this provides a compelling, all-new approach to the Instant Pot, from Lentils and Bulgur with Caramelized Onions, based on the Lebanese dish called mujaddara, to Jamaican-Style Yellow Split Pea Soup. It's a new world of home cooking.

Enjoy.

FAST AND SLOW: COOKING AT YOUR OWN SPEED

At Milk Street, we use the Instant Pot to cook at the speed we need. Its marriage of sauté pan, pressure cooker and slow cooker allows us to control the pace of cooking, while keeping flavors fresh and bright. Most of the recipes in this book offer you the choice of fast or slow, with instructions for both pressure cooking and slow cooking.

Conventional wisdom is that the Instant Pot is a better pressure cooker than slow cooker. We loved both functions, and developed these recipes to make the most of each. Partnered with the sauté mode—which streamlines browning and kickstarts the cooking—we found the slow cooker produced reliably great food.

The recipes in this book were developed using a 6-quart Instant Pot. We also tested our recipes in several alternative brands of multicookers and found they worked just as well. Check the user manuals to adapt the instructions.

Whether we want it fast or slow, the Instant Pot lets us decide.

PRESSURE POINTERS

Tips and Tricks for Getting the Most Out of the Instant Pot

At Milk Street, we spent hundreds of hours working with the Instant Pot to perfect the recipes for this book. Here are some key lessons learned along the way.

BEFORE YOU START TO COOK

For this book we developed our recipes for a 6-quart Instant Pot, using the included accessories. Though Instant Pots include a variety of preset functions, we found we got the best results using manual settings for pressure cooking, slow cooking and sautéing. Though the buttons can vary slightly between models, our recipes use directions that are universal to Instant Pots.

We also tested an 8-quart Instant Pot and several other popular brands of multicookers. We found they worked just as well, but timings may need to be adjusted. We found larger capacity

multicookers, including larger Instant Pot models, cooked a bit more quickly than the 6-quart model.

The instruction booklet for an Instant Pot—or any multicooker—will advise checking all gaskets and valves to make sure everything is seated properly and moving freely before starting to cook. This is important!

Before each cooking session **check your lid** and:

1. Make sure the lid gasket is properly inserted.

2. Make sure the pressure valve is all the way popped in and that there is no food residue clogging its holes.

3. Make sure the locking mechanism (the silver pin to the right of the pressure valve on the inside of the lid) slides easily. If any of these things isn't seated or moving as it should be, the pot cannot seal properly and won't come up to pressure.

DURING PREP

Pay attention to size specifications when prepping ingredients. Sizes don't have to be exact, but if a size is specified try to stay as close to it as possible to ensure the food cooks in the appropriate time and to the correct texture. Broadly speaking, it's better to err on the side of too large since undercooked ingredients can be cooked longer once the lid comes off, but overcooked ingredients can't be reversed.

Take advantage of hands-off cooking. Pressure cooking and slow cooking in the Instant Pot don't require inter-

mittent stirring or much babysitting at all. Read the recipe before you begin cooking to identify any ingredients that aren't needed until pressure cooking or slow cooking is complete. Once the lid goes on and the timer is set, you're free to prep those ingredients.

When braising, go low on liquid. For a rich, meaty braise, it's not necessary to add much liquid. The meat and any vegetables will produce their own moisture. Adding too much liquid dilutes the flavors of the finished dish.

Divide and conquer larger cuts. When cooking large cuts, such as a pot roast, it's best to divide the meat into smaller, evenly sized pieces that cook more quickly and more evenly. Tying the pieces ensures they are compact (so they fit in the pot) and won't fall apart during cooking.

PRESSURE COOKING TIPS

Pressure cooking is faster than conventional cooking because, under pressure, water can be heated above its natural boiling point of 212°F. The higher temperature in the pot means that food cooks faster. Meats and other sturdy proteins, beans, some grains, hardy vegetables and even pasta are excellent candidates for pressure cooking.

When switching from sauté mode to pressure cook, be sure to **scrape up every bit of stuck-on browned bits from the bottom of the pot before** beginning the pressure cycle. Stuck-on food can scorch, which will trigger the burn sensor and automatically shut off the pot.

During cooking, intense pressure builds up in the pot. When cooking is complete, the pot cannot be opened until the pressure is released. This can be done two ways: quickly, by opening the venting valve, or slowly, by allowing the pressure to naturally subside on its own.

Quick release is best for foods that overcook easily, or that would become mushy if not immediately removed from the pot. **To avoid steam burns when quick-releasing pressure in the pot, use a pair of tongs or a long spoon to open the pressure valve.** Make sure your hand or arm is not positioned over the vent when the valve is opened, as steam can cause burns.

Natural release is best for sturdy ingredients, particularly meats. The slow release allows the muscle fibers to relax and reabsorb some of the liquid they expelled during cooking. We also sometimes use a combination, starting with natural and then quick releasing at the end. This allows us to finish the cooking with the more gentle residual heat of the pot.

Check the pressure release valve after removing and returning the lid. If the lid is removed and then returned for further cooking, make sure the pressure release valve is in the correct position. It swings easily between sealing and venting when the lid is tilted or flipped.

SUCCESSFUL SLOW COOKING

During slow cooking, the Instant Pot heats gradually and maintains a temperature between 180°F and 210°F (depending on the setting) for a set duration. Meats, hardy vegetables and beans do well with slow cooking. Pastas, seafood and delicate grains and vegetables do not.

The Instant Pot tends to come to temperature more slowly than conventional slow cookers. This can considerably extend cooking time. To overcome this we **bring the contents to a boil using the sauté setting before switching to the slow cook function.** This jump-starts the heating so the total cooking time is shorter. Our start-to-finish cooking times reflect that.

If, at the end of the indicated cooking time, the dish isn't quite done and you

want to continue with slow cooking, turn the pot off, press **More/Sauté** and bring the contents to a boil. Press **Cancel,** lock on the lid, select **Slow Cook,** making sure the pressure valve is set to **Venting,** then cook until done. Heat is lost when the pot is uncovered during slow cooking and it takes some time to recover. Bringing the liquid to a boil speeds heat recovery.

Feel free to combo cook. If a dish isn't quite done at the end of the recommended slow cook time but you'd like to hurry it along, you can switch to the sauté or pressure cook function to get it across the finish line. Keep in mind that when pressure cooking the pot will take time to pressurize, so if only a few more minutes of cooking is needed the sauté function may be the better option.

A FEW MORE USEFUL TIPS

Take note of residual heat. When using the sauté function, the heating element will continue to generate heat through the base of the pot. It can maintain a simmer for about another 5 minutes after cutting power. If something goes wrong and you are concerned about scorching or overcooking, don't just turn the machine off. Also remove

the inner pot from the housing and transfer to a heat-safe surface. Similarly, if the inner pot is removed in the process of serving food, don't put the empty pot back in the hot machine. The residual heat may scorch any remaining food, making for a challenging cleanup.

Also, **take advantage of residual heat.** Even after turn-off, the pot retains a fair amount of heat, which can be used to gently cook or warm through delicate items such as shrimp.

Pay attention to stirring instructions. Cooking is more even if the pot's contents are evenly distributed and solids make good contact with liquids. So before locking on the lid, make sure that, for instance, the beef chunks in a stew aren't piled on one side of the pot. In some recipes that call for tomatoes and where liquid is scant,

we add the tomatoes on top of the other ingredients and do not stir them in. Tomatoes, if not diluted, have a tendency to burn on the bottom, so keeping them on top prevents this.

Use a kitchen towel or tongs to protect your hands when using a steam rack with handles. The rack makes it easy to add and remove large single items, such as a whole head of cauliflower or whole chicken, but the handles are hot after cooking. We find that a potholder or oven mitt can be too bulky.

If you open the pot and the dish appears too thin and watery, **let it rest for a few minutes to give the ingredients a chance to absorb some of the liquid.** If after 5 or 10 minutes the mixture still is too dilute, use the sauté function to bring it to a simmer, then cook until the excess moisture evaporates and the consistency has thickened.

VEGETABLES

CONTENTS

Caramelized Carrot Soup with Fennel Seeds and Cumin (p. 8)

VEGETABLES

Many people buy an Instant Pot with visions of making hearty, beefy stews without spending a lot of time in the kitchen. And it certainly is a great tool for turning out near-effortless braises and ragus. But we were pleasantly surprised to find that vegetables shine just as brightly as heavier fare. The Instant Pot brings the same fast, no-fuss approach to hearty root vegetables that it does to chunks of meat, and it can really tease out the full, rich flavors of classics such as collard greens. On the lighter side, it's also a good choice for brightly flavored vegetable chowders and soups.

To make the most of vegetables we **steam with a scant amount of liquid.** Our mashed Yukon Gold potatoes cook in just ½ cup water. The result: the potatoes really taste like potatoes because the flavor doesn't go down the drain with the cooking water. (Added bonus: We also skip the bother of draining.) We came up with some flavorful variations, including a cabbage and caraway version and another that balances the rich creaminess of two types of cheese with sharp black pepper. Our steamed cauliflower also uses ½ cup water and comes with three seasoning pastes, including a salty-savory blend of miso and honey.

For textural contrast, **we toast nuts and seeds to intensify crunch and flavor.** No need for an extra skillet; we do this right in the Instant Pot. Toasted almonds help garnish our carrot soup; toasted sesame seeds add flavor to our mushroom noodle dish. And we **balance sweet with heat.** Warm curry spices and the sharp heat of jalapeños add contrast to our sweet potatoes with cashews and cilantro. Cumin, paprika and cinnamon bring spicy depth to our eggplant, tomato and chickpea tagine inspired by the stews of North Africa.

To amplify flavor, we **add baking soda to accelerate caramelization,** a technique we picked up from the crew at "Modernist Cuisine." We use it in a carrot soup and find it really amplifies the flavor. Adding a small amount of alkaline baking soda to carrots during cooking speeds up cooking, creates more browning and deepens flavor.

Vegetables may be the best-kept secret of the Instant Pot. Taking inspiration from cooks around the world, we look for easy ways to concentrate flavor and use high-impact ingredients like spice mixes that deliver complex—but not complicated—flavor.

SPICED BUTTERNUT SQUASH SOUP

Active time: 30 minutes

Fast start to finish: 1¼ hours

Slow start to finish: 4½ to 5 hours

Servings: 4 to 6

2 tablespoons coconut oil, preferably unrefined

1 large yellow onion, halved and thinly sliced

Kosher salt and ground black pepper

2 tablespoons finely grated fresh ginger

1 tablespoon curry powder

2 teaspoons garam masala

2-pound butternut squash, peeled, seeded and cut into 1-inch chunks (4 cups)

1 quart low-sodium chicken broth

½ cup plain whole-milk yogurt, plus more to serve

½ cup toasted pumpkin seeds (see note)

This aromatic, colorful soup, inspired by a recipe in "Bollywood Kitchen" by Sri Rao, gets its rich flavor from two spice blends (garam masala and curry powder), plus coconut oil and whole-milk yogurt. If you like, substitute vegetable broth for the chicken broth to make the dish vegetarian. Toasted pumpkin seeds sprinkled on just before serving add color contrast, nutty flavor and crunchy texture. You can use store-bought roasted pumpkin seeds (plain or spiced) or you can toast raw ones in the Instant Pot before you begin cooking the soup. Simply cook them on **More/High Sauté**, stirring occasionally, until lightly browned and fragrant, about 4 minutes, then transfer to a small bowl; the seeds will crisp as they cool.

Don't add the yogurt directly to the hot puree, as the heat will cause the yogurt to separate. Gently warming the yogurt by whisking it with about 1 cup of the puree, then adding the mixture to the pot will prevent it from curdling.

START: On a 6-quart Instant Pot, select **More/High Sauté**. Add the coconut oil and heat until shimmering. Add the onion and 1 teaspoon salt, then cook, stirring occasionally, until the onion begins to brown, about 7 minutes. Stir in the ginger and cook until fragrant, about 30 seconds. Stir in the curry powder and garam masala, add the squash and broth. Stir to combine, then distribute in an even layer.

FAST

Press **Cancel**, lock the lid in place and move the pressure valve to **Sealing**. Select **Pressure Cook** or **Manual**; make sure the pressure level is set to **High**. Set the cooking time for 10 minutes. When pressure cooking is complete, allow the pressure to reduce naturally for 10 minutes, then release the remaining steam by moving the pressure valve to **Venting**. Press **Cancel**, then carefully open the pot.

SLOW

With the pot still on **More/High Sauté**, bring the mixture to a boil. Press **Cancel**, lock the lid in place and move the pressure valve to **Venting**. Select **Slow Cook** and set the temperature to **More/High**. Set the cooking time for 4 to 4½ hours; the squash is done when a skewer inserted into the largest piece meets no resistance. Press **Cancel**, then carefully open the pot.

FINISH: In a blender and working in 2 batches, puree the mixture until smooth, about 30 seconds, transferring the first batch to a bowl; return both batches to the pot. (Alternatively, use an immersion blender to puree the mixture directly in the pot). Select **More/High Sauté** and bring to a simmer, stirring occasionally, then press **Cancel** to turn off the pot. Remove the insert from the pot. In a small bowl, whisk together the yogurt and about 1 cup of the puree, then stir into the soup. Taste and season with salt and pepper. Serve topped with a dollop of yogurt and sprinkled with the pumpkin seeds and additional pepper.

BASQUE LEEK AND POTATO SOUP

Active time: 25 minutes

Fast start to finish: 50 minutes

Slow start to finish: 3 to 3½ hours

Servings: 4

3 tablespoons extra-virgin olive oil, plus more to serve

3 medium leeks, white and light green parts halved lengthwise, sliced ½ inch thick, rinsed and drained

4 bay leaves

1½ pounds Yukon Gold potatoes, peeled and cut into 1- to 1½-inch chunks

3 medium carrots, peeled and sliced ¼ inch thick

6 medium garlic cloves, finely chopped

¼ teaspoon red pepper flakes, plus more to serve

Kosher salt and ground black pepper

Porrusalda, a rustic soup from Spain's Basque country, takes a few humble ingredients and transforms them into a light but satisfying vegetarian meal. Leeks' many layers tend to trap dirt and sand, so make sure to thoroughly rinse the sliced leeks, then drain them well in a colander so excess water doesn't dilute the soup. Sliced crusty bread drizzled with olive oil and toasted until golden is a great accompaniment. Or to make the soup more substantial (although no longer vegetarian) garnish bowls with flaked smoked trout, a nod to traditional versions made with bacalao, or salted cod.

Don't substitute russet potatoes for the Yukon Golds. High-starch russets will turn mealy as they break down. If Yukon Golds aren't an option, use red potatoes instead.

START: On a 6-quart Instant Pot, select **Normal/Medium Sauté**. Add the oil and heat until shimmering. Add the leeks and bay and cook, stirring occasionally, until the leeks are softened, about 3 minutes. Stir in the potatoes, carrots, garlic, pepper flakes, 1 tablespoon salt, ½ teaspoon black pepper and 5 cups water, then distribute in an even layer.

FAST

Press **Cancel**, lock the lid in place and move the pressure valve to **Sealing**. Select **Pressure Cook** or **Manual**; make sure the pressure level is set to **High**. Set the cooking time for 3 minutes. When pressure cooking is complete, quick-release the steam by moving the pressure valve to **Venting**. Press **Cancel**, then carefully open the pot.

SLOW

Select **More/High Sauté** and bring the mixture to a boil. Press **Cancel**, lock the lid in place and move the pressure valve to **Venting**. Select **Slow Cook** and set the temperature to **More/High**. Set the cooking time for 2½ to 3 hours; the soup is done when a skewer inserted into a chunk of potato meets no resistance. Press **Cancel**, then carefully open the pot.

FINISH: Remove and discard the bay. If you prefer a thicker consistency, use a wooden spoon to gently crush some of the potatoes against the side of the pot, then stir to combine. Taste, then season with salt and black pepper. Serve drizzled with additional oil and sprinkled with additional pepper flakes.

CARAMELIZED CARROT SOUP WITH FENNEL SEEDS AND CUMIN

Active time: 20 minutes

Fast start to finish: 1 hour

Slow start to finish: 3¾ to 4¼ hours

Servings: 4

4 tablespoons (½ stick) salted butter, cut into 4 pieces, divided

½ cup sliced almonds

3½ cups carrot juice

1½ pounds carrots, peeled and cut into 1-inch sections

½ cup chopped fresh cilantro, plus cilantro leaves, to serve

1 tablespoon fennel seeds

2½ teaspoons ground cumin

½ teaspoon baking soda

Kosher salt and ground black pepper

2 tablespoons lime juice, plus lime wedges, to serve

This soup is simple to make but gets amazing depth of flavor thanks to a technique from the encyclopedic cookbook "Modernist Cuisine." The recipe uses baking soda, an alkali, to accelerate the caramelization process of the carrots' natural sugars; the soup takes on a sienna hue because of this browning. The fennel seeds and cumin add complexity without taking the spotlight away from the carrots. Garnishes of butter-toasted almonds and cilantro add texture and freshness; if you like, for added creaminess and a touch of tartness, top each serving with a spoonful of plain whole-milk yogurt.

Don't substitute water or broth for the carrot juice. The juice bolsters the carrots' sweet, earthy flavor as well as their vibrant color. Use shelf-stable bottled carrot juice or fresh-pressed sold in the refrigerator case; both yield good results.

START: On a 6-quart Instant Pot, select **Normal/Medium Sauté**. Add 1 tablespoon of butter and let melt. Add the almonds and cook, stirring often, until golden brown, 3 to 5 minutes. Press **Cancel**. Using a large spoon, transfer to a small bowl or plate. To the pot, add the carrot juice, carrots, cilantro, fennel seeds, cumin, baking soda and 1½ teaspoons salt. Stir to combine, then distribute in an even layer.

FAST

Lock the lid in place and move the pressure valve to **Sealing**. Select **Pressure Cook** or **Manual**; make sure the pressure level is set to **High**. Set the cooking time for 20 minutes. When pressure cooking is complete, allow the pressure to release naturally for 10 minutes, then release the remaining steam by moving the pressure valve to **Venting**. Press **Cancel**, then carefully open the pot.

SLOW

Select **More/High Sauté** and bring the mixture to a boil. Press **Cancel**, lock the lid in place and move the pressure valve to **Venting**. Select **Slow Cook** and set the temperature to **More/High**. Set the cooking time for 3½ to 4 hours; the carrots are done when they are tender enough to smash with a fork. Press **Cancel**, then carefully open the pot.

FINISH: In a blender and working in 2 batches, puree the mixture until smooth, about 30 seconds, transferring the first batch to a bowl; return both batches to the pot. (Alternatively, use an immersion blender to puree the mixture directly in the pot). Select **More/High Sauté** and bring to a simmer, stirring occasionally, then press **Cancel** to turn off the pot. Add the remaining 3 tablespoons butter and the lime juice; stir until the butter melts. Taste and season with salt and pepper. Serve sprinkled with the toasted almonds, cilantro leaves and additional pepper, with lime wedges on the side.

TWO-CORN CHOWDER WITH GREEN CHILI AND SCALLIONS

Active time: 30 minutes

Fast start to finish: 1 hour

Slow start to finish:
3 to 3½ hours

Servings: 4 to 6

3 ears fresh corn, husks and silk removed

4 tablespoons (½ stick) salted butter

1 bunch scallions, thinly sliced, white and green parts reserved separately

2 medium garlic cloves, finely chopped

1 poblano chili, stemmed, seeded and chopped

28-ounce can hominy, rinsed and drained

1 pound Yukon Gold potatoes, unpeeled, cut into 1-inch chunks

3 cups low-sodium chicken broth

Kosher salt and ground black pepper

½ cup heavy cream

Our light, bright take on a classic summer chowder uses corn in two forms: fresh kernels and canned hominy (dried kernels treated with alkali, then cooked until tender) to amplify the corn flavor. Peak-season fresh corn is ideal—after cutting away the kernels, we use the stripped cobs to infuse the broth with even more flavor. But if fresh corn is out of season, the chowder still is delicious made with a 12-ounce bag of frozen corn kernels and without the addition of the cobs (no need to thaw the frozen corn before use). Yellow corn, as opposed to white, gives the chowder the best color.

Don't forget to reserve the scallion whites and greens separately, as they are used at different times. Also, don't use half-and-half or milk, which lack richness and body and will break when cooked.

START: One at a time, stand each cob in a wide bowl. Using a chef's knife, cut the kernels from the ears of corn; you should have about 3 cups. Use the back of the knife to scrape each cob from top to bottom all around, allowing the liquid to fall into the bowl. Cut each cob in half and reserve separately.

On a 6-quart Instant Pot, select **More/High Sauté**. Add the butter and let melt. Add the scallion whites, garlic, chili, and corn kernels and liquid. Cook, stirring occasionally, until the chili is softened, about 7 minutes. Stir in the hominy, potatoes, broth, 1½ teaspoons salt and ½ teaspoon pepper, then distribute in an even layer. Add the corn cobs to the pot.

FAST

Press **Cancel**, lock the lid in place and move the pressure valve to **Sealing**. Select **Pressure Cook** or **Manual**; make sure the pressure level is set to **High**. Set the cooking time for 7 minutes. When pressure cooking is complete, allow the pressure to reduce naturally for 10 minutes, then release the remaining steam by moving the pressure valve to **Venting**. Press **Cancel**, then carefully open the pot.

SLOW

With the pot still on **More/High Sauté**, bring the mixture to a boil. Press **Cancel**, lock the lid in place and move the pressure valve to **Venting**. Select **Slow Cook** and set the temperature to **More/High**. Set the cooking time for 2½ to 3 hours; a skewer inserted into a piece of potato should meet no resistance. Press **Cancel**, then carefully open the pot.

FINISH: Remove and discard the corn cobs. Select **More/High Sauté**, then stir in the cream and half the scallion greens and cook, stirring occasionally, until heated through, about 3 minutes. Taste and season with salt and pepper. Serve sprinkled with the remaining scallion greens and pepper.

MASHED POTATOES WITH CABBAGE,
CARAWAY AND DILL

MASHED POTATOES AND CELERY
ROOT WITH TARRAGON

MASHED POTATOES WITH FONTINA,
ASIAGO AND BLACK PEPPER

MASHED YUKON GOLD POTATOES

Active time: 15 minutes

Fast start to finish:
35 minutes

Servings: 4

2 pounds Yukon Gold potatoes, unpeeled

6 tablespoons (¾ stick) salted butter, cut into 6 pieces, divided

Kosher salt and ground black pepper

½ cup half-and-half

The Instant Pot makes easy work of great mashed potatoes. So little water is needed for cooking that even sliced potatoes don't end up watery and washed out. They also don't require draining after cooking. We prefer Yukon Golds over russets for their buttery color and flavor and slightly lower starch content, and we leave the skins on for ease since they tenderize quite nicely under pressure. We do, however, add the potatoes to water as they're sliced, then give them a quick rinse to remove excess starch that would otherwise make the cooked potatoes a little gluey. For flavorful spins on these basic mashed potatoes, see the following recipes.

Don't add the half-and-half to the potatoes until all of the liquid in the pot has been cooked off. Also, don't remove the potatoes from the pot to mash them because the pot's residual heat will keep them warm even after the half-and-half and butter are added.

START: Fill a large bowl with water. Quarter the potatoes lengthwise, then slice about ½ inch thick; add the slices to the water as you go. After all the potatoes have been sliced, drain in a colander set in the sink and rinse briefly under cool water. Drain well, shaking the colander to remove as much water as possible. On a 6-quart Instant Pot, select **More/High Sauté**. Add 4 tablespoons of butter and let melt. Add the potatoes and 1 teaspoon salt, then stir until the potatoes are well coated. Stir in ½ cup water, then distribute in an even layer.

FAST

Press **Cancel**, lock the lid in place and move the pressure valve to **Sealing**. Select **Pressure Cook** or **Manual**; make sure the pressure level is set to **High**. Set the cooking time for 9 minutes. When pressure cooking is complete, quick-release the steam by moving the pressure valve to **Venting**. Press **Cancel**, then carefully open the pot.

FINISH: If there is liquid remaining in the pot, select **More/High Sauté** and cook, stirring often, until no moisture remains. Press **Cancel** to turn off the pot. Using a potato masher, mash the potatoes directly in the pot until mostly smooth with some large bits. Add the half-and-half and continue to mash to the desired consistency. Fold in the remaining 2 tablespoons butter until melted. Taste and season with salt and pepper.

MASHED POTATOES WITH CABBAGE, CARAWAY AND DILL

Active time: 20 minutes
Start to finish: 35 minutes
Servings: 4

6 tablespoons (¾ stick) salted butter, divided

2 pounds Yukon Gold potatoes, unpeeled, quartered lengthwise and sliced ½ inch thick

8 ounces green cabbage, cored and chopped (about 3 cups)

1 teaspoon caraway seeds

Kosher salt and ground black pepper

½ cup half-and-half

¼ cup finely chopped fresh dill

Follow the recipe through melting 4 tablespoons of butter. Add the potatoes, cabbage, caraway and 1 teaspoon salt, then stir until the vegetables are coated. Stir in ½ cup water, then distribute in an even layer. Continue with the recipe to cook and finish the potatoes, stirring in the dill before seasoning with salt and pepper.

MASHED POTATOES WITH FONTINA, ASIAGO AND BLACK PEPPER

Active time: 20 minutes
Start to finish: 35 minutes
Servings: 4

4 tablespoons (½ stick) salted butter

2 pounds Yukon Gold potatoes, unpeeled, quartered lengthwise and sliced ½ inch thick

Kosher salt and ground black pepper

½ cup half-and-half

2 ounces fontina cheese, shredded (½ cup)

2 ounces asiago cheese, shredded (½ cup)

Follow the recipe, melting all 4 tablespoons of butter. Add the potatoes and 1 teaspoon salt, then stir until the potatoes are coated. Stir in ½ cup water, then distribute in an even layer. Continue with the recipe to cook and finish the potatoes, stirring in the cheeses and 1 teaspoon pepper instead of the remaining butter.

MASHED POTATOES WITH CELERY ROOT AND TARRAGON

Active time: 20 minutes
Start to finish: 35 minutes
Servings: 4

6 tablespoons (¾ stick) salted butter, divided

1½ pounds Yukon Gold potatoes, unpeeled, quartered lengthwise and sliced ½ inch thick

1 pound celery root, peeled and cut into ½-inch chunks

Kosher salt and ground black pepper

½ cup sour cream

¼ cup finely chopped fresh tarragon

Follow the recipe through melting 4 tablespoons of butter. Add the potatoes, celery root and 1 teaspoon salt, then stir until the vegetables are coated. Stir in ½ cup water, then distribute in an even layer. Continue with the recipe to cook and finish the potatoes, stirring in the sour cream along with the remaining 2 tablespoons butter and adding the tarragon before seasoning with salt and pepper.

SPICY COLLARD GREENS WITH TOMATOES AND PEANUTS

Active time: 35 minutes

Fast start to finish: 1¼ hours

Slow start to finish:
9 to 9½ hours

Servings: 4

1 tablespoon coconut oil, preferably unrefined

1 medium yellow onion, chopped

1 pound tomatoes, cored and chopped

Kosher salt and ground black pepper

2 habanero chilies

1 bunch (1 pound) collard greens, stemmed and cut into 1-inch pieces (3 cups)

3 tablespoons crunchy peanut butter

15½-ounce can black-eyed peas, rinsed and drained

Hardy greens stewed with tomatoes and peanuts and spiked with chili is a staple food in parts of Africa. For our version of the dish called muriwo unedovi, we use collards, as they hold up well under the intensity of pressure cooking and the prolonged heat of slow cooking. The peanuts are in the form of chunky peanut butter; it lends the cooking liquid creaminess while also adding rich roasted nut flavor. Black-eyed peas aren't customary, but they make the greens substantial enough that they can be served as a vegetarian main. Rice or cornbread are excellent sides to these greens.

Don't be afraid of the habanero chilies. They're left whole so they contribute their characteristic fruitiness without releasing overwhelmingly spicy heat.

START: On a 6-quart Instant Pot, select **More/High Sauté**. Add the coconut oil and heat until shimmering. Add the onion, half the tomatoes, 1½ teaspoons salt and ½ teaspoon pepper, then cook, stirring occasionally, until the vegetables are lightly browned, 6 to 8 minutes. Add the chilies, 1½ cups water and the collards; stir to combine, then distribute in an even layer.

FAST

Press **Cancel**, lock the lid in place and move the pressure valve to **Sealing**. Select **Pressure Cook** or **Manual**; make sure the pressure level is set to **High**. Set the cooking time for 15 minutes. When pressure cooking is complete, let the pressure reduce naturally for 15 minutes, then release the remaining steam by moving the pressure valve to **Venting**. Press **Cancel**, then carefully open the pot.

SLOW

With the pot still on **More/High Sauté**, bring the mixture to a boil. Press **Cancel**, lock the lid in place and move the pressure valve to **Venting**. Select **Slow Cook** and set the temperature to **More/High**. Set the cooking time for 8½ to 9 hours; the collards are done when they are fully tender. Press **Cancel**, then carefully open the pot.

FINISH: Select **More/High Sauté** and bring the mixture to a simmer. Stir in the remaining tomatoes and the peanut butter, then cook, stirring occasionally, until the tomatoes have broken down and the sauce is creamy, 7 to 9 minutes. Press **Cancel** to turn off the pot. Remove and discard the chilies. Add the black-eyed peas and stir until heated through, 1 to 2 minutes. Taste and season with salt and pepper.

MUSHROOM AND TOASTED SESAME NOODLES

Active time: 35 minutes

Fast start to finish: 1 hour

Servings: 4

10 ounces dried Asian wheat noodles (see note), cooked, drained and rinsed

2 tablespoons plus 2 teaspoons toasted sesame oil

¼ cup sesame seeds, toasted

4 medium shallots, peeled and thinly sliced

1 bunch scallions, thinly sliced, whites and greens reserved separately

4 medium garlic cloves, finely chopped

¼ cup oyster sauce

3 tablespoons hoisin sauce

2 to 3 tablespoons chili-garlic sauce, divided

1 pound cremini mushrooms, trimmed and chopped

1 tablespoon finely grated fresh ginger

Chili oil, to serve (optional)

This meatless noodle dish is packed with flavor, thanks to the cremini mushrooms, as well as oyster sauce and hoisin. Dried udon noodles, which are thick and chewy, work well here, but if you can't find udon, substitute with an equal amount of linguine. Whichever type you use, make sure to rinse the noodles after draining to wash off excess starch. If you can find pre-toasted sesame seeds (look for them in the Asian aisle of the supermarket), you can use them straight from the container and skip the step of toasting. Adjust the spiciness by adding as little or as much chili-garlic sauce as you like. And a drizzle of chili oil to finish will not only up the heat a little, it'll also add nice color.

Don't chop the mushrooms too finely. *Uniformity isn't essential, but aim for pieces that are about ½ inch. This will give the sauce a heartier, meatier texture.*

START: Drizzle the rinsed udon noodles with the 2 teaspoons sesame oil, then toss until evenly coated; set aside.

On a 6-quart Instant Pot, select **More/High Sauté**. Add the sesame seeds and toast, stirring often, until golden brown and fragrant, about 10 minutes. Press **Cancel** to turn off the pot. Using potholders, carefully remove the insert from the housing and pour the seeds into a small bowl; return the insert to the housing.

Select **More/High Sauté**. Add the remaining 2 tablespoons oil, shallots and the scallion whites. Cook, stirring often, until the shallots are lightly browned, 3 to 5 minutes. Add the garlic and cook, stirring, until fragrant, about 30 seconds. Stir in the sesame seeds, oyster sauce, hoisin and 1 tablespoon of chili-garlic sauce, scraping up any browned bits. Add the mushrooms and stir to combine, then distribute in an even layer.

FAST

Press **Cancel**, lock the lid in place and move the pressure valve to **Sealing**. Select **Pressure Cook** or **Manual**; make sure the pressure level is set to **High**. Set the cooking time for 12 minutes. When pressure cooking is complete, quick-release the remaining steam by moving the pressure valve to **Venting**. Press **Cancel**, then carefully open the pot.

FINISH: Select **More/High Sauté** and bring the mixture to a boil. Cook, stirring often, until the mixture begins to sizzle, about 5 minutes. Stir in the ginger and the remaining 1 to 2 tablespoons chili-garlic sauce, then cook until fragrant, about 30 seconds. Press **Cancel** to turn off the pot. Stir in half of the scallion greens, then let stand for 5 minutes. Meanwhile, divide the noodles among individual serving bowls. Spoon on the sauce, then sprinkle with the remaining scallion greens and drizzle with chili oil (if using).

EGGPLANT, TOMATO AND CHICKPEA TAGINE

Active time: 25 minutes

Fast cook time: 45 minutes

Slow cook time:
5½ to 6½ hours

Servings: 4 to 6

¼ cup extra-virgin olive oil, plus more to serve

4 medium garlic cloves, finely chopped

1 medium yellow onion, roughly chopped

2 pints grape or cherry tomatoes, halved

4 teaspoons finely grated fresh ginger

1½ teaspoons ground cumin

1 teaspoon sweet paprika

¼ teaspoon ground cinnamon

Kosher salt and ground black pepper

2 pounds eggplant, trimmed and cut into 1-inch chunks

15½-ounce can chickpeas, rinsed and drained

1 tablespoon lemon juice, plus lemon wedges to serve

1 cup lightly packed fresh cilantro, finely chopped

A tagine is a North African stew cooked in a shallow, conical clay pot that goes by the same name. This particular chunky vegetable dish is warmly spiced like a tagine and features the common North African pairing of sweet and tart flavors. For extra depth and a touch of spiciness, swirl a spoonful of harissa into the tagine just before serving or offer some at the table for spooning on to taste. Serve with crusty bread, warmed flatbread or couscous to soak up the delicious sauce.

Don't shortcut the prep by leaving the tomatoes whole. Slicing 2 pints of grape tomatoes may take some time, but this step helps the tomatoes break down and cook at the same rate as the eggplant.

START: On a 6-quart Instant Pot, select **Normal/Medium Sauté**. Add the oil and garlic, then cook, stirring often, until the garlic is golden brown, about 4 minutes. Add the onion, tomatoes, ginger, cumin, paprika, cinnamon, 2½ teaspoons salt and 1 teaspoon pepper. Cook, stirring occasionally, until the tomatoes begin to release some of their juices, 2 to 4 minutes. Press **Cancel**, then stir in ¼ cup water, scraping up any browned bits. Gently stir in the eggplant, then distribute in an even layer.

FAST

Lock the lid in place and move the pressure valve to **Sealing**. Select **Pressure Cook** or **Manual**; adjust the pressure level to **Low**. Set the cooking time for 3 minutes. When pressure cooking is complete, quick-release the steam by moving the pressure valve to **Venting**. Press **Cancel**, then carefully open the pot.

SLOW

Select **More/High Sauté** and bring the mixture to a boil. Press **Cancel**, lock the lid in place and move the pressure valve to **Venting**. Select **Slow Cook** and set the temperature to **Less/Low**. Set the cooking time for 5 to 6 hours; the tagine is done when the tomatoes have broken down and the eggplant is very tender. Press **Cancel**, then carefully open the pot.

FINISH: Gently stir in the chickpeas and lemon juice, then taste and season with salt and pepper. Stir in the cilantro. Serve drizzled with additional oil and with lemon wedges on the side.

POTATO AND GREEN PEA CURRY

Active time: 25 minutes

**Fast start to finish:
55 minutes**

Servings: 4

¼ cup coconut oil

1 medium red onion,
finely chopped

1 tablespoon finely grated
fresh ginger

4 medium garlic cloves,
finely chopped

1 tablespoon sweet paprika

1 tablespoon ground
turmeric

1 tablespoon garam masala

¼ teaspoon cayenne pepper

2½ pounds russet potatoes,
peeled and cut into 1-inch
chunks

Kosher salt and ground
black pepper

14½-ounce can diced
tomatoes

1½ cups frozen peas,
thawed

¼ cup finely chopped
fresh cilantro

This classic Indian curry, called aloo matar, balances the sweetness of tomatoes and green peas with pungent aromatics and warm spices, all tempered by the mild flavor and starchiness of potatoes. The peas usually are drab army green from the acidity of the tomatoes; we add them at the end so they retain their bright color. The cilantro also is added at the end, so to save time, prep it while the curry rests for 10 minutes. Serve with basmati rice and cooling plain whole-milk yogurt, if desired.

Don't forget to thaw the peas before use. They are added off heat, when cooking is complete, so if they are still frozen, they will cool the curry. After adding the tomatoes, don't stir them into the potato mixture; if mixed in, they tend to sink to the bottom of the pot and burn.

START: On a 6-quart Instant Pot, select **More/High Sauté**. Add the oil and onion, then cook, stirring occasionally, until the onion begins to brown, about 5 minutes. Add the ginger and garlic, then cook, stirring, until fragrant, about 30 seconds. Stir in the paprika, turmeric, garam masala and cayenne. Pour in 1½ cups water, scraping up any browned bits. Add the potatoes and 1½ teaspoons salt; stir to combine, then distribute in an even layer. Add the tomatoes with their juice in an even layer on top of the potatoes; do not stir.

FAST

Press **Cancel**, lock the lid in place and move the pressure release valve to **Sealing**. Select **Pressure Cook** or **Manual**; make sure the pressure level is set to **High**. Set the cooking time for 4 minutes. When pressure cooking is complete, quick-release the steam by moving the pressure valve to **Venting**. Press **Cancel**, then carefully open the pot.

FINISH: Select **More/High Sauté** and cook, stirring often, until a skewer inserted into the potatoes meets no resistance and the sauce clings lightly, 3 to 4 minutes. Press **Cancel** to turn off the pot. Using potholders, carefully remove the insert from the housing. Let stand for 10 minutes. Stir in the peas and cilantro, then taste and season with salt and pepper.

BRAISED RED CABBAGE WITH APPLES

Active time: 25 minutes

Fast start to finish: 1 hour

Slow start to finish:
6 to 6½ hours

Servings: 4

4 tablespoons (½ stick) salted butter, cut into 4 pieces, divided

1 medium red onion, halved and thinly sliced

1 teaspoon ground allspice

1 teaspoon caraway seeds

Kosher salt and ground black pepper

2½- to 3-pound head red cabbage, outer leaves discarded, cut into 8 wedges, cored and cut crosswise into 1-inch sections

1 tablespoon packed brown sugar

¾ cup unfiltered apple juice or apple cider

3 tablespoons cider vinegar, divided

2 medium tart apples, such as Granny Smith

Our take on classic German Rotkohl (also called Blaukraut or Rotkraut) gets a little sweetness and fruitiness from apple cider along with grated fresh apples, and tanginess from cider vinegar. We prefer to use Granny Smith apples, not only for their crisp texture, but also for their sweet-tart flavor. Served as is, this is a wonderful vegetarian dish. But the flavors also work well with roasted or grilled pork chops, turkey and sausages.

Don't shred the apples far in advance of adding them to the pot because they may discolor. If convenient, they can be shredded, tossed with the vinegar and salt, then stored at room temperature with plastic wrap pressed directly against the surface for up to 15 minutes.

START: On a 6-quart Instant Pot, select **Normal/Medium Sauté**. Add 3 tablespoons of the butter and let melt. Add the onion, allspice, caraway and 2 teaspoons salt, then cook, stirring occasionally, until the onion is softened and beginning to brown, 6 to 8 minutes. Stir in the cabbage and sugar. Stir in the apple juice, 2 tablespoons of vinegar and ¼ cup water, then distribute in an even layer.

FAST

Press **Cancel**, lock the lid in place and move the pressure valve to **Sealing**. Select **Pressure Cook** or **Manual**; make sure the pressure level is set to **High**. Set the cooking time for 4 minutes. When pressure cooking is complete, let the pressure reduce naturally for 15 minutes, then release the remaining steam by moving the pressure valve to **Venting**. Press **Cancel**, then carefully open the pot.

SLOW

Select **More/High Sauté** and bring the mixture to a boil. Press **Cancel**, lock the lid in place and move the pressure valve to **Venting**. Select **Slow Cook** and set the temperature to **Less/Low**. Set the cooking time for 5½ to 6 hours; the cabbage is done when tender but the pieces still hold their shape. Press **Cancel**, then carefully open the pot.

FINISH: On the large holes of a box grater set in a medium bowl, shred each apple down to the core, rotating as needed; discard the cores. Add the remaining 1 tablespoon vinegar and 1 teaspoon salt to the grated apples and toss. Select **Normal/Medium Sauté** and bring the cabbage to a simmer. Add the apples and cook, stirring occasionally, until the apples are tender, 5 to 7 minutes. Press **Cancel** to turn off the pot. Add the remaining 1 tablespoon butter and stir until melted. Taste and season with salt and pepper.

SPICED SWEET POTATOES
WITH CASHEWS AND CILANTRO

Active time: 20 minutes

**Fast start to finish:
35 minutes**

Servings: 4

2 tablespoons grapeseed
or other neutral oil

½ cup unsweetened
wide-flake coconut

¼ cup unsalted roasted
cashews, chopped

2 tablespoons sesame seeds

1 tablespoon yellow
mustard seeds

1 tablespoon cumin seeds

6 medium garlic cloves,
4 finely chopped, 2 smashed
and peeled

2 jalapeño chilies,
1 stemmed, seeded and
finely chopped, 1 stemmed
and quartered lengthwise

2 pounds orange-flesh
sweet potatoes, peeled and
cut into 1-inch chunks

Kosher salt and ground
black pepper

1 cup lightly packed fresh
cilantro, chopped

In the Indian kitchen, sabzi are cooked vegetable dishes typically flavored with curry spices. For our take on sweet potato sabzi, we first toast nuts, spices, seeds and aromatics then set the mix aside for tossing with chunks of sweet potatoes after they've been pressure-cooked. The result is a delicious contrast of sweet, savory and spicy flavors, as well as creamy and crunchy textures. If you're a fan of chili heat, leave the seeds in the jalapeño that's finely chopped. Serve this vibrant dish as a side to grilled or roasted chicken, lamb or pork, or offer it as a vegetarian main with basmati rice or warmed naan. And if you like, offer plain yogurt on the side—it's a cooling contrast to the warm spices and adds creamy richness.

Don't use sweetened coconut, which will overwhelm with its sugariness. If you can't find unsweetened wide-flake coconut, use regular unsweetened shredded coconut—the fine shreds won't offer as much texture or visual appeal but the dish still will taste great.

START: On a 6-quart Instant Pot, select **Normal/Medium Sauté**. Add the oil and heat until shimmering. Add the coconut, cashews and sesame seeds, then cook, stirring often, until light golden brown, about 3 minutes. Add the mustard seeds, cumin seeds, finely chopped garlic and chopped jalapeño. Continue to cook, stirring often, until the nuts and seeds are golden brown and the mixture has a toasty aroma, another 2 to 3 minutes. Press **Cancel** to turn off the pot. Using potholders, carefully remove the insert from the housing and pour the mixture into a large bowl; return the insert to the housing. Add the sweet potatoes, smashed garlic cloves, quartered jalapeño, 2 teaspoons salt and ½ cup water to the pot; stir to combine, then distribute in an even layer.

FAST

Lock the lid in place and move the pressure release valve to **Sealing**. Select **Pressure Cook** or **Manual**; adjust the pressure level to **Low**. Set the cooking time for 4 minutes.

When pressure cooking is complete, quick-release the steam by moving the pressure valve to **Venting**. Press **Cancel**, then carefully open the pot.

FINISH: Using a slotted spoon, transfer the potatoes to the large bowl with the nut-spice mixture, removing and discarding the garlic cloves and jalapeño quarters. Gently toss to coat the potatoes, then fold in the cilantro. Taste and season with salt and pepper.

STEAMED WHOLE CAULIFLOWER
WITH MUSTARD, PARSLEY AND FETA

STEAMED WHOLE CAULIFLOWER
WITH HARISSA AND MINT

STEAMED WHOLE CAULIFLOWER
WITH MISO AND HONEY

STEAMED WHOLE CAULIFLOWER

Active time: 5 minutes

Fast start to finish: 40 minutes

Servings: 4

2-pound head cauliflower, trimmed (see note)

1 tablespoon extra-virgin olive oil

Kosher salt and ground black pepper

Steaming a whole head of cauliflower is easy (no need to cut it into florets) and pressure-cooking makes the process hands-off. Make sure to trim the base of the head so it sits flat, and remove any large, thick-stemmed green leaves; the small inner leaves become tender with cooking. This recipe is for basic salt-and-pepper seasoned cauliflower, but we've included a few simple high-impact flavor options, too. To make this, you will need the steam rack with handles that was included with the Instant Pot.

Don't use a large head of cauliflower. Up to 2½ pounds is fine, but a larger head will not cook evenly in the time indicated; the center of the core will be underdone.

START: Pour ½ cup water into a 6-quart Instant Pot. Place the cauliflower on a steam rack with handles, then brush with the oil and sprinkle with 1 teaspoon salt and ¼ teaspoon pepper. Lower the rack with the cauliflower into the pot.

FAST

Lock the lid in place and move the pressure valve to **Sealing**. Select **Pressure Cook** or **Manual**; adjust the pressure level to **Low**. Set the cooking time for 12 minutes. When pressure cooking is complete, allow the pressure to reduce naturally for 15 minutes, then release the remaining steam by moving the valve to **Venting**. Press **Cancel**, then carefully open the pot.

FINISH: Using a kitchen towel or two pairs of tongs, carefully grab the handles and lift out the rack with the cauliflower. With a wide metal spatula, transfer the cauliflower to a platter. To serve, cut into 4 wedges.

STEAMED WHOLE CAULIFLOWER WITH MISO AND HONEY

⅓ cup white miso

4 teaspoons unseasoned rice vinegar

2 teaspoons honey

2-pound head cauliflower, trimmed

Ground white pepper

Chopped fresh cilantro and/ or roasted pistachios, to serve

Pour ½ cup water into a 6-quart Instant Pot. In a small bowl, whisk together the miso, vinegar, honey and ¼ teaspoon white pepper. Place the cauliflower on a steam rack with handles, then brush with the miso mixture. Lower the rack with the cauliflower into the pot and cook as directed. After transferring to the platter, sprinkle with cilantro and/or pistachios.

STEAMED WHOLE CAULIFLOWER WITH MUSTARD, PARSLEY AND FETA

¼ cup yellow mustard

2 tablespoons extra-virgin olive oil

2 medium garlic cloves, finely chopped

2 teaspoons honey

Kosher salt

2-pound head cauliflower, trimmed

Chopped fresh flat-leaf parsley, to serve

Crumbled feta cheese, to serve

Pour ½ cup water into a 6-quart Instant Pot. In a small bowl, whisk together the mustard, oil, garlic, honey and 1 teaspoon salt. Place the cauliflower on a steam rack with handles, then brush with the mustard mixture. Lower the rack with the cauliflower into the pot and cook as directed. After transferring to the platter, sprinkle with parsley and feta.

STEAMED WHOLE CAULIFLOWER WITH HARISSA AND MINT

¼ cup mayonnaise

2 tablespoons harissa

2 teaspoons honey

Kosher salt

2-pound head cauliflower, trimmed

Chopped fresh mint, to serve

Pour ½ cup water into a 6-quart Instant Pot. In a small bowl, whisk together the mayonnaise, harissa, honey and 1 teaspoon salt. Place the cauliflower on a steam rack with handles, then brush with the mayonnaise mixture. Lower the rack with the cauliflower into the pot and cook as directed. After transferring to the platter, sprinkle with mint.

GRAINS

CONTENTS

Peruvian-Style Arroz con Pollo (p. 57)

GRAINS

To make sure our grains aren't stodgy or bland, we **use spice blends and simple but high-impact techniques to add flavor and texture.** Our take on steel-cut oats, for instance, starts by coaxing out rich and nutty flavor by toasting them in browned butter with a bit of allspice. Some water, apples and salt go in and the pressure cooker does the rest, no stirring while simmering—and no risk of the porridge boiling over.

Grains aren't sturdy like chunks of beef and shouldn't be treated the same way, so we **don't always use the high setting for pressure-cooking and slow-cooking** to keep our grains from blowing out and turning to mush. For the same reason, we tend to **skip the slow-cooker function in many cases,** and use only the pressure-cooker option.

Along with full meals, like our simplified take on "clay pot" chicken and rice, we've included recipes that can be served as sides or offered as light mains, especially with embellishments like a fried-egg topping or a simple salad alongside. Our polenta takes just 10 minute hands-on effort and works great as a side or as a light meal with one of the three toppings we came up with. Risottos, too, are a snap using the Instant Pot; we've included one with tender sausage and another with mushrooms and herbs.

Multicookers retain a fair amount of heat after being turned off and we **utilize residual heat to cook delicate foods.** The shrimp and corn in our rice pilaf with sweet corn and shrimp don't go in until after switch-off so they cook gently and evenly. Likewise, we wait until the end to add the shrimp in our West African-inspired jollof rice. And even when we're not using residual heat to cook extra ingredients, we **give grains a brief rest before serving.** This allows them to finish cooking and absorb any remaining moisture or liquid so the dish is not wet and soupy.

The Instant Pot lets us reach beyond standard steamed rice and get slower cooking grains like steel-cut oats and polenta on the table fast and fuss free. And it shakes up the risotto routine— no lengthy standing and stirring required.

BREAKFAST FARRO WITH CARDAMOM AND DRIED APRICOTS

Active time: **10 minutes**

Fast start to finish: **40 minutes**

Servings: **6**

2 tablespoons salted butter

1½ cups pearled farro (see note)

1 teaspoon ground cardamom

½ cup dried apricots, chopped

½ teaspoon kosher salt

Honey, to serve

Yogurt, to serve

Farro, a type of wheat, is available as whole-grain, semi-pearled (bran partially removed) and pearled (bran completely removed). The latter varieties are quicker-cooking; we found either type works better than whole-grain for pressure cooking and slow cooking. When cooked until the grains are creamy-tender yet still plump, farro makes a comforting hot breakfast and is a nice change from standard oatmeal. And cooking pearled farro in the Instant Pot means no need to stand over the pot and stir regularly. Cardamom brings out the floral notes in apricots; the combination pairs beautifully with the wheaty, nutty flavor of the farro. Top individual portions with yogurt for richness and honey for sweetness.

*Don't use whole-grain farro, as it won't cook through properly. Semi-pearled farro will work but may require a few additional minutes of cooking (Bob's Red Mill refers to their semi-pearled farro as "lightly scratched"). After opening the pot and stirring the farro, give the grains a taste. If still too firm, select **Medium/Normal Sauté**, bring to a simmer and cook, stirring often, until tender; press **Cancel** to turn off the pot, then continue with the recipe.*

START: On a 6-quart Instant Pot, select **More/High Sauté**. Add the butter and let melt. Add the farro and cardamom, then cook, stirring occasionally, until fragrant and toasted, about 3 minutes. Stir in 3½ cups water, the apricots and salt, then distribute in an even layer.

FAST

Press **Cancel**, lock the lid in place and move the pressure valve to **Sealing**. Select **Pressure Cook** or **Manual**; make sure the pressure level is set to **High**. Set the cooking time for 12 minutes. When pressure cooking is complete, quick-release the steam by moving the pressure valve to **Venting**. Press **Cancel**, then carefully open the pot.

FINISH: Stir the mixture well, then re-cover without locking the lid in place. Let stand for 10 minutes. Stir vigorously until thick and creamy, about 30 seconds. Serve with honey and yogurt.

BUTTER-TOASTED STEEL-CUT OATS WITH DRIED APPLES

Active time: 10 minutes

Fast start to finish: 35 minutes

Servings: 6

2 tablespoons salted butter

1½ cups steel-cut oats

½ teaspoon ground allspice

½ cup dried apples, chopped

½ teaspoon kosher salt

Maple syrup or brown sugar, to serve

Milk or cream, to serve

Cooking steel-cut oats in a pressure cooker means the grains tenderize quickly, without stirring and without risk of boiling over, making this breakfast staple a breeze to prepare. To build rich flavor, we start by cooking a couple tablespoons of butter until fragrant and nutty, then toast the oats, along with a small measure of allspice, in the browned butter to bring out notes of butterscotch and caramel. Dried apples add tangy, fruity flavor; their texture softens as they cook with the oats.

Don't use rolled oats, not even slower-cooking old-fashioned rolled oats, as they will turn mushy. Steel-cut oats are sturdier and can stand up to pressure cooking. Also, keep a close eye on the butter as it cooks because it goes quickly from brown and nutty to scorched.

START: On a 6-quart Instant Pot, select **More/High Sauté**. Add the butter and cook, stirring often, until it begins to smell nutty and the milk solids at the bottom begin to brown, about 3 minutes. Stir in the oats and allspice, then cook, stirring occasionally, until fragrant and toasted, about 3 minutes. Add 5½ cups water, the apples and salt; stir to combine, then distribute in an even layer.

FAST

Press **Cancel**, lock the lid in place and move the pressure valve to **Sealing**. Select **Pressure Cook** or **Manual**; make sure the pressure level is set to **High**. Set the cooking time for 5 minutes. When pressure cooking is complete, quick-release the steam by moving the pressure valve to **Venting**. Press **Cancel**, then carefully open the pot.

FINISH: Stir the mixture well, then re-cover without locking the lid in place. Let stand for 10 minutes. Stir vigorously until thick and creamy, about 30 seconds. Serve with maple syrup and milk.

Active time: 10 minutes

Fast start to finish:
1¼ hours

Slow start to finish:
5½ to 6½ hours

Servings: 4

SOFT POLENTA
WITH EASY TOPPINGS

1½ cups coarse stoneground yellow cornmeal

Kosher salt and ground black pepper

Thick, creamy polenta is a breeze to make in a pressure cooker, as the cooking is completely hands-off. This polenta is not enriched with butter or cheese, so the sweetness of the corn is front and center. A simple topping (recipes follow; each makes enough for four servings) can turn a bowl of plain polenta into a light meal or a delicious first course. Polenta also is a perfect accompaniment to many stews and braises. Served plain, this polenta is vegan, and two of the toppings are vegetarian.

Don't use fine yellow cornmeal, which cooks up pasty and gluey. For the best flavor and texture, use coarse stoneground cornmeal; steel-ground cornmeal has less flavor. We especially liked Bob's Red Mill Organic Polenta Corn Grits (cornmeal).

START: In a 6-quart Instant Pot, whisk together 7½ cups water, the polenta and 2½ teaspoons salt.

FAST

Lock the lid in place and move the pressure valve to **Sealing**. Select **Pressure Cook** or **Manual**; make sure the pressure level is set to **High**. Set the cooking time for 20 minutes. When pressure cooking is complete, let the pressure reduce naturally for 20 minutes, then release the remaining steam by moving the pressure valve to **Venting**. Press **Cancel**, then carefully open the pot.

SLOW

Select **Normal/Medium Sauté** and bring to a simmer, stirring often. Press **Cancel**, lock the lid in place and move the pressure valve to **Venting**. Select **Slow Cook** and set the temperature to **Less/Low**. Set the cooking time for 5 to 6 hours. Press **Cancel**, then carefully open the pot.

FINISH: Whisk the polenta until creamy, then taste and season with salt and pepper. Let stand for about 10 minutes to thicken slightly, then stir again and serve.

EASY TOPPINGS FOR SOFT POLENTA

PISTACHIOS, APRICOTS AND PARMESAN

In a small bowl, stir together ⅓ cup salted roasted pistachios (chopped), ⅓ cup dried apricots (chopped), 2 tablespoons white balsamic vinegar and 2 tablespoons extra-virgin olive oil. Spoon onto individual bowls of polenta, then sprinkle with finely grated Parmesan cheese and drizzle with olive oil.

FIG JAM AND PROSCIUTTO

In a small bowl, whisk together ¼ cup fig jam, 1 tablespoon extra-virgin olive oil and ½ teaspoon ground black pepper. Spoon onto individual bowls of polenta, then top with 3 ounces thinly sliced prosciutto (cut into thin strips) and 2 ounces manchego or Parmesan cheese (shaved with a vegetable peeler), then drizzle with olive oil.

GORGONZOLA AND ROSEMARY HONEY

In a small microwave-safe bowl, combine ¼ cup honey and a 5-inch sprig fresh rosemary, making sure the rosemary is fully submerged. Microwave on high until the honey is bubbling, about 1 minute. Divide 3 ounces gorgonzola (crumbled) evenly among individual bowls of polenta, then drizzle with the rosemary honey. Sprinkle with ground black pepper and drizzle with extra-virgin olive oil.

PERUVIAN QUINOA STEW WITH QUESO FRESCO

Active time: 30 minutes

**Fast start to finish:
1 hour 10 minutes**

Slow start to finish:
4½ to 5½ hours

Servings: 4 to 6

3 tablespoons grapeseed or other neutral oil

1 medium yellow onion, finely chopped

4 medium garlic cloves, smashed and peeled

3 plum tomatoes, cored and chopped

Kosher salt and ground black pepper

1 yellow bell pepper, stemmed, seeded and chopped

1 habanero chili, halved (see note)

2½ teaspoons sweet paprika

2½ teaspoons ground cumin

1 teaspoon dried oregano

1½ cups red, white or tricolor (rainbow) quinoa, rinsed and drained

4 ounces queso fresco, cut into ½-inch cubes (about 1 cup)

Chopped fresh cilantro, to serve

The Peruvian quinoa stew called quinua atamalada is thick and hearty and typically is seasoned with ají amarillo, a yellow-orange chili widely used in Peruvian cuisine. For our version, we approximated ají amarillo's flavor by using a yellow bell pepper plus a habanero. The habanero provides only subtle heat because the pod is merely cut in half, not minced, but if you wish to minimize spiciness, remove the seeds from the chili halves. Queso fresco is a salty, milky Mexican cheese with a firm, slightly crumbly texture; its savoriness contrasts nicely with the sweetness of the vegetables and lends the stew a delicious richness. If you like, garnish with finely chopped onion tossed with fresh lime juice.

Don't undercook the onion and tomato mixture. The goal is to evaporate the moisture and create a concentrated flavor base for seasoning the stew.

START: On a 6-quart Instant Pot select **More/High Sauté**. Heat the oil until shimmering. Add the onion, garlic, tomatoes, 1½ teaspoons salt and ¼ teaspoon pepper. Cook, stirring occasionally, until the moisture evaporates and the onion is softened and translucent, about 10 minutes. Add the bell pepper, chili, paprika, cumin and oregano, then cook, stirring often, until the spices begin to stick to the bottom of the pot, 1 to 2 minutes. Stir in the quinoa and 2 cups water, scraping up any browned bits; distribute the mixture in an even layer.

FAST

Press **Cancel**, lock the lid in place and move the pressure valve to **Sealing**. Select **Pressure Cook** or **Manual**; adjust the pressure level to **Low**. Set the cooking time for 12 minutes. When pressure cooking is complete, let the pressure reduce naturally for 10 minutes, then release the remaining steam by moving the pressure valve to **Venting**. Press **Cancel**, then carefully open the pot. Fluff the quinoa with a fork, removing and discarding the chili halves. Add the queso fresco and stir until it begins to melt. Stir in 2 cups water and re-cover without locking the lid in place, then let stand for 5 minutes.

SLOW

With the pot still on **More/High Sauté**, bring the mixture to a boil. Press **Cancel**, lock the lid in place and move the pressure valve to **Venting**. Select **Slow Cook** and set the temperature to **Less/Low**. Set the cooking time for 4 to 5 hours; the mixture is done when the quinoa has absorbed the liquid. Press **Cancel**, then carefully open the pot. Fluff the quinoa with a fork, removing and discarding the chili halves. Add the queso fresco and stir until it begins to melt. Stir in 2 cups water, then select **Normal/Medium Sauté** and bring the mixture to a simmer, stirring once or twice. Press **Cancel** to turn off the pot, re-cover without locking the lid in place and let stand for 5 minutes.

FINISH: Taste and season with salt and pepper. Serve sprinkled with cilantro.

PERSIAN BARLEY-LENTIL SOUP WITH SPINACH

Active time: 20 minutes

**Fast start to finish:
50 minutes**

Slow start to finish:
5¼ to 6¼ hours

Servings: 4

2 tablespoons extra-virgin olive oil, plus more to serve

1 medium yellow onion, chopped

6 medium garlic cloves, finely chopped

2 medium carrots, peeled, quartered lengthwise and sliced ½-inch thick

2 tablespoons tomato paste

4 bay leaves

Kosher salt and ground black pepper

1 tablespoon grated lime zest, plus 3 tablespoons lime juice, plus lime wedges to serve

¾ cup pearled barley

½ cup brown or green lentils

1½ quarts low-sodium vegetable broth

4 cups (3 ounces) lightly packed baby spinach, chopped

1 cup lightly packed fresh cilantro, chopped

This hearty vegetarian soup was inspired by a recipe in "Bottom of the Pot" by Naz Deravian, who explains that she created the dish by combining two classic Persian soups: lentil and barley. She uses dried limes common in Persian cuisine to infuse the broth with unique citrus notes. We opted for easier-to-find fresh limes and use the zest for fragrance and flavor and the juice to add tanginess. For efficiency, prep the spinach and cilantro while the barley and lentils cook. And to round out the meal, serve with warmed bread or flatbread and a dollop of plain yogurt for richness.

Don't use hulled barley instead of pearled barley. Hulled barley has had its inedible outer hull removed but retains its bran. Pearled barley, on the other hand, has been polished to remove the bran, which makes it quicker to tenderize; in this recipe, it cooks at the same rate as the lentils.

START: On a 6-quart Instant Pot, select **More/High Sauté**. Add the oil and heat until shimmering. Add the onion, garlic, carrots, tomato paste, bay and 1 teaspoon salt. Cook, stirring occasionally, until the vegetables begin to brown, about 5 minutes. Stir in the lime zest and juice, barley, lentils and broth, scraping up any browned bits, then distribute in an even layer.

FAST

Press **Cancel**, lock the lid in place and move the pressure valve to **Sealing**. Select **Pressure Cook** or **Manual**; set the pressure level to **High**. Set the cooking time for 15 minutes. When pressure cooking is complete, quick-release the steam by moving the pressure valve to **Venting**. Press **Cancel**, then carefully open the pot.

SLOW

With the pot still on **More/High Sauté**, bring the mixture to a boil. Press **Cancel**, lock the lid in place and move the pressure valve to **Venting**. Select **Slow Cook** and set the temperature to **Less/Low**. Set the cooking time for 5 to 6 hours; the soup is done when the barley and lentils are fully tender. Press **Cancel**, then carefully open the pot.

FINISH: Remove and discard the bay, then stir in the spinach and cilantro. Taste and season with salt and pepper. Serve drizzled with oil and with lime wedges on the side.

FARRO WITH CREMINI MUSHROOMS AND ARUGULA

Active time: 35 minutes
Fast start to finish: 1 hour
Servings: 4

4 tablespoons extra-virgin olive oil, divided

1 pound cremini mushrooms, trimmed and quartered

Kosher salt and ground black pepper

1 large yellow onion, finely chopped

4 medium garlic cloves, finely chopped

1½ cups farro (see note)

½ cup dry white wine

3 tablespoons salted butter, cut into 3 pieces

5-ounce container baby arugula, roughly chopped

½ teaspoon minced fresh rosemary

1½ ounces Parmesan cheese, finely grated (¾ cup)

We recommend semi-pearled farro (bran partially removed) or pearled (bran completely removed) for this recipe. If by chance you have a piece of Parmesan rind, toss it into the pot after adding the water, then remove and discard it just before serving; it will add extra depth of flavor and a touch more umami to the dish. Serve the farro as a light main course or offer it as a side to braised or roasted chicken or pork.

Don't use whole-grain farro, as it won't cook through properly in the times indicated. Bob's Red Mill sells farro that is "lightly scratched." It works in this recipe but retains a chewier texture than semi-pearled or pearled.

START: On a 6-quart Instant Pot, select **More/High Sauté**. Add 2 tablespoons of oil and heat until shimmering. Add the mushrooms and ½ teaspoon salt, then cook, stirring occasionally, until well browned and most of the liquid released by the mushrooms has evaporated, 6 to 8 minutes. Transfer to a small bowl and set aside. With the pot still on **More/High Sauté**, add the remaining 2 tablespoons oil and the onion. Cook, stirring occasionally, until lightly browned, 5 to 7 minutes. Stir in the garlic and cook until fragrant, about 30 seconds. Add the farro, 2 teaspoons salt and ¾ teaspoon pepper, stirring to coat the grains with oil. Add the wine and cook, scraping up any browned bits, until most of the liquid evaporates, 1 to 2 minutes. Pour in 3 cups water; stir to combine, then distribute the mixture in an even layer.

FAST

Press **Cancel**, lock the lid in place and move the pressure valve to **Sealing**. Select **Pressure Cook** or **Manual**; make sure the pressure level is set to **High**. Set the cooking time for 12 minutes. When pressure cooking is complete, quick-release the steam by moving the pressure valve to **Venting**. Press **Cancel**, then carefully open the pot.

FINISH: Stir the farro, then select **Normal/Medium Sauté**. Cook, stirring vigorously and scraping the corners of the pot, until the farro is thick and creamy, about 4 minutes; if needed to thin the consistency, stir in up to ½ cup water. Add the cooked mushrooms, the butter, arugula, rosemary and half of the Parmesan, then stir until the butter has melted. Taste and season with salt and pepper. Serve with the remaining Parmesan on the side.

BULGUR PILAF WITH CHICKPEAS AND HERBS

Active time: 20 minutes

**Fast start to finish:
40 minutes**

Slow start to finish:
6 to 6½ hours

Servings: 4

4 tablespoons (½ stick) salted butter

2½ teaspoons garam masala

1 bunch scallions, thinly sliced, whites and greens reserved separately

1 cup coarse bulgur, rinsed and drained

Kosher salt and ground black pepper

Two 15½-ounce cans chickpeas, rinsed and drained

1 cup lightly packed fresh dill, roughly chopped

1 cup lightly packed fresh flat-leaf parsley, roughly chopped

¼ cup toasted pistachios, chopped

This simple but hearty pilaf combines fast-cooking bulgur and canned chickpeas, so it comes together easily and quickly. A generous measure of butter adds richness. For flavoring, we reached for garam masala, an Indian spice blend, as it offers the complexity of a handful of spices in a single jar. This dish makes a satisfying vegetarian main or great accompaniment for just about any roasted or grilled meat or seafood. It can be served warm, but also is good at room temperature.

Don't use fine bulgur, which typically is the variety used in boxed tabbouleh mixes; it will cook too quickly and wind up mushy. Don't forget to rinse the bulgur to remove excess starch, but make sure to drain it well so extra water doesn't go into the pot. Don't forget to quick-release the pressure when pressure cooking is done. If left to stand, moisture and heat trapped in the pot will make the bulgur soft and gummy.

START: On a 6-quart Instant Pot, select **More/High Sauté**. Add the butter and let melt. Add the garam masala and scallion whites, then cook, stirring, until fragrant, about 1 minute. Stir in the bulgur, coating the grains with butter. Stir in 1½ cups water, 2 teaspoons salt and ½ teaspoon pepper, then distribute the mixture in an even layer.

FAST

Press **Cancel**, lock the lid in place and move the pressure valve to **Sealing**. Select **Pressure Cook** or **Manual**; adjust the pressure level to **Low**. Set the cooking time for 5 minutes. When pressure cooking is complete, quick-release the steam by moving the pressure valve to **Venting**. Press **Cancel**, then let stand for 5 minutes. Carefully open the pot.

SLOW

With the pot still on **More/High Sauté**, bring the mixture to a boil. Press **Cancel**, lock the lid in place and move the pressure valve to **Venting**. Select **Slow Cook** and set the temperature to **Less/Low**. Set the cooking time for 5½ to 6 hours; the mixture is done when the liquid is absorbed and the bulgur is tender. Press **Cancel**, then let stand for 5 minutes. Carefully open the pot.

FINISH: Stir in the chickpeas and about half of the scallion greens, half of the dill and half of the parsley. Taste and season with salt and pepper. Transfer to a serving dish, sprinkle with the remaining scallion greens, the remaining dill and the remaining parsley, then top with the pistachios.

COCONUT RICE WITH RED BEANS AND SCALLIONS

Active time: 15 minutes

**Fast start to finish:
50 minutes**

Slow start to finish:
2¾ to 3¼ hours

Servings: 6

3 tablespoons coconut oil (preferably unrefined), melted

1½ cups long-grain white rice, rinsed and drained

1 bunch scallions, thinly sliced

4 medium garlic cloves, finely chopped

1 small red bell pepper, stemmed, seeded and chopped

2 tablespoons minced fresh cilantro stems, plus ½ cup chopped fresh cilantro leaves, reserved separately

2½ cups coconut water

1 teaspoon ground cumin

1 teaspoon white sugar

Kosher salt and ground black pepper

15½-ounce can small red beans or kidney beans, rinsed and drained

This flavorful, colorful side was inspired by resanbinsi, a rice and red bean dish from the Caribbean coast of Honduras and Nicaragua. We approximate the delicate sweetness and subtle richness of fresh coconut milk with a combination of coconut oil and coconut water; unrefined coconut oil lends the fullest flavor, but regular refined oil works, too. This is an excellent accompaniment to grilled seafood, chicken or pork, or turn it into dinner by topping the rice with fried eggs and offering lime wedges and hot sauce alongside.

Don't substitute coconut milk for the coconut water. The richness of coconut milk—even light coconut milk—will result in a heavy, almost gummy texture. When cooking is done, don't leave the inner pot in the housing. The residual heat had a tendency to overcook the grains; it's best to remove the insert before allowing the rice to rest.

START: In a 6-quart Instant Pot, stir together the oil, rice, scallions, garlic, bell pepper and cilantro stems. Add the coconut water, cumin, sugar, 2 teaspoons salt and 1 teaspoon pepper. Stir to combine, then distribute the mixture in an even layer.

FAST

Lock the lid in place and move the pressure valve to **Sealing**. Select **Pressure Cook** or **Manual**; adjust the pressure level to **Low**. Set the cooking time for 10 minutes. When pressure cooking is complete, quick-release the steam by moving the pressure valve to **Venting**. Press **Cancel**, then carefully open the pot.

SLOW

Select **More/High Sauté** and bring the mixture to a boil. Press **Cancel**, then lock the lid in place and move the pressure valve to **Venting**. Select **Slow Cook** and set the temperature to **Less/Low**. Set the cooking time for 2 to 2½ hours; the rice is done when the liquid is absorbed and the grains are tender. Press **Cancel**, then carefully open the pot.

FINISH: Using potholders, carefully remove the insert from the housing. Without fluffing the rice, scatter the beans over the surface, then drape a kitchen towel across the top and re-cover without locking the lid in place. Let stand for 10 minutes. Uncover and add the cilantro leaves, then fluff the rice, stirring in the beans and cilantro. Taste and season with salt and pepper.

BROWN BASMATI RICE PILAF
WITH SPICED BEEF AND GREEN BEANS

Active time: 25 minutes

Fast start to finish:
1 hour 10 minutes

Servings: 4

8 ounces 85 percent lean ground beef

2 tablespoons tomato paste

1¾ teaspoons ground cinnamon

1¾ teaspoons ground turmeric

Kosher salt and ground black pepper

2 tablespoons extra-virgin olive oil, divided

8 ounces green beans, trimmed and cut into 1-inch pieces

1½ cups brown basmati rice, rinsed and drained

¼ cup golden raisins

1 cup chopped fresh cilantro

The Persian dish known as loobia polow, or green beans and rice, served as the inspiration for this recipe. White basmati rice would be the classic choice, but we opted for brown basmati. The grains hold up well to pressure cooking and their nutty flavor pairs well with the earthy spices and the sweetness from the golden raisins. This is a one-pot meal, though a salad of tomatoes and cucumbers with a simple lemon and olive oil vinaigrette would be a nice accompaniment, as would plain yogurt for dolloping on the pilaf.

Don't use extra-lean ground beef. The small amount of fat from 85 percent lean ground beef adds richness and also carries flavor so the spicy, sweet and herbal notes taste fuller and more complex.

START: In a medium bowl, mix together the beef, tomato paste, cinnamon, turmeric, 1¾ teaspoons salt and 1 teaspoon pepper; set aside. On a 6-quart Instant Pot, select **Normal/Medium Sauté**. Add 1 tablespoon of the oil and the green beans, then cook, stirring occasionally, until browned in spots, 8 to 9 minutes. Transfer to a plate and set aside. Add the remaining 1 tablespoon oil and the beef mixture. Cook, stirring to break up the meat into small pieces, until the beef is no longer pink, 2 to 4 minutes. Press **Cancel**, then stir in the rice and half the raisins. Pour in 1½ cups water; stir to combine, then distribute the mixture in an even layer.

FAST

Lock the lid in place and move the pressure valve to **Sealing**. Select **Pressure Cook** or **Manual**; make sure the pressure level is set to **High**. Set the cooking time for 22 minutes.

When pressure cooking is complete, quick-release the steam by moving the pressure valve to **Venting**. Press **Cancel**, then carefully open the pot.

FINISH: Scatter the green beans and remaining raisins over the surface of the rice mixture. Drape a kitchen towel across the pot and re-cover without locking the lid in place. Let stand for 10 minutes. Fluff the pilaf, stirring in the beans and raisins, then stir in the cilantro. Taste and season with salt and pepper.

JOLLOF RICE WITH SHRIMP

Active time: 30 minutes

Fast start to finish: 1 hour

Servings: 4

2 tablespoons extra-virgin olive oil

1 large yellow onion, chopped

2 medium carrots, peeled, halved lengthwise and thinly sliced

1 medium red bell pepper, stemmed, seeded and chopped

Kosher salt and ground black pepper

2 medium garlic cloves, smashed and peeled

2 tablespoons curry powder

14½-ounce can diced tomatoes

1½ cups basmati rice, rinsed and drained

2 cups low-sodium chicken broth

1 teaspoon dried thyme

12 ounces extra-large (21/25 per pound) shrimp, peeled (tails removed), deveined, halved crosswise and patted dry

1 cup frozen green peas

Jollof is a tomato and rice dish popular throughout West Africa. For our version, we use fragrant basmati rice and flavor it with garlic, curry powder and dried thyme. Shrimp give the dish substance and make it a light meal. If you prefer, you can use an equal amount of medium (41/50 per pound) shrimp; their smaller size means they can be used whole (no need to cut them in half after shelling and deveining).

Don't drain the tomatoes. *Their liquid is necessary for properly cooking the rice. But don't forget to pat the shrimp dry before seasoning them with salt and pepper; excess moisture may make the rice soggy.*

START: On a 6-quart Instant Pot, select **More/High Sauté**. Add the oil and heat until shimmering. Add the onion, carrots, bell pepper and 1 teaspoon salt, then cook, stirring, until the onion is softened and golden brown at the edges, 5 to 7 minutes. Stir in the garlic and curry powder, then cook until fragrant, about 30 seconds. Add the tomatoes with their juices, the rice, broth and thyme; stir to combine then distribute in an even layer.

FAST

Press **Cancel**, lock the lid in place and move the pressure valve to **Sealing**. Select **Pressure Cook** or **Manual**; adjust the pressure level to **Low**. Set the cooking time for 10 minutes. Meanwhile, season the shrimp with salt and black pepper; set aside. When pressure-cooking is complete, quick-release the steam by moving the pressure valve to **Venting**. Press **Cancel**, then carefully open the pot.

FINISH: Scatter the shrimp and peas evenly on the rice, then re-cover without locking the lid in place. Let stand until the shrimp are opaque throughout, about 10 minutes. Fluff the rice, stirring in the shrimp and peas. Taste and season with salt and pepper.

PERUVIAN-STYLE ARROZ CON POLLO

Active time: 20 minutes
Fast start to finish: 1 hour
Servings: 4

2 tablespoons grapeseed or other neutral oil

1½ pounds boneless, skinless chicken thighs, trimmed and quartered

1½ cups long-grain white rice, rinsed and drained

1 small red bell pepper, stemmed, seeded and finely chopped

1 medium carrot, peeled, quartered lengthwise and sliced ¼ inch thick

4 medium garlic cloves, finely chopped

3 scallions, thinly sliced

½ teaspoon ground cumin

Kosher salt

15-ounce can hominy, rinsed and drained (1 cup)

½ cup frozen peas

2 cups lightly packed fresh cilantro leaves and tender stems

2 jalapeño chilies, stemmed, seeded and roughly chopped

Throughout Latin America, there are many versions of arroz con pollo (which translates from Spanish as "rice with chicken"). This is our simplified, Instant Pot take on Peruvian arroz con pollo. The dish gets fresh flavor and bright color from a cilantro-jalapeño puree added only after cooking is complete. Choclo—big, starchy kernels of corn—is traditional, but since it's difficult to find here, we opted for canned hominy, which approximates the flavor and texture of choclo. If you like, serve with sliced red onions for a bit of tang and crunch, and bottled hot sauce for added spiciness.

Don't leave the inner pot in the housing after the pressure has been released and the lid has been removed. We found that the pot's residual heat had a tendency to overcook the grains, so it's best to remove the insert before allowing the rice to rest.

START: In a 6-quart Instant Pot, combine the oil, chicken, rice, bell pepper, carrot, garlic, scallions, cumin, 2 teaspoons salt and 1⅓ cups water. Stir to combine, then distribute in an even layer.

FAST

Lock the lid in place and move the pressure valve to **Sealing**. Select **Pressure Cook** or **Manual**; adjust the pressure level to **Low**. Set the cooking time for 10 minutes. When pressure cooking is complete, quick-release the steam by moving the pressure valve to **Venting**. Press **Cancel**, then carefully open the pot.

FINISH: Using potholders, carefully remove the insert from the housing. Without fluffing the rice, scatter the hominy and peas over the top, then drape a kitchen towel across the top and re-cover without locking the lid in place. Let stand for 10 minutes. Meanwhile, in a blender, combine 3 tablespoons water, the cilantro, jalapeños and 1 teaspoon salt. Blend until smooth, about 1 minute, scraping down the blender as needed. Fluff the rice, stirring in the peas and hominy. Add the cilantro puree and fold with a silicone spatula until evenly distributed. Taste and season with salt.

RICE PILAF WITH SWEET CORN AND SHRIMP

Active time: 20 minutes

Fast start to finish: 40 minutes

Servings: 4

4 tablespoons (½ stick) salted butter

2 large shallots, halved and thinly sliced

¾ teaspoon red pepper flakes

2 teaspoons grated lemon zest, plus 2 teaspoons lemon juice

Kosher salt

1½ cups long-grain white rice, rinsed and drained

1 cup fresh or frozen corn kernels

1½ cups low-sodium chicken broth or water

1 pound extra-large (21/25 per pound) or large (26/30 per pound) shrimp, peeled (tails removed), deveined and chopped into ¾-inch pieces

2 cups lightly packed baby arugula (about 1 ounce), roughly chopped

½ cup roasted red peppers, patted dry and diced

This colorful rice pilaf balances sweetness from corn and roasted peppers with briny shrimp and peppery arugula. You can use either fresh or frozen corn. If you prefer fresh, you'll need to cut the kernels from one large or two medium ears to get the 1 cup the recipe calls for. The shrimp, arugula and roasted peppers aren't needed until after pressure cooking is complete; to be efficient, prep these ingredients while the rice-corn mixture cooks. The pilaf is a perfect light main dish for summer.

Don't bother thawing the corn if frozen. The kernels will quickly thaw once added to the pot. Also, don't forget to stir the shrimp into the hot rice mixture after standing for 10 minutes, then let stand for another 5 minutes before finishing the dish. This allows the shrimp to cook evenly.

START: In a 6-quart Instant Pot, select **Normal/Medium Sauté**. Add the butter and let melt. Add the shallots, pepper flakes, lemon zest and 1 teaspoon salt, then cook, stirring occasionally, until the shallots are softened, about 3 minutes. Add the rice and cook, stirring, until the grains turn translucent, about 2 minutes. Add the corn and broth; stir to combine, then distribute in an even layer.

FAST

Press **Cancel**, lock the lid in place and move the pressure valve to **Sealing**. Select **Pressure Cook** or **Manual**; adjust the pressure level to **Low**. Set the cooking time for 13 minutes. When pressure cooking is complete, quick-release the steam by moving the pressure valve to **Venting**. Press **Cancel**, then carefully open the pot.

FINISH: Scatter the shrimp in an even layer on the rice, then drape a kitchen towel across the pot and re-cover without locking the lid in place. Let stand for 10 minutes. Stir the shrimp into the rice mixture, then re-cover with the towel and lid for another 5 minutes. Fluff the mixture, stirring in the arugula, roasted peppers and lemon juice. Taste and season with salt.

MUSHROOM AND HERB RISOTTO

Active time: 25 minutes

**Fast start to finish:
40 minutes**

Servings: 4

6 tablespoons (¾ stick)
salted butter, cut into
1-tablespoon pieces, divided

2 medium shallots, chopped

8 ounces mixed fresh
mushrooms (see note),
tough stems removed,
thinly sliced

1 cup Arborio or
carnaroli rice

2 tablespoons finely
chopped fresh sage

1 cup low-sodium vegetable
broth

1½ ounces Parmesan
cheese, finely grated
(¾ cup), plus more to serve

Kosher salt and ground
black pepper

4 tablespoons sliced fresh
chives (½-inch lengths),
divided

4 teaspoons white balsamic
vinegar

Earthy, meaty mushrooms and fresh herbs pair perfectly with salty, savory Parmesan cheese and the rich creaminess of risotto. We especially liked this dish made with a combination of fresh mushrooms—a mix of shiitakes and oysters was our favorite—but even basic cremini mushrooms yielded delicious results. Serve this as a first course or, with a lemon vinaigrette-dressed salad alongside, as a satisfying light main dish. It also is terrific as an accompaniment to simple roasted or sautéed chicken.

Don't forget to quick-release the pressure. If the pressure is allowed to release naturally, the rice will overcook and turn mushy and gummy.

START: On a 6-quart Instant Pot, select **Normal/Medium Sauté**. Add 2 tablespoons of the butter and let melt. Add the shallots and mushrooms, then cook, stirring occasionally, until the mushrooms have released all of their moisture, about 5 minutes. Add the rice and cook, stirring, until the grains are translucent at the edges, 1 to 2 minutes. Stir in the sage, broth and 1½ cups water, then distribute the mixture in an even layer.

FAST

Press **Cancel**, lock the lid in place and move the pressure valve to **Sealing**. Select **Pressure Cook** or **Manual**; adjust the pressure level to **Low**. Set the cooking time for 3 minutes. When pressure cooking is complete, quick-release the steam by moving the pressure valve to **Venting**. Press **Cancel**, then carefully open the pot.

FINISH: Vigorously stir in the Parmesan and the remaining 4 tablespoons butter, adding the butter one piece at a time. Taste and season with salt, then stir in 3 tablespoons of the chives and the vinegar. Serve sprinkled with the remaining 1 tablespoon chives and with additional Parmesan on the side.

"CLAY POT" CHICKEN AND RICE WITH SHIITAKE MUSHROOMS

Active time: 15 minutes

Fast start to finish: 1 hour 20 minutes

Servings: 4

5 dried shiitake mushrooms (about ½ ounce)

Boiling water

1 pound boneless, skinless chicken thighs, trimmed and cut into 1-inch pieces

3 tablespoons oyster sauce

2 tablespoons soy sauce, plus more to serve

2 teaspoons finely grated fresh ginger

2 teaspoons white sugar

Kosher salt and ground black pepper

1 cup long-grain white rice, rinsed and drained

2 teaspoons grapeseed or other neutral oil

1 cup low-sodium chicken broth

3 scallions, cut into 1-inch lengths on the diagonal

This is a simplified version of a Chinese dish that's traditionally cooked in and served from a clay pot. An Instant Pot makes quick work of cooking the rice and chicken and can even produce a lightly crisped layer of rice on the bottom. Oyster sauce, soy sauce and dried shiitakes add tons of umami, so the dish is rich and satisfying. The mushrooms must soak for about 30 minutes to rehydrate; use this time to complete the other prep. For a complete meal, serve the rice with steamed or stir-fried bok choy.

Don't stir after layering the chicken on top of the rice; this allows the chicken to gently steam rather than simmer directly in the liquid, which would overcook it. Also, don't forget to quick-release the steam immediately after pressure cooking, then remove the pot insert from the unit and let the rice rest before serving. These steps ensure the grains have the proper texture and are not wet and soggy.

START: Place the shiitakes in a small heat-safe bowl and cover with boiling water. Soak until softened, about 30 minutes. Remove the shiitakes, reserving ¼ cup of the liquid. Remove and discard the stems; thinly slice the caps. While the mushrooms soak, in a medium bowl, stir together the chicken, oyster sauce, soy sauce, ginger, sugar, ½ teaspoon each salt and pepper. Set aside.

FAST

In a 6-quart Instant Pot, stir together the rice and oil. Stir in the broth, the reserved mushroom liquid and the sliced mushroom caps. Add the chicken and its marinade in an even layer over the top; do not stir. Lock the lid in place and move the pressure valve to **Sealing**. Select **Pressure Cook** or **Manual**; adjust the pressure level to **Low**. Set the cooking time for 10 minutes. When pressure cooking is complete, quick-release the steam by moving the pressure valve to **Venting**. Press **Cancel**, then carefully open the pot.

FINISH: Select **Less/Low Sauté**. Let the rice cook, undisturbed, until you hear sizzling, 9 to 12 minutes. Press **Cancel** to turn off the pot. Using potholders, carefully remove the insert from the housing. Scatter the scallions over the rice, cover with a kitchen towel and let stand for 10 minutes. Fluff the mixture, stirring in the scallions and chicken. Taste and season with additional soy sauce and pepper.

RISOTTO WITH SAUSAGE AND ARUGULA

Active time: 15 minutes

Fast start to finish: 25 minutes

Servings: 4

5 tablespoons salted butter, cut into 1-tablespoon pieces, divided

1 cup Arborio or carnaroli rice

4 medium garlic cloves, finely chopped

8 ounces sweet or hot Italian sausage, casing removed, sausage broken into ½-inch pieces

1½ ounces Parmesan cheese, finely grated (¾ cup), plus more to serve

Kosher salt and ground black pepper

4 cups (2½ ounces) lightly packed baby arugula, roughly chopped

4 teaspoons white balsamic vinegar

For this easy risotto, the sausage isn't browned, allowing its texture to remain tender even after pressure cooking. Use whichever you prefer, hot or sweet Italian sausage, and if you can purchase it in bulk rather than links, even better, as there's no casing to remove. You can serve this as a first course, but it contains both sausage and arugula, so it also is satisfying as a light main dish. A summer tomato or shaved zucchini salad would be an excellent complement, as would ribbons of radicchio tossed with sliced fresh fennel and a simple vinaigrette.

Don't break the sausage into bits smaller than ½ inch, otherwise it will overcook and dry out.

START: On a 6-quart Instant Pot, select **Normal/Medium Sauté**. Add 1 tablespoon of butter and let melt. Add the rice and garlic, then cook, stirring, until the grains are translucent at the edges, 1 to 2 minutes. Stir in the sausage and 2½ cups water, scraping up any bits stuck to the bottom of the pot, then distribute the mixture in an even layer.

FAST

Press **Cancel**, lock the lid in place and move the pressure valve to **Sealing**. Select **Pressure Cook** or **Manual**; adjust the pressure level to **Low**. Set the cooking time for 3 minutes. When pressure cooking is complete, quick-release the steam by moving the pressure valve to **Venting**. Press **Cancel**, then carefully open the pot.

FINISH: Vigorously stir in the Parmesan, 1 teaspoon pepper and the remaining 4 tablespoons butter, adding the butter one piece at a time. Add the arugula and stir until slightly wilted, about 30 seconds. Taste and season with salt, then stir in the vinegar. Serve sprinkled with pepper and with additional Parmesan on the side.

BEANS

CONTENTS

White Bean Salad with Avocado and Fresh Herbs (p. 79)

BEANS

The thought of soaking, simmering and supervising dried beans has us reaching for a can opener. Using an Instant Pot shaves hours off the process and, just as importantly, means plump, well-seasoned beans are mostly hands-off. No need to stir. No need to make sure the beans are simmering at the proper rate. No need to keep checking that the liquid isn't running low. Switch to slow cook and it's the same carefree routine. Do the prep, lock the lid and return to a perfectly cooked pot of beans.

Beans can be side, starter or supper, and we play up that versatility by starting with simple but flavorful master recipes for black beans, chickpeas and white beans, along with easy variations for their use. They shine refried, made into soups, tucked into hearty salads or turned into dips.

Legumes are a staple in culinary traditions around the world—where they're likely to be the focus of the meal, not served on the side—and we found options that go well beyond basic baked beans. Our recipes include a take on Jamaican split pea stew, Indian-inspired curried chickpeas, and a hearty dish of pinto beans and pork drawn from a dish popular on Mexico's Yucatan Peninsula.

To get beans right, we **balance their mild earthiness with assertive seasonings.** We bloom spices in hot oil to ramp up the flavor in our Indian-spiced kidney bean stew. And bacon and chipotle chilies bring smoky spice to our Mexican-style black beans. We **boost flavor by cooking beans in broth and other flavor-packed liquids.** The beans in our cranberry beans with Spanish chorizo and red cabbage are cooked in chicken broth. And we use tangy cider to add flavor to our lentils with leeks and chives. Meanwhile, we **balance the creamy smoothness of beans with crunchy, tangy texture.** Earthy lentils and bulgur meet crisply caramelized onions, a classic combination from the Levant, while quick-pickled tomatoes provide a fresh, cool contrast to braised cranberry beans.

Using the Instant Pot means **we don't soak overnight.** Some legumes—think lentils and black beans—can go into the pot dry, no pretreatment required. Others, like cranberry or certain types of white beans, do require extra attention. To make sure they're fully cooked we **give thicker-skinned beans five minutes in the pressure cooker,** then drain and rinse them before using. Meanwhile, we **add baking soda to the cooking liquid for softer skins and creamier interiors.** Just a little bit of baking soda pays off handsomely. First, during the 5-minute starter session, the baking soda and salt in the cooking liquid combine with the pectin in the skins to make them more elastic so they can expand without breaking (called blowout). Second, heated baking soda is a strong alkali that strengthens the cell walls of the beans, resulting in beans that are soft and creamy and cook more quickly.

Beans cooked from scratch join the weeknight line-up thanks to the Instant Pot. We skip the long soak and load up on flavor, using broth or water, bold seasonings and a bit of crunch to complement their smooth creaminess.

SIMPLE BLACK BEANS

Active time: 15 minutes

Fast cook time: 1½ hours

Slow cook time:
7¼ to 8¼ hours

Makes 6 cups

2 cups (1 pound) dried black beans, rinsed and drained

1 large white or yellow onion, chopped

1 pint grape or cherry tomatoes

1 head garlic, outer papery skins removed, top third sliced off and discarded

1 tablespoon chili powder

3 bay leaves

Kosher salt

These black beans, inspired by beans we tasted in Oaxaca, Mexico, are flavorful enough to be served as a side dish, or you can use them as a filling for tacos or burritos. The tomatoes melt into the mix, lending sweetness and acidity, as well as a dose of umami that makes the dish taste full and complex. For additional ideas on how to use the beans, see the following recipes.

Don't forget to squeeze the softened garlic cloves from the head into the beans when cooking is complete. Not only does the garlic boost flavor, its creamy consistency gives the beans a little thickness and body.

START: In a 6-quart Instant Pot, combine the beans, onion, tomatoes, garlic, chili powder, bay, 1 teaspoon salt and 5 cups water. Stir to combine, then distribute in an even layer.

FAST

Lock the lid in place and move the pressure valve to **Sealing**. Select **Pressure Cook** or **Manual**; make sure the pressure level is set to **High**. Set the cooking time for 35 minutes. When pressure cooking is complete, allow the pressure to reduce naturally for 20 minutes, then release the remaining steam by moving the pressure valve to **Venting**. Press **Cancel**, then carefully open the pot.

SLOW

Select **More/High Sauté** and bring the mixture to a boil. Press **Cancel**, lock the lid in place and move the pressure valve to **Venting**. Select **Slow Cook** and set the temperature to **Less/Low**. Set the cooking time for 7 to 8 hours; the beans are done when they are fully tender but still hold their shape. Press **Cancel**, then carefully open the pot.

FINISH: Remove and discard the bay. Using tongs, squeeze the garlic cloves from the head into the beans and stir to combine. Taste and season with salt.

BLACK BEAN SOUP

Start to finish: 15 minutes
Servings: 4

We turn basic black beans into a lightly spicy, subtly smoky vegetarian soup. Cornbread or warmed tortillas are excellent accompaniments.

4 cups drained Simple Black Beans, plus 3 cups cooking liquid

1 chipotle chili in adobo, minced

½ cup finely chopped fresh cilantro

2 tablespoons lime juice

Kosher salt and ground black pepper

In a large saucepan over medium, combine the beans, the 3 cups cooking liquid and the chipotle chili. Cook, stirring often, until heated through, 5 to 8 minutes. Off heat, stir in the cilantro and lime juice. Taste and season with salt and pepper.

BLACK BEAN SOUP

REFRIED BLACK BEANS

BLACK BEANS WITH
SWEET CORN

REFRIED BLACK BEANS

Start to finish: 20 minutes
Servings: 4

This recipe takes a full pot of cooked black beans and turns them into full-flavored refried beans; make sure you save the cooking liquid when draining the beans. We prefer the rustic, slightly coarse texture of beans mashed by hand, not pureed in a blender or food processor. Crumbled cotija cheese and chopped fresh cilantro are delicious garnishes.

6 cups Simple Black Beans, drained (cooking liquid reserved), beans returned to the Instant Pot insert

2 tablespoons coconut oil or lard

5 medium garlic cloves, finely chopped

4 teaspoons ground cumin

4 teaspoons ground coriander

1 tablespoon chili powder

Kosher salt and ground black pepper

Using a potato masher or the back of a large spoon, mash the beans until mostly smooth. Add ½ cup of the reserved cooking liquid and vigorously stir until the beans are as smooth as possible.

In a nonstick 12-inch skillet over medium, heat the oil until shimmering. Add the garlic, cumin, coriander and chili powder, then cook, stirring, until fragrant, about 30 seconds. Stir in the mashed beans and cook, stirring often, until beginning to brown, 8 to 10 minutes. Continue to cook and stir, adding additional reserved cooking liquid as needed, until the mixture is thick and creamy, about 5 minutes. Taste and season with salt and pepper.

BLACK BEANS WITH SWEET CORN

Start to finish: 5 minutes
Makes 3 cups

This colorful combination of ingredients can be tucked into tacos, stuffed into quesadillas or used as a topping, along with ripe avocado, on a leafy green salad. These are great warm or at room temperature.

2 cups drained Simple Black Beans

2 roasted red or green peppers, patted dry and thinly sliced

½ cup frozen corn kernels, thawed and patted dry

Kosher salt and ground black pepper

In a medium bowl, stir together the beans, peppers and corn. Taste and season with salt and pepper.

SIMPLE CHICKPEAS

Active time: 15 minutes

Fast start to finish:
1¼ hours

Slow start to finish:
7¼ to 7¾ hours

Makes 6 cups

2 cups (1 pound) dried chickpeas, rinsed and drained

Kosher salt and ground black pepper

½ teaspoon baking soda

4 medium garlic cloves, smashed and peeled

3 bay leaves

We consider basic cooked chickpeas to be a kitchen staple. They can be made into salads, added to soups or stews, stirred into cooked grains or braised vegetables, or even mashed or pureed. This recipe yields a simply seasoned but flavorful pot of tender chickpeas intended for use in other dishes. For a few ideas on how to use the chickpeas, see the following recipes; note that if making the mashed chickpeas, you will need to reserve ½ cup of the chickpea cooking liquid before draining.

Don't season too aggressively with salt and pepper after draining at the end, as the chickpeas likely will be seasoned with additional salt and pepper in whatever dish they are used in.

START: In a 6-quart Instant Pot, stir together the chickpeas, 2 teaspoons salt, the baking soda and 6 cups water, then distribute in an even layer. Lock the lid in place and move the pressure valve to **Sealing**. Select **Pressure Cook** or **Manual**; make sure the pressure level is set to **High**. Set the cooking time for 5 minutes. When pressure cooking is complete, quick-release the steam by moving the pressure valve to **Venting**. Press **Cancel**, then carefully open the pot. Using potholders, carefully remove the insert from the housing and drain the chickpeas in a colander; return the insert to the housing. Rinse the chickpeas under cool water, then return them to the pot. Add the garlic, bay and 6 cups water; stir to combine, then distribute in an even layer.

FAST

Lock the lid in place and move the pressure valve to **Sealing**. Select **Pressure Cook** or **Manual**; make sure the pressure level is set to **High**. Set the cooking time for 20 minutes. When pressure cooking is complete, allow the pressure to reduce naturally for 20 minutes, then release the remaining steam by moving the pressure valve to **Venting**. Press **Cancel**, then carefully open the pot.

SLOW

Select **More/High Sauté** and bring the mixture to a boil. Press **Cancel**, lock the lid in place and move the pressure valve to **Venting**. Select **Slow Cook** and set the temperature to **More/High**. Set the cooking time for 6½ to 7 hours; the chickpeas are done when they are fully tender but still hold their shape. Press **Cancel**, then carefully open the pot.

FINISH: Using potholders, carefully remove the insert from the housing and drain the chickpeas in a colander. Remove and discard the bay and garlic. Taste and season with salt and pepper.

CHICKPEA AND PITA SALAD WITH YOGURT AND MINT

Start to finish: 25 minutes
Servings: 4 to 6

This salad is a simplified version of Levantine fatteh, which typically is made with stale pita bread (we use pita chips instead) and often is eaten for breakfast. If you like, instead of mint, use flat-leaf parsley or a combination of the two herbs.

2 cups Simple Chickpeas

1½ teaspoons ground cumin, divided

Kosher salt and ground black pepper

1 cup plain whole-milk yogurt

¼ cup tahini

2 medium garlic cloves, finely chopped

1 teaspoon grated lemon zest, plus
1 tablespoon lemon juice

¼ cup pine nuts

3 tablespoons salted butter, cut
into 3 pieces

4 cups (6 ounces) pita chips

1½ cups lightly packed fresh mint,
torn if large

In a medium bowl, toss the chickpeas with 1 teaspoon of cumin and 1 teaspoon salt. In a small bowl, whisk together the yogurt, tahini, garlic, lemon zest and juice, ½ teaspoon salt and ¼ teaspoon pepper.

In a small skillet over medium, toast the pine nuts, stirring often, until light golden brown and fragrant, 3 to 4 minutes. Remove from the heat and add the butter, the remaining ½ teaspoon cumin and ¼ teaspoon each salt and pepper, then stir until the butter is melted. Set aside.

Place the pita chips in a shallow serving bowl, then scatter on the chickpeas. Spoon on the yogurt mixture, then top with mint and the pine nut–butter mixture.

CHICKPEAS AND CUCUMBERS WITH CHUTNEY VINAIGRETTE

Start to finish: 20 minutes
Servings: 6

This is our version of the South Asian street food known as chickpea (chana) chaat. It's a good appetizer or side to grilled meats or seafood. For convenience, for the dressing we use store-bought tamarind chutney (look in the international aisle) and spike it with brown sugar, lime juice and hot sauce.

6 cups Simple Chickpeas

1 small red onion, finely chopped

2 teaspoons curry powder

Kosher salt and ground black pepper

⅓ cup tamarind chutney

1½ tablespoons hot sauce (such as Tabasco), plus more as needed

3 tablespoons lime juice, plus lime wedges, to serve

2 tablespoons packed brown sugar

3 cups (4 ounces) fried wonton strips

1 English cucumber, quartered lengthwise and cut crosswise into ¼-inch pieces

1 cup lightly packed fresh cilantro leaves

In a large bowl, toss the chickpeas with the onion, curry powder, 2 teaspoons salt and 1 teaspoon pepper; set aside. In a small bowl, combine the chutney, hot sauce, lime juice and sugar, then whisk until the sugar dissolves. Taste and season with more hot sauce, if desired.

Pour the chutney mixture over the chickpeas and stir. Toss in the wonton strips, cucumber and half the cilantro. Taste and season with salt and pepper. Sprinkle with the remaining cilantro and serve with lime wedges.

CHICKPEAS AND CUCUMBERS
WITH CHUTNEY VINAIGRETTE

CHICKPEA AND PITA SALAD
WITH YOGURT AND MINT

MASHED CHICKPEAS
WITH SCALLIONS AND LEMON

MASHED CHICKPEAS WITH SCALLIONS AND LEMON

Start to finish: 25 minutes
Servings: 6

Spiced with garam masala and turmeric, this is an excellent side dish to grilled or roasted chicken, lamb or seafood. Make sure to reserve ½ cup of the cooking liquid before draining, as it's used to thin the chickpeas after they're mashed and heated.

6 cups Simple Chickpeas, plus
½ cup reserved cooking liquid

1 tablespoon garam masala

2 teaspoons ground turmeric

¼ teaspoon cayenne pepper

1 bunch scallions, thinly sliced, white and green parts reserved separately

4 tablespoons extra-virgin olive oil, divided, plus more to serve

2 teaspoons grated lemon zest, plus ¼ cup lemon juice, plus lemon wedges to serve

Kosher salt and ground black pepper

In a large bowl, use a potato masher to mash 1 cup of the chickpeas. Stir in the remaining whole chickpeas, the garam masala, turmeric, cayenne and scallion whites.

In a nonstick 12-inch skillet over medium-high, heat 2 tablespoons of oil until barely smoking. Add about half of the chickpea mixture and cook, stirring occasionally, until heated through, 2 to 3 minutes. Transfer to a large bowl and cover with foil to keep warm. Repeat with remaining oil and the remaining chickpea mixture.

Add the reserved chickpea cooking liquid and lemon juice and zest, then stir to combine. Taste and season with salt and pepper. Sprinkle with the scallion greens and drizzle with additional oil.

SIMPLE WHITE BEANS

Active time: 20 minutes

Fast start to finish: 1½ hours

Slow start to finish: 7¼ to 7¾ hours

Makes 6 cups

2½ cups (1 pound) dried cannellini beans (see note), rinsed and drained

Kosher salt and ground black pepper

½ teaspoon baking soda

2 tablespoons extra-virgin olive olive oil

1 medium yellow onion, chopped

4 medium garlic cloves, smashed and peeled

3 bay leaves

2 tablespoons chopped fresh sage

Firm yet creamy cooked white beans are amazingly versatile. With a mild, subtly sweet flavor they can be made into salads or sides, are excellent additions to soups and stews, add substance to pasta dishes or can be pureed into silky-smooth dips. Cannellini, one of the larger and more common white bean varieties, is our favorite and the type we call for in this recipe. But small white beans such as navy and great northern work, too. Smaller beans require the same pre-treatment as larger beans, but if pressure cooking, set the cooking time for 12 minutes, or if slow cooking, set the cooking time for 6 to 6½ hours. For a few easy ways to use the cooked beans, see the following recipes.

Don't season too aggressively with salt and pepper after draining at the end, as the beans *likely will be seasoned with additional salt and pepper in whatever dish they are used in.*

START: In a 6-quart Instant Pot, stir together the beans, 2 teaspoons salt, the baking soda and 6 cups water, then distribute in an even layer. Lock the lid in place and move the pressure valve to **Sealing**. Select **Pressure Cook** or **Manual**; make sure the pressure level is set to **High**. Set the cooking time for 5 minutes. When pressure cooking is complete, quick-release the steam by moving the pressure valve to **Venting**. Press **Cancel**, then carefully open the pot. Using potholders, carefully remove the insert from the housing and drain the beans in a colander; return the insert to the housing. Rinse the beans under cool water; set aside.

Select **More/High Sauté** on the Instant Pot. Add the oil and heat until shimmering. Add the onion, garlic, bay, sage and 1 teaspoon salt, then cook, stirring occasionally, until the onion is softened, about 5 minutes. Return the beans to the pot and add 6 cups water; stir, then distribute in an even layer.

FAST

Press **Cancel**, lock the lid in place and move the pressure valve to **Sealing**. Select **Pressure Cook** or **Manual**; make sure the pressure level is set to **High**. Set the cooking time for 16 minutes. When pressure cooking is complete, allow the pressure to reduce naturally for 20 minutes, then release the remaining steam by moving the pressure valve to **Venting**. Press **Cancel**, then carefully open the pot.

SLOW

With the pot still on **More/High Sauté**, bring the mixture to a boil. Press **Cancel**, lock the lid in place and move the pressure valve to **Venting**. Select **Slow Cook** and set the temperature to **More/High**. Set the cooking time for 6½ to 7 hours; the beans are done when they are fully tender but still hold their shape. Press **Cancel**, then carefully open the pot.

FINISH: Using potholders, carefully remove the insert from the housing and drain the beans in a colander. Remove and discard the garlic and bay. Taste and season with salt and pepper.

WHITE BEAN SALAD WITH AVOCADO AND FRESH HERBS

Start to finish: 20 minutes
Servings: 4 to 6

This colorful salad pairs the creaminess of white beans and avocado with the crunch of red onion and the grassy notes of fresh herbs. Make sure the beans are still hot when they're dressed; this helps them better absorb the seasonings, and their heat will soften the onion slightly.

6 cups Simple White Beans, still hot

2 medium garlic cloves, finely chopped

1 small red onion, halved and thinly sliced

⅓ cup red wine vinegar

3 tablespoons extra-virgin olive oil, plus more to serve

Kosher salt and ground black pepper

1 ripe avocado, halved, pitted, peeled and chopped

1 cup lightly packed flat-leaf parsley, torn if large

½ cup lightly packed fresh dill, chopped

1 teaspoon grated lemon zest, plus 1 teaspoon lemon juice

To the hot beans, add the garlic, onion, vinegar, oil, 2 teaspoons salt and ¾ teaspoon pepper; toss to combine. Let stand for 5 minutes. Stir the beans, then stir in the avocado, parsley, dill and lemon zest and juice. Taste and season with salt and pepper. Transfer to a serving bowl and drizzle with additional oil.

WHITE BEAN DIP
WITH ROASTED RED PEPPERS

Start to finish: 15 minutes
Makes 2 cups

Be sure to pat dry the roasted peppers before adding them to the food processor; this will prevent excess moisture from diluting the dip. Serve with pita chips or crudités.

1 tablespoon chopped fresh mint

1 tablespoon chopped fresh flat-leaf parsley

2 cups Simple White Beans

2 teaspoons grated lemon zest, plus 2 tablespoons lemon juice

½ cup drained roasted red peppers, patted dry

2 tablespoons extra-virgin olive oil, plus more to serve

2 medium garlic cloves

½ teaspoon sweet paprika, plus more to serve

Kosher salt and ground black pepper

In a small bowl, toss together the mint, parsley and lemon zest. In a food processor, combine the beans, lemon juice, roasted peppers, oil, garlic, paprika, 2 teaspoons salt and ¼ teaspoon pepper, then puree until smooth, about 30 seconds, scraping the bowl as needed. Transfer to a serving bowl. Sprinkle with additional paprika, drizzle with oil and top with the herbs.

WHITE BEAN SALAD WITH AVOCADO AND FRESH HERBS

WHITE BEAN DIP WITH ROASTED RED PEPPERS

**WHITE BEANS WITH
CHERRY TOMATOES AND DILL**

WHITE BEANS WITH
CHERRY TOMATOES AND DILL

Start to finish: 15 minutes
Servings: 4 to 6

This dish can be served as a side to simply prepared chicken, lamb or shrimp. Or offer it as a light vegetarian main with crusty bread and a leafy salad alongside.

3 tablespoons extra-virgin olive oil,
plus more to serve

1 medium yellow onion, chopped

2 carrots, peeled, halved and thinly sliced

1 pint cherry or grape tomatoes

Kosher salt and ground black pepper

4 medium garlic cloves, finely chopped

½ teaspoon red pepper flakes

2 cups Simple White Beans

¼ cup finely chopped fresh dill

2 ounces feta cheese, crumbled (½ cup)

Lemon wedges, to serve

In a nonstick 12-inch skillet over medium-high, heat the oil until shimmering. Stir in the onion, carrots, tomatoes and 1 teaspoon salt. Cover and cook, stirring occasionally, until the tomatoes begin to burst and the vegetables are tender, about 10 minutes. Add the garlic and pepper flakes, then cook, stirring, until fragrant, about 30 seconds. Reduce to medium, stir in the beans and cook, stirring occasionally, until heated through, about 2 minutes. Remove from the heat, then stir in half the dill. Taste and season with salt and black pepper, then transfer to a serving bowl. Top with the feta and the remaining dill and drizzle with additional oil. Serve with lemon wedges.

CIDER-BRAISED LENTILS
WITH LEEKS AND CHIVES

Active time: 30 minutes

**Fast start to finish:
1¼ hours**

Slow start to finish:
4½ to 5½ hours

Servings: 6

4 tablespoons (½ stick) salted butter

3 medium-large leeks, white and light green parts thinly sliced, rinsed and dried

2 medium garlic cloves, finely chopped

1½ teaspoons fresh thyme leaves, minced

1 medium Granny Smith apple, peeled, cored and finely chopped

Kosher salt and ground black pepper

2½ cups lentils du Puy, rinsed and drained

3 cups apple cider

1 bunch chives, thinly sliced

1 to 2 tablespoons balsamic vinegar (optional)

Lentils du Puy, also called French green lentils, are the variety to use in this hearty side dish. They hold their shape and retain a firm yet tender texture even under the intensity of pressure cooking. We cook them in apple cider, with a fresh Granny Smith thrown in for brightness and acidity; leeks and chives balance the dish with savory onion notes. These lentils are a terrific accompaniment to grilled or roasted salmon, pork or sausages.

Don't forget to wash and dry the leeks after slicing them; their many layers trap sand and grit.

START: On a 6-quart Instant Pot, select **More/High Sauté**. Add the butter and melt. Add the leeks and cook, stirring occasionally, until lightly browned, 5 to 7 minutes. Stir in the garlic, thyme, apple, 2 teaspoons salt and ¼ teaspoon pepper. Cook, stirring, until fragrant, about 30 seconds. Add the lentils, cider and 2 cups water; stir to combine, then distribute in an even layer.

FAST

Press **Cancel**, lock the lid in place and move the pressure valve to **Sealing**. Select **Pressure Cook** or **Manual**; make sure the pressure level is set to **High**. Set the cooking time for 8 minutes. When pressure cooking is complete, allow the pressure to reduce naturally for 10 minutes, then release the remaining steam by moving the pressure valve to **Venting**. Press **Cancel**, then carefully open the pot.

SLOW

With the pot still on **More/High Sauté**, bring the mixture to a boil. Lock the lid in place and move the pressure valve to **Venting**. Select **Slow Cook** and set the temperature to **Less/Low**. Set the cooking time for 4 to 5 hours; the lentils are done when they are fully tender but still hold their shape. Press **Cancel**, then carefully open the pot.

FINISH: Stir in the chives and balsamic vinegar (if using), then taste and season with salt and pepper. Serve hot, warm or at room temperature.

JAMAICAN-STYLE YELLOW SPLIT PEA SOUP

Active time: 20 minutes

Fast start to finish: 1 hour

Slow start to finish: 6¼ to 7¼ hours

Servings: 4 to 6

2 tablespoons coconut oil, preferably unrefined

1 large yellow onion, finely chopped

6 medium garlic cloves, finely chopped

1 teaspoon dried thyme

1 teaspoon ground allspice

1 habanero or Scotch bonnet chili, stemmed

1½ quarts low-sodium chicken broth

1½ cups yellow split peas, rinsed and drained

3 medium carrots, peeled, halved lengthwise and thinly sliced

Kosher salt and ground black pepper

1 tablespoon ground turmeric

¼ cup finely chopped fresh cilantro

Lime wedges, to serve

This mildly spicy soup is a lighter, brighter version of a Jamaican split pea stew typically flavored with salted pork. Unrefined coconut oil lends subtle coconut notes, but regular refined coconut oil works fine. To make the dish vegetarian, use water instead of chicken broth. Though unconventional, we liked the soup garnished with a spoonful of plain yogurt.

Don't chop or mince the chili *or the soup will be too spicy. Don't forget to remove and discard the chili before serving.*

START: On a 6-quart Instant Pot, select **More/High Sauté**. Add the oil and heat until shimmering. Add the onion and cook, stirring often, until softened and golden brown at the edges, 5 to 7 minutes. Stir in the garlic, thyme and allspice, then cook until fragrant, about 30 seconds. Add the chili, broth and split peas; stir to combine, then distribute in an even layer.

FAST

Press **Cancel**, lock the lid in place and move the pressure valve to **Sealing**. Select **Pressure Cook** or **Manual**; make sure the pressure level is set to **High**. Set the cooking time for 18 minutes. When pressure cooking is complete, quick-release the steam by moving the pressure valve to **Venting**. Press **Cancel**, then carefully open the pot.

SLOW

With the pot still on **More/High Sauté**, bring the mixture to a boil. Press **Cancel**, lock the lid in place and move the pressure valve to **Venting**. Select **Slow Cook** and set the temperature to **More/High**. Set the cooking time for 6 to 7 hours; the soup is done when the split peas have completely broken down. Press **Cancel**, then carefully open the pot.

FINISH: Stir the split pea mixture, scraping the bottom of the pot, then stir in the carrots. Select **More/High Sauté** and cook, stirring occasionally, until the carrots are tender, about 5 minutes. Press **Cancel** to turn off the pot. Let stand for 10 minutes, then whisk in the turmeric and cilantro. Remove and discard the chili. Taste and season with salt and pepper.

TUNISIAN BRAISED CHICKPEAS WITH SWISS CHARD

Active time: 35 minutes

Fast start to finish:
2 hours

Slow start to finish:
7 to 7½ hours

Servings: 4 to 6

2 tablespoons extra-virgin olive oil, plus more to serve

1 medium yellow onion, chopped

2 tablespoons tomato paste

6 medium garlic cloves, smashed and peeled

1 tablespoon ground coriander

1 tablespoon cumin seeds

½ teaspoon ground allspice

½ teaspoon red pepper flakes

3 cups low-sodium chicken broth, or water

28-ounce can whole peeled tomatoes, crushed by hand

2 cups (1 pound) dried chickpeas, rinsed and drained

1 bunch Swiss chard, stems finely chopped, leaves roughly chopped

Kosher salt and ground black pepper

Lemon wedges, to serve

This wholesome but hearty dish was inspired by a recipe in "Mediterranean Cooking" by Paula Wolfert, an expert on North African and Mediterranean cuisines. We don't pre-soak the dried chickpeas for this recipe; they take a little longer to cook, but their texture remains slightly firmer and offers a more appealing textural contrast to the tender Swiss chard. Use rainbow chard if you can find it—the vibrant stems add color to the dish. This is an excellent side to roasted or grilled chicken or lamb, or serve it as a main along with warmed flatbread and couscous or rice.

Don't leave lots of water clinging to the chard after washing the leaves. Drain well so there won't be excess moisture to dilute the flavor and consistency of the stew.

START: On a 6-quart Instant Pot, select **More/High Sauté**. Add the oil and heat until shimmering, then add the onion and cook, stirring occasionally, until softened, about 3 minutes. Add the tomato paste and cook, stirring, until the paste begins to brown, about 2 minutes. Stir in the garlic, coriander, cumin, allspice and pepper flakes, then cook until fragrant, about 30 seconds. Stir in the broth, the tomatoes with their juices and the chickpeas, then distribute in an even layer.

FAST

Press **Cancel**, lock the lid in place and move the pressure valve to **Sealing**. Select **Pressure Cook** or **Manual**; make sure the pressure level is set to **High**. Set the cooking time for 50 minutes. When pressure cooking is complete, allow the pressure to reduce naturally for 15 minutes, then release the remaining steam by moving the pressure valve to **Venting**. Press **Cancel**, then carefully open the pot.

SLOW

With the pot still on **More/High Sauté**, bring the mixture to a boil. Press **Cancel**, lock the lid in place and move the pressure valve to **Venting**. Select **Slow Cook** and set the temperature to **More/High**. Set the cooking time for 6½ to 7 hours; the chickpeas are done when they are fully tender but still hold their shape. Press **Cancel**, then carefully open the pot.

FINISH: Select **More/High Sauté**, bring the mixture to a simmer and cook, stirring occasionally, until slightly thickened, about 5 minutes. Add the chard and continue to cook, stirring occasionally, until the chard is tender, about 5 minutes. Press **Cancel** to turn off the pot, then taste and season with salt and pepper. Serve with lemon wedges.

HUMMUS

Active time: 15 minutes

**Fast start to finish:
1½ hours**

Slow start to finish:
6¾ to 7¼ hours

Makes 4 cups

1 cup (about 8 ounces) dried chickpeas, rinsed and drained

½ teaspoon baking soda

Kosher salt

¾ cup toasted tahini (see note), room temperature

3 tablespoons lemon juice

1 to 2 tablespoons extra-virgin olive oil

1 tablespoon chopped fresh flat-leaf parsley

½ teaspoon ground cumin

½ teaspoon sweet paprika

Our Israeli-style hummus has a smooth, almost sour cream-like texture, and since it is not seasoned with raw garlic or laden with excessive olive oil, the headline flavor is the nuttiness of the chickpeas and tahini. Tahini can be found near the peanut butter or in the international aisle at most supermarkets. Look for a brand made from toasted sesame seeds; we like Kevala, but Soom and Aleppo are good, too. Make sure to stir the tahini well before measuring. Like natural peanut butter, it separates on standing. For a few flavorful twists on hummus, see the three recipes for simple toppings that follow.

Don't allow the chickpeas to cool before processing; they puree better warm. And don't stop short of processing for the full 3 minutes during the first stage.

START: In a 6-quart Instant Pot, combine the chickpeas, baking soda, 2 teaspoons salt and 6 cups water. Lock the lid in place and move the pressure valve to **Sealing**. Select **Pressure Cook** or **Manual**; make sure the pressure level is set to **High**. Set the cooking time for 5 minutes. When pressure cooking is complete, quick-release the steam by moving the pressure valve to **Venting**. Press **Cancel**, then carefully open the pot. Using potholders, carefully remove the insert from the housing and drain the chickpeas in a colander; return the insert to the housing. Rinse the chickpeas under cool water and drain well, then return to the pot. Add 6 cups water and distribute the chickpeas in an even layer.

FAST

Lock the lid in place and move the pressure valve to **Sealing**. Select **Pressure Cook** or **Manual**; make sure the pressure level is set to **High**. Set the cooking time for 25 minutes. When pressure cooking is compete, allow the pressure to reduce naturally for 20 minutes, then release the remaining steam by moving the pressure valve to **Venting**. Press **Cancel**, then carefully open the pot.

SLOW

Select **More/High Sauté** and bring to a boil. Press **Cancel**, lock the lid in place and move the pressure valve to **Venting**. Select **Slow Cook** and set the temperature to **More/High**. Set the cooking time for 6½ to 7 hours; the chickpeas are done when they are fully tender but still hold their shape. Press **Cancel**, then carefully open the pot.

FINISH: Set a colander in a large bowl. Using potholders, carefully remove the insert from the housing and pour the chickpeas and liquid into the colander. Reserve ¾ cup of the cooking liquid, then discard the remainder. Let the chickpeas drain for about 1 minute, then transfer them, still warm, to a food processor. Add 1 teaspoon salt, then process for 3 minutes. Stop the machine and add the tahini. Continue to process until the mixture is lightened and very smooth, about 1 minute longer. Scrape the sides and bottom of the processor bowl. With the machine running, pour in the reserved ¾ cup cooking liquid and the lemon juice, then process until combined, 45 to 60 seconds. Taste and season with salt. Transfer the hummus to a shallow serving bowl. Use the back of a spoon to swirl a well in the center. Drizzle with the oil, then sprinkle with the parsley, cumin and paprika.

HUMMUS TOPPINGS

HUMMUS WITH BLACK OLIVES, OREGANO AND LEMON

In a small bowl, combine ½ cup pitted Kalamata olives (chopped), 2 tablespoons fresh oregano (minced), 1 tablespoon grated lemon zest and ½ teaspoon black pepper. After transferring the hummus to a serving bowl, use the back of a spoon to swirl a well in the center. Drizzle with 1 to 2 tablespoons extra-virgin olive oil, then top with the olive mixture.

HUMMUS WITH ROASTED RED PEPPERS AND CAPERS

In a small bowl, combine 1 cup drained roasted red peppers (patted dry and chopped), ¼ cup drained capers (patted dry and chopped) and 1 tablespoon red wine vinegar. Taste and season with kosher salt and black pepper. After transferring the hummus to a serving bowl, use the back of a spoon to swirl a well in the center. Drizzle with 1 to 2 tablespoons extra-virgin olive oil, then top with the roasted pepper mixture.

HUMMUS WITH GRAPES, FETA AND MINT

In a small bowl, stir together 8 ounces seedless red grapes (halved), 1 tablespoon hot sauce, 1 tablespoon white vinegar and 1 teaspoon kosher salt; let stand 15 minutes, then drain. In another small bowl, combine 2 ounces crumbled feta cheese (½ cup), 2 tablespoons extra-virgin olive oil, 1 teaspoon za'atar and ¼ cup finely chopped fresh mint. After transferring the hummus to a serving bowl, use the back of a spoon to swirl a well in the center. Drizzle with 1 to 2 tablespoons extra-virgin olive oil, then top with the grapes, followed by the feta mixture.

CANNELLINI BEANS WITH TOMATOES, BASIL AND PARMESAN

Active time: 20 minutes

Fast start to finish:
2 hours

Slow start to finish:
7 to 7½ hours

Servings: 4 to 6

1 pound (2½ cups) dried cannellini beans (see note), rinsed and drained

Kosher salt and ground black pepper

½ teaspoon baking soda

3 tablespoons extra-virgin olive oil, plus more to serve

1 medium yellow onion, chopped

4 medium garlic cloves, thinly sliced

1 tablespoon fennel seeds

½ teaspoon red pepper flakes

14½-ounce can diced tomatoes

1 piece Parmesan cheese rind (optional), plus shaved Parmesan to serve

½ cup lightly packed fresh basil, torn

These flavorful, creamy beans are comforting and rich, and vegetarian, too. We like to include a chunk of Parmesan rind with the beans as they cook; it infuses the dish with rich, complex flavor. If you don't have a piece of rind, don't worry—the shaved cheese at the end adds plenty of savoriness. We prefer cannellini beans, but smaller white beans such as navy and great northern work, too. Smaller beans require the same pre-treatment as larger beans, but set the cooking time for only 12 minutes if pressure cooking or 6 to 6½ hours if slow cooking. Serve the beans as a side to simply cooked chicken, pork or lamb, or make them into a meal by offering a salad and crusty bread alongside.

Don't prep the basil in advance or it will wilt and discolor. Since it's added at the very end, prep it after the beans are done cooking, while they rest for 10 minutes.

START: In a 6-quart Instant Pot, stir together the beans, 2 teaspoons salt, the baking soda and 6 cups water, then distribute in an even layer. Lock the lid in place and move the pressure valve to **Sealing**. Select **Pressure Cook** or **Manual**; make sure the pressure level is set to **High**. Set the cooking time for 5 minutes. When pressure cooking is complete, quick-release the steam by moving the pressure valve to **Venting**. Press **Cancel**, then carefully open the pot. Using potholders, carefully remove the insert from the housing and drain the beans in a colander; return the insert to the housing. Rinse the beans under cool water, set aside.

Select **More/High Sauté** on the Instant Pot. Add the oil and heat until shimmering. Add the onion, garlic, fennel seeds, pepper flakes and 1 teaspoon salt, then cook, stirring occasionally, until the onion begins to soften, about 3 minutes. Add the tomatoes with their juices and cook, stirring occasionally, until the liquid has almost evaporated, 6 to 7 minutes. Add the beans and Parmesan rind (if using), then stir in 3 cups water; distribute in an even layer.

FAST

Press **Cancel**, lock the lid in place and move the pressure valve to **Sealing**. Select **Pressure Cook** or **Manual**; make sure the pressure level is set to **High**. Set the cooking time for 16 minutes. When pressure cooking is complete, allow the pressure to reduce naturally for 20 minutes, then release the remaining steam by moving the pressure valve to **Venting**. Press **Cancel**, then carefully open the pot.

SLOW

With the pot still on **More/High Sauté**, bring the mixture to a boil. Press **Cancel**, lock the lid in place and move the pressure valve to **Venting**. Select **Slow Cook** and set the temperature to **More/High**. Set the cooking time for 6½ to 7 hours; the beans are done when they are fully tender but still hold their shape. Press **Cancel**, then carefully open the pot.

FINISH: Let stand for about 15 minutes, then remove and discard the Parmesan rind (if used). Taste and season with salt and pepper, then stir in half of the basil. Serve topped with the remaining basil, shaved Parmesan, black pepper and additional oil.

INDIAN-SPICED KIDNEY BEAN STEW

Active time: 25 minutes

Fast start to finish: 1½ hours

Slow start to finish: 7½ to 8 hours

Servings: 4 to 6

2½ cups (1 pound) dried red kidney beans, rinsed and drained

Kosher salt and ground black pepper

½ teaspoon baking soda

3 tablespoons extra-virgin olive oil

1 large yellow onion, halved and thinly sliced

6 medium garlic cloves, finely chopped

3 tablespoons finely grated fresh ginger

2 tablespoons garam masala

1 tablespoon ground cumin

2 teaspoons curry powder

28-ounce can whole peeled tomatoes, drained, 1 cup juices reserved, tomatoes crushed by hand

½ cup finely chopped fresh cilantro

This is our version of the aromatic kidney bean curry called rajma. We season the dish with two spice blends—garam masala and curry powder—along with a good dose of cumin to add earthy notes, so its flavor is complex and robust. Blooming the spices in the oil brings depth and fullness to the dish. You can offer the stew as a part of an Indian meal, but it's hearty enough to be a vegetarian main. If you like, garnish with plain yogurt and serve basmati rice or warmed naan alongside.

Don't adjust the seasoning with salt and pepper until after the bean mixture has simmered for 5 to 8 minutes to reduce and thicken. If seasoned before simmering, the beans may wind up too salty, as the seasonings become more concentrated with reduction.

START: In a 6-quart Instant Pot, stir together the beans, 2 teaspoons salt, the baking soda and 6 cups water. Lock the lid in place and move the pressure valve to **Sealing**. Select **Pressure Cook** or **Manual**; make sure the pressure level is set to **High**. Set the cooking time for 5 minutes. When pressure cooking is complete, quick-release the steam by moving the pressure valve to **Venting**. Press **Cancel**, then carefully open the pot. Using potholders, carefully remove the insert from the housing and drain the beans in a colander; return the insert to the housing. Rinse the beans under cool water; set aside.

Select **More/High Sauté** on the Instant Pot. Add the oil and onion, then cook, stirring occasionally, until the onion begins to brown, about 5 minutes. Add the garlic, ginger, garam masala, cumin and curry powder, then cook, stirring, until fragrant, about 30 seconds. Stir in the tomatoes and reserved juices, scraping up any browned bits. Stir in 3 cups water, the beans and 1½ teaspoons salt, then distribute in an even layer.

FAST

Press **Cancel**, lock the lid in place and move the pressure valve to **Sealing**. Select **Pressure Cook** or **Manual**; make sure the pressure level is set to **High**. Set the cooking time for 15 minutes. When pressure cooking is complete, allow the pressure to reduce naturally for 20 minutes, then release the remaining steam by moving the pressure valve to **Venting**. Press **Cancel**, then carefully open the pot.

SLOW

With the pot still on **More/High Sauté**, bring the mixture to a boil. Press **Cancel**, lock the lid in place and move the pressure valve to **Venting**. Select **Slow Cook** and set the temperature to **More/High**. Set the cooking time for 6½ to 7 hours; the beans are done when they are fully tender but still hold their shape. Press **Cancel**, then carefully open the pot.

FINISH: Stir the beans, then select **More/High Sauté**. Cook, stirring occasionally, until slightly thickened, 5 to 8 minutes. Press **Cancel** to turn off the pot. Let stand for 10 minutes, then stir in the cilantro. Taste and season with salt and pepper.

RED LENTIL AND BULGUR SOUP WITH BROWNED BUTTER AND YOGURT

Active time: 15 minutes

Fast start to finish: 50 minutes

Slow start to finish: 6¼ to 7¼ hours

Servings: 4

¾ cup plain whole-milk yogurt

2 teaspoons grated lemon zest, plus lemon wedges to serve

1 cup lightly packed fresh mint leaves, finely chopped, divided

Kosher salt and ground black pepper

6 tablespoons (¾ stick) salted butter, cut into 1 tablespoon-pieces, divided

1½ cups red lentils, rinsed and drained

¼ cup coarse bulgur

1 large yellow onion, finely chopped

2 medium garlic cloves, finely chopped

3 tablespoons tomato paste

2 tablespoons harissa, plus more to serve

2 tablespoons sweet paprika

Red lentils, which soften and break down during cooking, give this vegetarian soup a rich, pleasantly thick body. The bulgur, on the other hand, keeps its chewiness while adding nutty notes that complement the lentils' earthy flavor. Harissa is a North African spiced chili paste; it lends the soup gentle heat and depth of flavor and also adds to its color. Look for harissa in the international aisle of the supermarket or in Middle Eastern grocery stores. The browned butter and lemon-mint yogurt garnishes are flourishes that transform this humble dish into something special. If the browned butter solidifies while the lentils and bulgur cook, simply melt it in the microwave just before use.

Don't use fine bulgur instead of coarse, as it cooks more quickly and doesn't have the same nutty, nubby texture.

START: In a small bowl, stir together the yogurt, lemon zest, half the mint and ¼ teaspoon each salt and pepper. Cover and refrigerate until ready to serve. On a 6-quart Instant Pot, select **Normal/Medium Sauté**. Add 3 tablespoons of butter and cook, stirring often, until it begins to smell nutty and the milk solids at the bottom begin to brown, 1 to 2 minutes. Press **Cancel** to turn off the pot. Using potholders, carefully remove the insert from the housing and pour the browned butter into a small microwave-safe bowl, scraping out the butter with a silicone spatula. Return the insert to the housing, then add the remaining 2 tablespoons butter, the lentils, bulgur, onion, garlic, tomato paste, harissa, paprika and 2 teaspoons salt. Stir, then pour in 7 cups water and distribute the mixture in an even layer.

FAST

Lock the lid in place and move the pressure valve to **Sealing**. Select **Pressure Cook** or **Manual**; make sure the pressure level is set to **High**. Set the cooking time for 15 minutes. When pressure cooking is complete, quick-release the steam by moving the pressure valve to **Venting**. Press **Cancel**, then carefully open the pot.

SLOW

Select **More/High Sauté** and bring the mixture to a boil. Press **Cancel**, lock the lid in place and move the pressure valve to **Venting**. Select **Slow Cook** and set the temperature to **More/High**. Set the cooking time for 6 to 6½ hours; the soup is done when the lentils are soft and have partially broken down. Press **Cancel**, then carefully open the pot.

FINISH: Stir the soup, scraping the bottom of the pot, then stir in the remaining mint. Taste and season with salt. If the browned butter has solidified, microwave on high until melted, 10 to 15 seconds. Ladle the soup into bowls, drizzle with browned butter and dollop with the yogurt mixture, then sprinkle with additional pepper. Offer lemon wedges and additional harissa on the side.

BRAISED CRANBERRY BEANS
WITH QUICK-PICKLED TOMATOES

Active time: 35 minutes

**Fast start to finish:
1¾ hours**

Slow start to finish:
8 to 8½ hours

Servings: 4 to 6

2 cups (12¾ ounces) dried cranberry beans (see note), rinsed and drained

Kosher salt and ground black pepper

½ teaspoon baking soda

1 pint grape or cherry tomatoes, roughly chopped

1 tablespoon lemon juice, plus lemon wedges to serve

3 tablespoons salted butter

¼ cup tomato paste

1 medium yellow onion, chopped

4 medium garlic cloves, smashed and peeled

2 medium carrots, halved lengthwise and sliced about ½ inch thick

3 medium celery stalks, sliced about ½ inch thick

3 bay leaves

1 cinnamon stick

2 teaspoons dried mint

This dish was inspired in part by a recipe in "Spice," by Ana Sortun, an expert in Mediterranean cuisine. Cranberry beans (also called Roman beans or borlotti beans) are cooked with butter and aromatics, then are finished with quick-pickled tomatoes that add acidity to brighten the earthiness of the beans. Plain yogurt and chopped fresh flat-leaf parsley or dill are excellent, but optional, garnishes. These beans are good as a side dish to roasted or grilled meats, or serve them as a vegetarian main with a cucumber salad and crusty bread alongside.

Don't use double-concentrated tomato paste (the type often sold in a tube), as its strong flavor will overwhelm the other ingredients. Opt instead for regular tomato paste sold in a can.

START: In a 6-quart Instant Pot, stir together the beans, 2 teaspoons salt, the baking soda and 6 cups water. Lock the lid in place and move the pressure valve to **Sealing**. Select **Pressure Cook** or **Manual**; make sure the pressure level is set to **High**. Set the cooking time for 5 minutes. When pressure cooking is complete, quick-release the steam by moving the pressure valve to **Venting**. Press **Cancel**, then carefully open the pot. Using potholders, carefully remove the insert from the housing and drain the beans in a colander; return the insert to the housing. Rinse the beans under cool water; set aside.

In a small bowl, stir together the tomatoes, lemon juice and 1 teaspoon salt; cover and refrigerate until ready to use. Select **Normal/Medium Sauté** on the Instant Pot. Add the butter and let melt. Add the tomato paste, onion, garlic, carrots, celery, bay and cinnamon. Cook, stirring occasionally, until the onion is softened, about 5 minutes. Add the mint, 1 tablespoon salt and 2 teaspoons pepper, scraping up any browned bits. Add the drained beans and 3 cups water; stir to combine, then distribute in an even layer.

FAST

Press **Cancel**, lock the lid in place and move the pressure valve to **Sealing**. Select **Pressure Cook** or **Manual**; make sure the pressure level is set to **High**. Set the cooking time for 25 minutes. When pressure cooking is complete, let the pressure reduce naturally for 20 minutes, then release any remaining steam by moving the pressure valve to **Venting**. Press **Cancel**, then carefully open the pot.

SLOW

Select **More/High Sauté** and bring the mixture to a boil. Press **Cancel**, lock the lid in place and move the pressure valve to **Venting**. Select **Slow Cook** and set the temperature to **More/High**. Set the cooking time for 6½ to 7 hours; the beans are done when they are fully tender but still hold their shape. Press **Cancel**, then carefully open the pot.

FINISH: Remove and discard the bay and cinnamon, then stir in the lemon-pickled tomatoes. Select **More/High Sauté**, bring to a simmer and cook, stirring occasionally, just until the tomatoes begin to soften, about 3 minutes. Press **Cancel** to turn off the pot. Taste and season with salt and pepper. Serve with lemon wedges.

PINTO BEAN AND PORK STEW WITH TOMATOES AND CITRUS

Active time: 20 minutes

Fast start to finish:
2 hours

Slow start to finish:
6½ to 7 hours

Servings: 6

2⅓ cups (1 pound) dried pinto beans, rinsed and drained

Kosher salt and ground black pepper

½ teaspoon baking soda

1 teaspoon ground cumin

4 medium garlic cloves, thinly sliced

1 habanero chili, pierced a few times with a paring knife

1 tablespoon grated lime zest, plus ¼ cup lime juice

2 tablespoons grated orange zest, plus ½ cup orange juice

28-ounce can diced fire-roasted tomatoes

3 tablespoons finely chopped cilantro stems, plus 1 cup lightly packed leaves, reserved separately

1½ pounds boneless country-style pork ribs, trimmed and cut into 1-inch chunks

Sliced radishes, to serve

In the hearty Yucatecan dish called frijoles con puerco, black beans are cooked with chunks of pork. We opted to use creamier-textured, lighter-colored pinto beans and added both lime and orange zests and juices to balance the heft of the stew. The habanero chili, pierced a few times with a knife, infuses the dish with just a touch of heat. If you prefer it spicier, halve the habanero instead; either way, remember to remove the chili before serving. Serve with warmed tortillas or rice, or for a bit of textural contrast, spoon it over tortilla chips. A crumble of queso fresco or a dollop of sour cream are nice finishing touches in addition to the cilantro and radishes.

Don't forget to zest the citrus before juicing. The zest is easier to remove when the fruits are whole. Also, don't use ribs that are very lean, otherwise the meat will end up dry and the stew will lack rich, meaty flavor. Instead, substitute with an equal amount of boneless pork shoulder.

START: In a 6-quart Instant Pot, stir together the beans, 2 teaspoons salt, the baking soda and 6 cups water, then distribute in an even layer. Lock the lid in place and move the pressure valve to **Sealing**. Select **Pressure Cook** or **Manual**; make sure the pressure level is set to **High**. Set the cooking time for 5 minutes. When pressure cooking is complete, quick-release the steam by moving the pressure valve to **Venting**. Press **Cancel**, then carefully open the pot. Using potholders, carefully remove the insert from the housing and drain the beans in a colander; return the insert to the housing. Rinse the beans under cool water and return to the pot. Stir in the cumin, garlic, habanero, lime zest and juice, orange zest and juice, the tomatoes with their juices, the cilantro stems and the pork. Add 2 cups water; stir to combine, then distribute in an even layer.

FAST

Lock the lid in place and move the pressure valve to **Sealing**. Select **Pressure Cook** or **Manual**; make sure the pressure level is set to **High**. Set the cooking time for 25 minutes. When pressure cooking is complete, allow the pressure to release naturally for 20 minutes, then release the remaining steam by moving the pressure valve to **Venting**. Press **Cancel**, then carefully open the pot.

SLOW

Select **More/High Sauté** and bring the mixture to a boil. Press **Cancel**, lock the lid in place and move the pressure valve to **Venting**. Select **Slow Cook** and set the temperature to **More/High**. Set the cooking time for 5½ to 6 hours; the meat and beans are done when a skewer inserted into a chunk of pork meets no resistance and the beans are fully tender but still hold their shape. Press **Cancel**, then carefully open the pot.

FINISH: Remove and discard the habanero. Let stand for about 10 minutes, then taste and season with salt and pepper. Serve topped with the cilantro leaves and sliced radishes.

CURRIED CHICKPEAS
WITH CILANTRO AND SCALLIONS

Active time: 35 minutes

**Fast start to finish:
1¾ hours**

Slow start to finish:
7¼ to 7¾ hours

Servings: 4 to 6

2 cups (1 pound) dried chickpeas, rinsed and drained

Kosher salt and ground black pepper

½ teaspoon baking soda

4-inch piece fresh ginger (about 3 ounces), peeled and cut into 4 pieces

1 serrano chili, stemmed, halved and seeded

6 medium garlic cloves, smashed and peeled

1 tablespoon ground coriander

1 tablespoon ground cumin

1 bunch cilantro, stems and leaves roughly chopped

4 scallions, roughly chopped

3 tablespoons coconut oil

3 tablespoons lime juice, plus lime wedges to serve

Whole-milk yogurt, to serve

This hearty, flavor-packed chickpea curry was inspired by a recipe in "Vegetarian India" by Madhur Jaffrey. A puree of aromatics and spices provides a flavorful base for cooking the chickpeas. But to keep the herbal notes bright and fresh, we add a cilantro-scallion puree only after the chickpeas are fully cooked and have rested for about 10 minutes. The consistency of the curry is best immediately after the herb puree and lime juice have been stirred in; it thickens upon standing and cooling, but it can be thinned with a little water. Serve dolloped with yogurt as a side dish, or offer it as a light vegetarian main along with basmati rice or warmed naan.

Don't bother washing the food processor bowl and blade after processing the ginger, chili, garlic and spices; they can be used straightaway for pureeing the herbs. Don't forget to cover the herb puree with plastic wrap pressed directly against the surface to prevent oxidation.

START: In a 6-quart Instant Pot, stir together the chickpeas, 2 teaspoons salt, the baking soda and 6 cups water, then distribute in an even layer. Lock the lid in place and move the pressure valve to **Sealing**. Select **Pressure Cook** or **Manual**; make sure the pressure level is set to **High**. Set the cooking time for 5 minutes. When pressure cooking is complete, quick-release the steam by moving the pressure valve to **Venting**. Press **Cancel**, then carefully open the pot. Using potholders, carefully remove the insert from the housing and drain the chickpeas in a colander; return the insert to the housing. Rinse the chickpeas under cool water; set aside.

In a food processor, combine the ginger, chili, garlic, coriander and cumin; process until finely chopped, about 1 minute, scraping the bowl as needed. Transfer the mixture to a small bowl. Add the cilantro, scallions and ½ cup water to the now-empty food processor, then process until smooth, about 30 seconds. Transfer to another small bowl, press plastic wrap directly against the surface and refrigerate until ready to use. Select **More/High Sauté** on the Instant Pot. Add the coconut oil and let melt, then add the chili mixture and cook, stirring, until fragrant, about 1 minute. Add the chickpeas, 1½ teaspoons salt and 4 cups water; stir to combine, then distribute in an even layer.

FAST

Press **Cancel**, lock the lid in place and move the pressure valve to **Sealing**. Select **Pressure Cook** or **Manual**; make sure the pressure level is set to **High**. Set the cooking time for 20 minutes. When pressure cooking is complete, allow the pressure to reduce naturally for 20 minutes, then release the remaining steam by moving the pressure valve to **Venting**. Press **Cancel**, then carefully open the pot.

SLOW

With the pot still on **More/High Sauté**, bring the mixture to a simmer. Press **Cancel**, lock the lid in place and move the pressure valve to **Venting**. Select **Slow Cook** and set the temperature to **More/High**. Set the cooking time for 6½ to 7 hours; the chickpeas are done when they are fully tender but still hold their shape. Press **Cancel**, then carefully open the pot.

FINISH: Stir the chickpeas, then select **More/High Sauté** and cook, stirring occasionally, until the liquid is slightly thickened, 8 to 10 minutes. Using potholders, carefully remove the insert from the housing and let stand for about 10 minutes. Stir in the cilantro puree and the lime juice. Taste and season with salt and pepper. Serve with lime wedges and yogurt.

LENTILS AND BULGUR
WITH CARAMELIZED ONIONS

Active time: 30 minutes

Fast start to finish:
1 hour

Slow start to finish:
6 to 6½ hours

Servings: 4 to 6

¼ cup extra-virgin olive oil

2 medium yellow onions, halved and thinly sliced

3 bay leaves

2½ teaspoons ground cumin

½ teaspoon ground allspice

Kosher salt and ground black pepper

1 cup coarse bulgur

1 cup brown lentils, rinsed and drained

4 scallions, thinly sliced

¼ cup chopped fresh flat-leaf parsley

Plain yogurt, to serve

Mujaddara is a Levantine dish that typically pairs fried onions and lentils with rice. In this version, instead of rice, we've used coarse bulgur, or cracked parcooked wheat, which lends a nutty flavor and texture. The onions are fried in olive oil until deeply caramelized—almost burnt—to coax out a savory bittersweet flavor. Served hot, warm or at room temperature, with a dollop of plain yogurt, this is a delicious accompaniment to grilled or roasted meats, but it's also hearty enough to be the center of a vegetarian meal.

Don't worry if the onions caramelize unevenly. A handful of pale slices won't affect the dish's final flavor, but the bulk should be deep, dark brown—almost mahogany. Underbrowned onions won't lend the dish the proper depth of flavor because they lack complex bittersweet notes.

START: On a 6-quart Instant Pot, select **More/High Sauté**. Add the oil and heat until shimmering. Add the onions and cook, stirring occasionally, until deeply browned, about 20 minutes. Transfer about half the onions to a paper towel–lined plate; set aside. Add the bay, cumin, allspice and 2 teaspoons salt to the pot, then cook, stirring, until fragrant, about 30 seconds. Pour in 3 cups water, scraping up any browned bits.

FAST

Stir in the bulgur and lentils, then distribute in an even layer. Press **Cancel**, lock the lid in place and move the pressure valve to **Sealing**. Select **Pressure Cook** or **Manual**; set the pressure level to **Low**. Set the cooking time for 10 minutes. When pressure cooking is complete, quick-release the steam by moving the pressure valve to **Venting**. Press **Cancel**, then carefully open the pot.

SLOW

Stir in the lentils. With the pot still on **More/High Sauté**, bring the mixture to a boil, then stir in the bulgur and distribute in an even layer. Press **Cancel**, lock the lid in place and move the pressure valve to **Venting**. Select **Slow Cook** and set the temperature to **Less/Low**. Set the cooking time for 5½ to 6 hours; the mixture is done when the liquid is absorbed and the lentils are tender. Press **Cancel**, then carefully open the pot.

FINISH: Drape a kitchen towel across the pot and re-cover without locking the lid in place. Let stand for 10 minutes. Open the pot, then fluff the mixture with a fork, removing and discarding the bay. Taste and season with salt and pepper. Transfer to a serving dish and sprinkle with the reserved onions, the scallions and parsley. Serve with yogurt.

BEANS 103

BLACK BEANS WITH
BACON AND TEQUILA

Active time: 30 minutes

Fast start to finish:
1¼ hours

Slow start to finish:
7½ to 8½ hours

Servings: 6

6 slices bacon, roughly
chopped

1 large yellow onion,
finely chopped

10 medium garlic cloves,
finely chopped

1 tablespoon ground cumin

4 chipotle chilies in adobo,
minced, plus 2 tablespoons
adobo sauce

¼ cup tequila (optional)

1¼ quarts low-sodium
chicken broth

2 cups (1 pound) dried black
beans, rinsed and drained

Kosher salt and ground
black pepper

3 tablespoons lime juice,
plus lime wedges to serve

1 tablespoon packed
brown sugar

Chopped fresh cilantro,
to serve

Bacon gives these beans a subtle smokiness, and chipotle chilies add both smoke and spice. If you decide to use the optional tequila, save your top-shelf bottle for sipping; any inexpensive tequila worked well here. Offer the beans as a side to any Tex-Mex or Mexican-style main, or use them as a filling in tacos and burritos. Or make a light meal out of them by serving with rice, sour cream and salsa. Refrigerate leftovers in an airtight container for up to three days; when reheating, thin with broth or water to the desired consistency.

Don't soak the black beans. In the Instant Pot, the unsoaked beans were plump and tender after only 35 minutes of pressure cooking and after 7 to 8 hours of slow cooking. Soaked beans will end up overdone if cooked for the same amount of time.

START: On a 6-quart Instant Pot, select **More/High Sauté**. Add the bacon and cook, stirring, until browned and crisp, 5 to 8 minutes. Using a slotted spoon, transfer to a paper towel–lined plate and set aside. Add the onion to the pot and cook, stirring occasionally, until lightly browned, 6 to 7 minutes. Stir in the garlic and cumin and cook until fragrant, about 30 seconds. Add the minced chipotle chilies and the tequila (if using) and cook, stirring occasionally, until most of the liquid has evaporated, about 3 minutes. Stir in the broth, beans and 1 teaspoon salt.

FAST

Press **Cancel**, lock the lid in place and move the pressure valve to **Sealing**. Select **Pressure Cook** or **Manual**; make sure the pressure level is set to **High**. Set the cooking time for 35 minutes. When pressure cooking is complete, allow the pressure to reduce naturally for 20 minutes, then release the remaining steam by moving the pressure valve to **Venting**. Press **Cancel**, then carefully open the pot.

SLOW

With the pot still on **More/High Sauté**, bring the mixture to a boil. Press **Cancel**, lock the lid in place and move the pressure valve to **Venting**. Select **Slow Cook** and set the temperature to **Less/Low**. Set the cooking time for 7 to 8 hours; the beans are done when they are fully tender. Press **Cancel**, then carefully open the pot.

FINISH: Select **Normal/Medium Sauté** and cook, stirring occasionally, until the liquid is slightly thickened, about 5 minutes. Stir in the adobo sauce, lime juice, sugar and reserved bacon. Taste and season with salt and pepper. Serve sprinkled with cilantro and with lime wedges on the side.

CRANBERRY BEANS WITH
SPANISH CHORIZO AND RED CABBAGE

Active time: 35 minutes

Fast start to finish:
1¾ hours

Slow start to finish:
7½ to 8 hours

Servings: 6

2½ cups (1 pound) dried cranberry beans (see note), rinsed and drained

Kosher salt and ground black pepper

½ teaspoon baking soda

2 tablespoons extra-virgin olive oil

6 ounces Spanish chorizo, casing removed, quartered lengthwise and sliced ¼ inch thick

1 large yellow onion, finely chopped

1 tablespoon sweet paprika

1 teaspoon smoked paprika

½ teaspoon red pepper flakes

1 teaspoon dried oregano

1½ quarts low-sodium chicken broth

½ small head red cabbage (8 ounces), cored and finely chopped (4 cups)

This is a simplified take on a Spanish dish called alubias rojas con sacramentos. Instead of using multiple varieties of cured pork, as is traditional, we use only chorizo and heighten the flavor of the beans by cooking them in chicken broth. We also add both sweet and smoked paprika. Cranberry beans are approximately the size of kidney beans, but with a mottled reddish brown and white coloration; they're also known as Roman beans or borlotti beans.

Don't use fresh Mexican chorizo, as it has a different flavor and texture. Dry-cured Spanish chorizo, which typically is sold in small links and is firm like salami, is the correct type of sausage for this recipe.

START: In a 6-quart Instant Pot, stir together the beans, 2 teaspoons salt, the baking soda and 6 cups water. Lock the lid in place and move the pressure valve to **Sealing**. Select **Pressure Cook** or **Manual**; make sure the pressure level is set to **High**. Set the cooking time for 5 minutes. When pressure cooking is complete, quick-release the steam by moving the pressure valve to **Venting**. Press **Cancel**, then carefully open the pot. Using potholders, carefully remove the insert from the housing and drain the beans in a colander; return the insert to the housing. Rinse the beans under cool water; set aside.

Select **More/High Sauté** on the Instant Pot. Add the oil and chorizo and cook, stirring occasionally, until the chorizo releases its fat and begins to brown, about 5 minutes. Add the onion and cook, stirring occasionally, until the onion is lightly browned, 6 to 8 minutes. Stir in both paprikas, the pepper flakes and oregano, then cook until fragrant, about 30 seconds. Stir in the broth and beans, then distribute in an even layer.

FAST

Press **Cancel**, lock the lid in place and move the pressure valve to **Sealing**. Select **Pressure Cook** or **Manual**; make sure the pressure level is set to **High**. Set the cooking time for 25 minutes. When pressure cooking is complete, allow the pressure to reduce naturally for 20 minutes, then release the remaining steam by moving the pressure valve to **Venting**. Press **Cancel**, then carefully open the pot

SLOW

With the pot still on **More/High Sauté**, bring the mixture to a boil. Press **Cancel**, lock the lid in place and move the pressure valve to **Venting**. Select **Slow Cook** and set the temperature to **More/High**. Set the cooking time for 6½ to 7 hours; the beans are done when they are fully tender but still hold their shape. Press **Cancel**, then carefully open the pot

FINISH: Stir the beans, then select **More/High Sauté**. Stir in the cabbage and cook, stirring occasionally, until the cabbage is tender, 5 to 8 minutes. Press **Cancel** to turn off the pot. Let stand for 15 minutes, then taste and season with salt and pepper.

ONE-POT PASTAS

CONTENTS

Orecchiette with Sardinian Sausage Ragu (p. 120)

ONE-POT PASTAS

When we use the Instant Pot to make pasta we're not necessarily saving time; stovetop pasta often is quite speedy. But we do get a big assist in flavor and efficiency. Because the noodles cook directly in the sauce they absorb flavor as they cook. Meanwhile, liquids and sauces reduce for boldness and a better consistency. We get less cleanup and no worries about timing noodles and sauce to finish together.

The **slow-cooker is a no-go for pasta,** the noodles fall apart over time. And when cooking pasta in a pressure cooker, **the pasta should be submerged in the liquid; long strands, like spaghetti, need to be broken in half and laid flat.** We **stay away from subbing one pasta shape for another;** that can throw off cooking times. If you do make a substitution, make sure the pasta has a similar cooking time to the variety of noodle specified in the recipe.

The best sauces provide a strong counterpoint to the warm and neutral foundation of the noodles, and we **opt for one-stroke flavor boosters** to get that contrast without a lot of effort. Capers and olives flavor our spaghetti puttanesca—we learned in Naples that those ingredients, not anchovies, are what give the sauce its briny punch. We take the same approach to our version of macaroni and cheese. Macaroni refers to pasta shaped like tubes and we use the cavatappi type; it's named after the Italian word for corkscrew. We load up on the cheese, using asiago, fontina and Parmesan and add a little cornstarch and heavy cream to create a rich sauce. Plenty of black pepper and some fresh basil add a fresh and mildly spicy finish.

Pasta and tomato sauce are natural partners and we make one using fresh cherry or grape tomatoes. No need to simmer the tomatoes—or boil the noodles in a separate pan—the pasta cooks at the same time the tomatoes gently break down to a tangy-sweet sauce.

We **pair legumes with pasta to create simple but satisfyingly hearty dishes.** Kidney beans add earthy heft to our toasted pearl couscous with butternut squash and feta, and lentils du Puy pair with short pasta in our pasta with spicy tomato-lentil sauce, inspired by Italy's pasta e lenticchie.

We **keep hands-on time to a minimum.** Most of our recipes require 30 minutes of active work and some are real speed demons. Our spaghetti with goat cheese, mint and peas takes just 15 minutes' effort.

Cooking pasta in the Instant Pot means more flavor,
less cleanup. We cook the noodles in the sauce—
no boiling, no draining, no problem.

SPAGHETTI PUTTANESCA

Active time: 25 minutes

Start to finish: 45 minutes

Servings: 4 to 6

3 tablespoons extra-virgin olive oil, divided

4 medium garlic cloves, finely chopped

1 teaspoon red pepper flakes

1 cup pitted Kalamata olives, roughly chopped

½ cup drained capers (two 4-ounce bottles)

28-ounce can whole peeled tomatoes, drained, 1 cup juices reserved, tomatoes crushed by hand

1 pound spaghetti, broken in half

½ cup chopped fresh basil

1 ounce Parmesan cheese, finely grated (½ cup)

Kosher salt and ground black pepper

Most of us think of puttanesca as a tomato sauce built on anchovies. But in Naples, where it originates, the bold savoriness comes from briny olives and pungent capers. We call for a generous amount of capers, which often are sold in small bottles or jars. When shopping, you will need to buy two 4-ounce bottles to get the ½ cup drained capers needed for this recipe.

Don't forget to save 1 cup of the juices when you drain the tomatoes. They, along with 4 cups of water, are the liquid that cooks the pasta.

START: On a 6-quart Instant Pot, select **More/High Sauté**. Add 2 tablespoons of oil, the garlic and pepper flakes, then cook, stirring, until fragrant, about 30 seconds. Add the olives and capers, then cook, stirring, until the capers begin to brown, about 1 minute. Add the tomatoes and cook, stirring occasionally, until most of the liquid has evaporated, about 8 minutes. Stir in the reserved tomato juices and 4 cups water, then distribute the mixture in an even layer. Add the pasta, placing the strands horizontally so they lay flat, then press them into the liquid until submerged.

FAST

Press **Cancel**, lock the lid in place and move the pressure valve to **Sealing**. Select **Pressure Cook** or **Manual**; make sure the pressure level is set to **High**. Set the cooking time for 3 minutes. When pressure cooking is complete, quick-release the steam by moving the pressure valve to **Venting**. Press **Cancel**, then carefully open the pot.

FINISH: Select **More/High Sauté**. Stir the mixture to combine, then cook until the pasta is al dente and most of the liquid has been absorbed, 3 to 4 minutes. Press **Cancel** to turn off the pot. Using potholders, carefully remove the insert from the housing. Let stand for 5 minutes. Stir in the basil, Parmesan and the remaining 1 tablespoon oil. Taste and season with salt and black pepper.

LEMONY ORZO WITH CHICKEN AND ARUGULA

Active time: 25 minutes
Start to finish: 45 minutes
Servings: 4

3 tablespoons extra-virgin olive oil

1 medium yellow onion, halved and thinly sliced

Kosher salt and ground black pepper

6 medium garlic cloves, finely chopped

½ cup dry white wine

12 ounces boneless, skinless chicken thighs, trimmed and cut into ¾-inch pieces

1 cup orzo pasta

1¾ cups low-sodium chicken broth

½ cup chopped fresh mint

3 cups lightly packed baby arugula (about 2 ounces), roughly chopped

1 tablespoon grated lemon zest, plus 1 tablespoon lemon juice

Crumbled feta cheese, to serve

Orzo means "barley" in Italian, but it also is the name of the pasta that resembles grains of rice. In this dish, we've paired orzo with chicken and greens, turning it into a light but complete one-pot meal. Feel free to substitute an equal amount of baby spinach for the arugula. And if you prefer tangy, creamy fresh goat cheese (chèvre) to briny feta, it's also a delicious way to top the pasta.

Don't use chicken breasts instead of thighs, as the meat will end up tough and dry. But don't cut the thighs into pieces larger than ¾ inch or they may not fully cook.

START: On a 6-quart Instant Pot, select **More/High Sauté**. Add the oil, onion and ½ teaspoon salt, then cook, stirring occasionally, until the onion begins to brown, 8 to 10 minutes. Stir in the garlic and cook until fragrant, about 30 seconds. Add the wine and cook, stirring, until almost fully evaporated, about 5 minutes. Add the chicken, orzo and broth; stir to combine, then distribute in an even layer.

FAST

Press **Cancel**, lock the lid in place and move the pressure valve to **Sealing**. Select **Pressure Cook** or **Manual**; make sure the pressure level is set to **High**. Set the cooking time for 6 minutes. When pressure cooking is complete, quick-release the steam by moving the pressure valve to **Venting**. Press **Cancel**, then carefully open the pot.

FINISH: Stir the mixture to combine, then re-cover without locking the lid in place and let stand for 5 minutes. Stir in the mint, arugula and lemon zest and juice. Taste and season with salt and pepper. Serve topped with feta.

PASTA ALL'AMATRICIANA

Active time: 35 minutes
Start to finish: 1 hour
Servings: 4 to 6

3 tablespoons extra-virgin olive oil, divided

3 ounces thinly sliced pancetta, finely chopped

10 medium garlic cloves, thinly sliced

½ teaspoon red pepper flakes

¾ cup dry white wine

28-ounce can whole peeled tomatoes, drained, 1 cup juices reserved, tomatoes crushed by hand

1 pound spaghetti, broken in half

1-ounce chunk pecorino Romano cheese without rind, plus more finely grated, to serve

Kosher salt and ground black pepper

This classic dish from the town of Amatrice in central Italy traditionally is prepared with guanciale (cured pork cheek), but more widely available pancetta is a good substitute. Be sure to purchase thinly sliced pancetta and chop it finely to ensure the pieces crisp with cooking. For a big boost of savory flavor, we cook a chunk of pecorino Romano cheese directly in the sauce; it softens with pressure-cooking, then is stirred until fully blended into the mix. Offer additional pecorino, finely grated, at the table for sprinkling to taste.

Don't forget to save 1 cup of the juices when you drain the tomatoes. The juices, along with 4 cups of water, are the liquid that cooks the pasta. Don't worry if the spaghetti isn't fully cooked when you open the pot; it will reach al dente during uncovered cooking.

START: On a 6-quart Instant Pot, select **More/High Sauté**. Add 1 tablespoon of oil and the pancetta. Cook, stirring occasionally, until the pancetta is well-browned and crisp, 5 to 6 minutes. Using a slotted spoon, transfer to a paper towel–lined plate; set aside. Add the garlic and pepper flakes, then cook, stirring, until fragrant, 30 to 60 seconds. Pour in the wine and cook until most of the liquid has evaporated, 7 to 9 minutes. Add the tomatoes and cook, stirring occasionally, until they begin to stick to the pot, about 8 minutes. Add the reserved tomato juices and 4 cups water; stir to combine, then distribute the mixture in an even layer. Add the pasta, placing the strands horizontally so they lay flat, then press them into the liquid until submerged. Set the pecorino chunk on top.

FAST

Press **Cancel**, lock the lid in place and move the pressure valve to **Sealing**. Select **Pressure Cook** or **Manual**; make sure the pressure level is set to **High**. Set the cooking time for 3 minutes. When pressure cooking is complete, quick-release the steam by moving the pressure valve to **Venting**. Press **Cancel**, then carefully open the pot.

FINISH: Select **More/High Sauté**. Cook, stirring to incorporate the melted pecorino, until the pasta is al dente and most of the liquid has been absorbed, 3 to 4 minutes. Press **Cancel** to turn off the pot. Using potholders, carefully remove the insert from the housing. Let stand for 5 minutes. Stir in the remaining 2 tablespoons oil, the pancetta and 1 teaspoon black pepper. Taste and season with salt. Serve with grated pecorino and additional black pepper.

THREE-CHEESE PASTA WITH BASIL AND BLACK PEPPER

Active time: 15 minutes
Start to finish: 40 minutes
Servings: 4 to 6

8 ounces asiago cheese, shredded (2 cups)

8 ounces fontina cheese, shredded (2 cups)

1½ teaspoons cornstarch

1 pound cavatappi pasta

2 tablespoons salted butter, cut into 2 pieces

½ cup heavy cream

½ cup finely chopped fresh basil

Ground black pepper

½ ounce Parmesan cheese, finely grated (¼ cup)

Three types of Italian cheese—asiago, fontina and Parmesan—give this version of macaroni and cheese plenty of depth, complemented by fresh basil and black pepper. The starch from the pasta, combined with a small measure of cornstarch and a dose of heavy cream, creates a rich sauce that lightly coats the pasta. We like curly cavatappi pasta, but campanelle or large elbows work, too.

Don't forget to add the butter *to the pot along with the water and pasta. The fat prevents the starchy liquid from bubbling up through the pressure-release valve.*

START: In a large bowl, toss together the asiago, fontina and cornstarch; set aside. In a 6-quart Instant Pot, combine 5 cups water, the pasta and butter; stir to combine, then distribute in an even layer.

FAST

Lock the lid in place and move the pressure valve to **Sealing**. Select **Pressure Cook** or **Manual**; make sure the pressure level is set to **High**. Set the cooking time for 3 minutes.

When pressure cooking is complete, quick-release the steam by moving the pressure valve to **Venting**. Press **Cancel**, then carefully open the pot.

FINISH: Select **Normal/Medium Sauté**, add the cream and bring to a simmer. One handful at a time, stir in the cheese mixture; after all the cheese has been added, continue to stir until fully melted. Return to a simmer and cook, stirring gently, until the mixture has thickened, about 1 minute. Press **Cancel** to turn off the pot. Using potholders, carefully remove the insert from the housing. Let stand for 5 minutes. Stir in the basil and ½ to 1 teaspoon pepper. Transfer to a serving bowl and sprinkle with Parmesan and additional black pepper.

ORECCHIETTE WITH
SARDINIAN SAUSAGE RAGU

Active time: 20 minutes
Start to finish: 40 minutes
Servings: 4 to 6

¼ cup extra-virgin olive oil

4 medium garlic cloves, finely chopped

½ cup dry white wine

¼ teaspoon saffron threads (optional)

14½-ounce can tomato puree (1½ cups)

1 pound orecchiette or small shell pasta (see note)

1 pound sweet or hot Italian sausage, casing removed, broken into ½-inch or smaller pieces

Kosher salt and ground black pepper

1 ounce pecorino Romano cheese, finely grated (½ cup), plus more to serve

¾ cup roughly chopped fresh basil, divided

Saffron gives this simple Sardinian ragu lots of character. The spice's unique, vaguely floral, slightly minerally flavor pairs beautifully with the sausage, tomatoes and salty pecorino Romano. But since saffron can be expensive, we've kept it optional. Even without, the dish is delicious. Our favorite pasta for this recipe is orecchiette, a small saucer-shaped noodle that does an excellent job of catching the bits of sausage. Small shells work well, too, or any other small pasta that cooks in about 10 minutes (check the package for the recommended cooking time).

Don't use canned tomato sauce instead of tomato puree. The former contains seasonings such as salt and garlic powder; the latter is made only from tomatoes. Also, don't heat the oil before adding the garlic. Starting the garlic in cold oil slows the rate at which it cooks so it browns evenly without scorching.

START: In a 6-quart Instant Pot, combine the oil and garlic. Select **Normal/Medium Sauté** and cook, stirring often, until the garlic is golden brown, about 4 minutes. Add the wine and saffron, if using, then cook, stirring occasionally, until the liquid is slightly syrupy, about 5 minutes. Stir in 2¾ cups water, the tomato puree, pasta, sausage and 1½ teaspoons salt, breaking up any pieces of pasta that stick together, then distribute in an even layer.

FAST

Press **Cancel**, lock the lid in place and move the pressure valve to **Sealing**. Select **Pressure Cook** or **Manual**; make sure the pressure level is set to **High**. Set the cooking time for 3 minutes. When pressure cooking is complete, quick-release the steam by moving the pressure valve to **Venting**. Press **Cancel**, then carefully open the pot.

FINISH: Stir the mixture to evenly distribute the sauce, then stir in the pecorino. Taste and season with salt and pepper. Stir in ½ cup of basil. Serve sprinkled with additional cheese and the remaining ¼ cup basil.

BUCATINI WITH CHERRY TOMATO SAUCE AND FRESH SAGE

Active time: 20 minutes
Start to finish: 45 minutes
Servings: 4 to 6

⅓ cup extra-virgin olive oil, plus more to serve

4 medium garlic cloves, thinly sliced

¼ teaspoon red pepper flakes

2 bay leaves

2 pints (1 pound) cherry or grape tomatoes, halved

½ teaspoon white sugar

Kosher salt

1 pound bucatini pasta, broken in half

2 tablespoons chopped fresh sage, divided

¾ teaspoon smoked paprika

Pecorino Romano cheese, shaved or finely grated, to serve

This dish takes inspiration from a recipe in "Simple" by Yotam Ottolenghi. But instead of conventional stovetop simmering, we pressure cook cherry or grape tomatoes—which tend to be dependably good no matter the season—into a tangy-sweet sauce. The pasta cooks in the pot at the same time, so there's no need to boil a separate pot of water. Fresh sage, smoked paprika and pecorino Romano cheese ratchet up the flavors. We especially liked this dish made with bucatini pasta, which is a thick, tubular spaghetti; linguini is a good alternative, but reduce the pressure-cooking time to 4 minutes.

Don't forget to break the pasta in half *so the strands can lay flat in the pot. And when adding the pasta, make sure no pieces poke above the surface of the liquid. All of the pasta must be submerged to cook properly.*

START: On a 6-quart Instant Pot, select **More/High Sauté**. Add the oil and heat until shimmering. Add the garlic, pepper flakes and bay, then cook, stirring, until the garlic is light golden brown, about 2 minutes. Stir in the tomatoes, sugar, 1 tablespoon salt and 3 cups water. Add the pasta, placing the strands horizontally so they lay flat, then press them into the liquid until submerged.

FAST

Press **Cancel**, lock the lid in place and move the pressure valve to **Sealing**. Select **Pressure Cook** or **Manual**; make sure the pressure level is set to **High**. Set the cooking time for 5 minutes. When pressure cooking is complete, quick-release the steam by moving the pressure valve to **Venting**. Press **Cancel**, then carefully open the pot.

FINISH: Using tongs, toss and stir the mixture to separate the strands of pasta, then stir in 1 tablespoon of sage and the paprika. Re-cover without locking the lid in place and let stand until the pasta is al dente, 3 to 5 minutes. Remove and discard the bay, then transfer to a serving dish and top with pecorino and the remaining 1 tablespoon sage.

TOASTED PEARL COUSCOUS WITH BUTTERNUT SQUASH, KIDNEY BEANS AND FETA

Active time: 30 minutes
Start to finish: 50 minutes
Servings: 4

3 tablespoons extra-virgin olive oil, divided

1 cup pearl couscous

1 medium yellow onion, chopped

4 medium garlic cloves, finely chopped

1 tablespoon ground cumin

Kosher salt and ground black pepper

1 pound butternut squash, peeled, seeded and cut into 1-inch chunks (about 3 cups)

15½-ounce can kidney beans, rinsed and drained

1 tablespoon lemon juice, plus lemon wedges to serve

3 tablespoons chopped fresh dill

3 ounces feta cheese, crumbled (about ½ cup)

Simple, yet satisfying, this vegetarian dish gets loads of flavor simply by toasting the pearl couscous to bring out notes of nuttiness and caramelization. Butternut squash adds color and subtle sweetness, while kidney beans and a good dose of cumin bring earthiness and savoriness. A sprinkling of sharp, salty feta cheese to finish is a perfect counterbalance. The lemon, dill and feta are added after cooking is complete, so if you're aiming to be efficient, prep these ingredients after programming the pot.

Don't skip the 5-minute rest after stirring in the kidney beans, lemon and dill. The couscous needs the time to finish cooking in the pot's residual heat.

START: On a 6-quart Instant Pot, select **Normal/Medium Sauté**. Add 1 tablespoon of the oil and heat until shimmering. Add the couscous and cook, stirring often, until golden brown, 6 to 9 minutes. Using a large spoon, transfer the couscous to a small bowl; set aside. Add the remaining 2 tablespoons oil, the onion, garlic, cumin and 1 teaspoon salt, then cook, stirring occasionally, until the onion begins to brown, 6 to 9 minutes. Add 2 cups water and scrape up any browned bits. Stir in the couscous, squash, 1½ teaspoons salt and ½ teaspoon pepper, then distribute in an even layer.

FAST

Press **Cancel**, lock the lid in place and move the pressure valve to **Sealing**. Select **Pressure Cook** or **Manual**; make sure the pressure level is set to **High**. Set the cooking time for 5 minutes. When pressure cooking is complete, quick-release the steam by moving the pressure valve to **Venting**. Press **Cancel**, then carefully open the pot.

FINISH: Stir in the kidney beans, lemon juice and half of the dill. Re-cover without locking the lid in place and let stand for 5 minutes. Taste and season with salt and pepper. Transfer to a serving bowl and sprinkle with the feta and the remaining dill. Serve with lemon wedges.

PASTA WITH SPICY TOMATO-LENTIL SAUCE

Active time: 30 minutes
Start to finish: 1 hour
Servings: 6

4 tablespoons extra-virgin olive oil, divided, plus more to serve

½ cup panko breadcrumbs

¾ teaspoon red pepper flakes, divided

Kosher salt and ground black pepper

1 tablespoon grated lemon zest, plus 1 tablespoon lemon juice

1 bunch flat-leaf parsley, leaves and tender stems, chopped

1 medium yellow onion, chopped

¾ cup lentils du Puy, rinsed and drained

8 ounces short, small pasta (see note), such as ditalini, shells or mezzi rigatoni

14½-ounce can tomato puree

Italian pasta e lenticchie features the unlikely pairing of two humble ingredients—pasta and lentils—to create a comforting, rib-sticking dish. Here we use French lentils du Puy, which hold their shape nicely, and give them a head start by simmering them for 10 minutes before adding the pasta and switching to pressure cooking. A generous amount of chopped parsley adds color and fresh, grassy notes, while toasted and seasoned panko breadcrumbs sprinkled over the finished dish adds a satisfying crispness. Though this dish already is rich with carbs, we liked serving it with crusty bread to mop up the flavorful sauce.

Don't use a pasta shape that cooks in under 10 minutes (check the cooking directions on the package for the recommended cooking time). Since the pasta is cooked directly in the sauce with the lentils, a fast-cooking shape will end up overdone by the time the lentils are tender. Also, don't used canned tomato sauce, which already is seasoned. Make sure to purchase canned tomato puree, which consists of only tomatoes and citric acid.

START: On a 6-quart Instant Pot, select **Normal/Medium Sauté**. Add 2 tablespoons of oil and heat until shimmering. Add the panko, ¼ teaspoon of pepper flakes and ½ teaspoon each salt and black pepper. Cook, stirring constantly, until the panko is deep golden brown, 3 to 4 minutes. Transfer to a small bowl. Add the lemon zest and ¼ cup parsley, then toss to combine; set aside. With the pot still on **Normal/Medium Sauté**, add the remaining 2 tablespoons oil. Heat until shimmering, then add the onion. Cook, stirring often, until softened, about 5 minutes. Stir in the remaining ½ teaspoon pepper flakes, 1½ teaspoons salt, 1 teaspoon black pepper, the lentils and 6 cups water. Select **More/High Sauté** and bring to a boil. Cook for 10 minutes, stirring occasionally, then stir in the pasta and tomato puree.

FAST

Press **Cancel**, lock the lid in place and move the pressure valve to **Sealing**. Select **Pressure Cook** or **Manual**; make sure the pressure level is set to **High**. Set the cooking time for 5 minutes. When pressure cooking is complete, quick-release the steam by moving the pressure valve to **Venting**. Press **Cancel**, then carefully open the pot.

FINISH: Stir in the remaining parsley and the lemon juice. Taste and season with salt and black pepper. Transfer to a serving bowl. Top with the toasted panko, drizzle with oil and sprinkle with black pepper.

SPAGHETTI WITH GOAT CHEESE, MINT AND PEAS

Active time: 15 minutes
Start to finish: 30 minutes
Servings: 4 to 6

2 cups frozen peas, thawed and patted dry, divided

8 ounces fresh goat cheese (chèvre)

⅓ cup plus 3 tablespoons extra-virgin olive oil

1 tablespoon grated lemon zest, plus 2 tablespoons lemon juice

½ cup chopped fresh mint

Kosher salt and ground black pepper

1 medium yellow onion, chopped

1 pound spaghetti or fine linguini, broken in half

This pasta dish is a simplified, pressure-cooked take on a recipe from "Rich Table" by Evan and Sarah Rich. The only knife work required is chopping an onion and fresh mint and halving a lemon to juice it. And since the pasta is cooked directly in the liquid that forms the base of the sauce, there's no need to boil a separate pot of water or to drain the noodles when done.

Don't forget to thaw the peas so that the ½ cup for mashing breaks down easily. Patting the peas dry with paper towels after they're thawed wicks away excess moisture.

START: Add 1 cup of peas to a medium bowl. Using a fork, mash to a coarse puree. Add the goat cheese, the ⅓ cup of oil, the lemon zest and juice, half the chopped mint, ½ teaspoon salt and ¾ teaspoon pepper. Mash well, then set aside. On a 6-quart Instant Pot, select **More/High Sauté**. Add the remaining 3 tablespoons oil, the onion and 1 teaspoon salt. Cook, stirring occasionally, until the onion begins to soften, about 2 minutes. Pour in 5 cups water, then stir to combine. Add the pasta, placing the strands horizontally so they lay flat, then press them into the liquid until submerged.

FAST

Press **Cancel**, lock the lid in place and move the pressure valve to **Sealing**. Select **Pressure Cook** or **Manual**; make sure the pressure level is set to **High**. Set the cooking time for 3 minutes. When pressure cooking is complete, quick-release the pressure by moving the pressure valve to **Venting**. Press **Cancel**, then carefully open the pot.

FINISH: Using tongs, toss and stir the mixture to separate the strands of pasta, then add the goat cheese mixture and the remaining peas. Toss well. Taste and season with salt and pepper, then transfer to a serving dish. Sprinkle with the remaining mint.

PEARL COUSCOUS WITH HERBS, ALMONDS AND PECORINO

Active time: 20 minutes

Start to finish: 35 minutes

Servings: 4

2 tablespoons extra-virgin olive oil, plus more to serve

2 ounces thinly sliced pancetta, finely chopped

1 small yellow onion, finely chopped

1 cup pearl couscous

1 tablespoon fennel seeds, ground

Kosher salt and ground black pepper

½ cup dry white wine

1 tablespoon lemon juice

2 ounces pecorino Romano cheese, finely grated (1 cup)

½ cup chopped fresh basil

½ cup chopped fresh mint

½ cup salted roasted almonds, chopped

This dish marries salty, savory flavors with fresh herbal notes and the nuttiness of roasted almonds. Fennel seeds add licorice undertones; grind the seeds to a powder in an electric spice grinder or with mortar and pestle (if you can find preground fennel seed at the store, use an equal amount). The herbs are less likely to discolor if chopped just before use; prep them while the couscous cooks. Serve as a light main course, or offer it as a side dish to grilled or roasted chicken or lamb.

Don't forget to scrape up the browned bits on the bottom of the pot after adding the wine. *Those bits build depth of flavor in the finished dish.*

START: On a 6-quart Instant Pot, select **Normal/Medium Sauté**. Add the oil and pancetta, then cook, stirring occasionally, until crisp, 2 to 3 minutes. Add the onion and cook, stirring occasionally, until softened, 3 to 5 minutes. Stir in the couscous, fennel seeds and 1 teaspoon pepper. Add the wine and cook, scraping up the browned bits, until reduced and syrupy, 1 to 2 minutes. Stir in 2 cups water, then distribute the couscous mixture in an even layer.

FAST

Press **Cancel**, lock the lid in place and move the pressure valve to **Sealing**. Select **Pressure Cook** or **Manual**; make sure the pressure level is set to **High**. Set the cooking time for 5 minutes. When pressure cooking is complete, quick-release the steam by moving the pressure valve to **Venting**. Press **Cancel**, then carefully open the pot.

FINISH: Stir in the lemon juice, half the pecorino, half of each herb and half the almonds. Taste and season with salt and pepper. Transfer to a serving bowl and sprinkle with the remaining cheese, the remaining herbs and the remaining almonds, then drizzle with oil.

TWO-CHEESE PASTA
WITH CAULIFLOWER

Active time: 25 minutes
Start to finish: 35 minutes
Servings: 4

3 tablespoons extra-virgin olive oil, plus more to serve

1 medium garlic clove, smashed and peeled

2-pound head cauliflower, trimmed and quartered, core intact, patted dry

Kosher salt and ground black pepper

8 ounces short, curly pasta, such as gemelli or fusilli

½ teaspoon red pepper flakes, plus more to serve

1½ ounces pecorino Romano cheese, finely grated (½ cup), plus more to serve

1½ ounces aged provolone cheese (see note), finely grated (½ cup), plus more to serve

In this dish from Naples, Italy, the cauliflower and pasta are given equal importance, and there's just enough cheese to balance the vegetable's natural sweetness. We use a combination of savory pecorino Romano cheese and aged provolone (also called provolone piccante, or sharp provolone). If you can't find aged provolone, regular provolone is an acceptable, though milder-tasting, substitute. A short, twisty pasta shape combines well with the cauliflower and stands up nicely to pressure cooking; we especially liked gemelli and fusilli.

Don't forget to dry the cauliflower; *the drier it is, the less splattering it will cause in the hot oil.*

START: On a 6-quart Instant Pot, select **Normal/Medium Sauté**. Add the oil and garlic, then cook, stirring, until the clove is golden brown, 2 to 3 minutes. Remove and discard the garlic, then add the cauliflower quarters. Cook, occasionally turning the cauliflower, until the pieces are well browned on all sides, 8 to 12 minutes. Add the pasta and pepper flakes, stirring to coat with the oil, then add 2¼ cups water, 1 teaspoon salt and ¼ teaspoon black pepper. Distribute the pasta in an even layer; it should be almost fully submerged in liquid (it's fine if the cauliflower is not fully submerged).

FAST

Press **Cancel**, lock the lid in place and move the pressure valve to **Sealing**. Select **Pressure Cook** or **Manual**; make sure the pressure level is set to **High**. Set the cooking time for 3 minutes. When pressure cooking is complete, quick-release the steam by moving the pressure valve to **Venting**. Press **Cancel**, then carefully open the pot.

FINISH: Stir the mixture, breaking the cauliflower into bite-size pieces. Sprinkle on the pecorino and stir until the cheese is evenly distributed and melted. Sprinkle on the provolone, then stir until the pasta is glossy and lightly coated with melted cheese. Taste and season with salt and black pepper. Serve drizzled with additional oil and sprinkled with additional cheese and pepper flakes.

SPAGHETTI WITH SAUSAGE, FENNEL SEED AND BROCCOLINI

Active time: 15 minutes
Start to finish: 40 minutes
Servings: 4 to 6

1 pound hot or sweet Italian sausage, casing removed

2 tablespoons extra-virgin olive oil, divided, plus more to serve

6 medium garlic cloves, finely chopped

2 tablespoons fennel seeds

½ teaspoon red pepper flakes

Kosher salt and ground black pepper

1 pound spaghetti, broken in half

8 ounces broccolini, trimmed and finely chopped

1 ounce Parmesan cheese, finely grated (½ cup), plus more to serve

For this one-pot pasta dish, use either hot or sweet Italian sausage, or a mixture if you prefer. And you can up the red pepper flakes for added spice. To give the pasta a meatier, more savory quality, substitute 1 quart of low-sodium chicken broth for 4 cups of the water, but also reduce the salt to ¼ teaspoon. The broccolini is added at the very end; prep it while the pot comes up to pressure.

Don't forget to break the spaghetti in half so the strands lay flat in the pot. And when adding the pasta, make sure no pieces poke above the surface of the liquid. All of the pasta must be submerged to cook properly.

START: In a medium bowl, combine the sausage with ⅓ cup water. Stir with a fork until well combined. On a 6-quart Instant Pot, select **More/High Sauté**. Add 1 tablespoon of oil and the sausage and cook, stirring and breaking the meat into small pieces, until the sausage is no longer pink, about 5 minutes. Stir in the garlic, fennel seeds and pepper flakes, then cook until fragrant, about 30 seconds. Add 5 cups water and 1 teaspoon salt; stir to combine, then distribute in an even layer. Add the pasta, placing the strands horizontally so they lay flat, then press them into the liquid until submerged.

FAST

Press **Cancel**, lock the lid in place and move the pressure valve to **Sealing**. Select **Pressure Cook** or **Manual**; make sure the pressure level is set to **High**. Set the cooking time for 3 minutes. When pressure cooking is complete, quick-release the steam by moving the pressure valve to **Venting**. Press **Cancel**, then carefully open the pot.

FINISH: Using tongs, toss and stir the mixture to separate the strands of pasta, then stir in the broccolini. Re-cover without locking the lid in place and let stand until the broccolini is tender and the pasta is al dente, about 5 minutes. Stir in the Parmesan and the remaining 1 tablespoon oil. Taste and season with salt and pepper, then transfer to a serving dish. Drizzle with oil and serve with additional Parmesan on the side.

PASTA WITH CREMINI MUSHROOMS AND MISO

Active time: 35 minutes
Start to finish: 50 minutes
Servings: 4 to 6

4 tablespoons (½ stick) salted butter

1 medium yellow onion, halved and thinly sliced

3 medium garlic cloves, thinly sliced

⅓ cup white miso

½ cup dry white vermouth

2 pounds cremini mushrooms, trimmed and quartered

1 pound cavatappi pasta (see note)

1 teaspoon minced fresh thyme

2 teaspoons lemon juice

Kosher salt and ground black pepper

¼ cup roughly chopped fresh flat-leaf parsley

½ ounce pecorino Romano cheese, finely grated (¼ cup)

Japanese miso may seem an unlikely ingredient to pair with Italian pasta, but it deepens the mushrooms' earthiness. Lightly browning the miso develops even more flavor intensity so the dish tastes surprisingly meaty and rich. We particularly liked cavatappi pasta because its twisty shape is a good match for the chunky mushrooms, but any short pasta shape with a similar cooking time, such as penne or fusilli, works well, too.

Don't forget to stir the pasta as it cooks. *The pot will be quite full, so frequent stirring will help ensure that the pasta cooks evenly.*

START: On a 6-quart Instant Pot, select **More/High Sauté**. Add the butter and let melt. Add the onion and garlic, then cook, stirring occasionally, until the onion begins to soften, about 5 minutes. Stir in the miso and cook until lightly browned, about 2 minutes. Add the vermouth and cook, stirring, until almost fully evaporated, about 5 minutes. Add 3 cups water and whisk until the miso dissolves. Stir in the mushrooms and bring to a boil, then distribute in an even layer.

FAST

Press **Cancel**, lock the lid in place and move the pressure valve to **Sealing**. Select **Pressure Cook** or **Manual**; make sure the pressure level is set to **High**. Set the cooking time for 5 minutes. When pressure cooking is complete, quick-release the steam by moving the pressure valve to **Venting**. Press **Cancel**, then carefully open the pot.

FINISH: Select **More/High Sauté**. Bring the mixture to a boil and add the pasta. Cook, stirring often, until the pasta is al dente and the sauce clings lightly, about 10 minutes. Press **Cancel** to turn off the pot. Stir in the thyme and lemon juice, then taste and season with salt and pepper. Transfer to a serving dish and sprinkle with the parsley and pecorino.

TOASTED PEARL COUSCOUS WITH CHICKEN AND CHICKPEAS

Start to finish: 1 hour
Active time: 35 minutes
Servings: 4

2 tablespoons grapeseed or other neutral oil, divided

1 cup pearl couscous

4 medium garlic cloves, finely chopped

1 medium yellow onion, chopped

3 large carrots, peeled and sliced ½ inch thick on the diagonal

2 bay leaves

Kosher salt and ground black pepper

1 tablespoon ground cumin

½ teaspoon ground allspice

1 pound boneless, skinless chicken thighs, trimmed and cut into 1-inch pieces

15½-ounce can chickpeas, rinsed and drained

1 teaspoon pomegranate molasses, plus more to serve

1 cup lightly packed fresh flat-leaf parsley, roughly chopped

A key step for achieving maximum flavor in this one-pot meal is to toast the pearl couscous, which deepens its wheaty flavor and yields a nutty aroma. A sauté of garlic, onion, cumin and allspice creates a heady base for simultaneously cooking boneless chicken thighs and the toasted couscous; cutting the chicken into bite-sized pieces allows everything to finish at the same same time. A spoonful of tangy-sweet pomegranate molasses brightens the flavors while balancing the warm, earthy spices.

Don't use regular couscous. Pearl couscous, sometimes referred to as Israeli couscous, is much larger so it cooks differently than regular couscous and retains a satisfying chew. Also, don't slice the carrots thinner than ½ inch or they will turn to mush.

START: On a 6-quart Instant Pot, select **Normal/Medium Sauté**. Add 1 tablespoon of oil and heat until shimmering. Add the couscous and cook, stirring often, until golden brown, 7 to 10 minutes. Using a large spoon, transfer the couscous to a small bowl; set aside. Add the remaining 1 tablespoon oil to the pot and heat until shimmering. Add the garlic and cook, stirring, until beginning to brown, about 1 minute, then add the onion, carrots, bay, 2 teaspoons salt and 1 teaspoon pepper. Cook, stirring occasionally, until the onion has softened, 2 to 4 minutes. Add the cumin and allspice, then cook, stirring, until fragrant, about 30 seconds. Pour in 1 cup water and scrape up any browned bits. Stir in the chicken, the toasted couscous and 1 teaspoon salt, then distribute in an even layer.

FAST

Press **Cancel**, lock the lid in place and move the pressure valve to **Sealing**. Select **Pressure Cook** or **Manual**; make sure the pressure level is set to **High**. Set the cooking time for 5 minutes. When pressure cooking is complete, quick-release the steam by moving the pressure valve to **Venting**. Press **Cancel**, then carefully open the pot.

FINISH: Stir in the chickpeas, pomegranate molasses and half the parsley. Re-cover without locking the lid in place and let stand for 5 minutes. Remove and discard the bay, then taste and season with salt and pepper. Transfer to a serving bowl and sprinkle with the remaining parsley. Serve with additional pomegranate molasses for drizzling.

CHICKEN

CONTENTS

Chicken Rogan Josh (p. 161)

CHICKEN

To make the most of one-pot ease, we cull all but essential ingredients. Far from feeling short-changed, we found that paring back made for lighter and brighter layers of flavor. Chicken biryani, the rich and layered dish from India and Pakistan for example, often comes with a dizzyingly long list of ingredients and the intensive prep to match. Our Instant Pot version requires just a dozen ingredients, only 30 minutes of effort and is ready to eat in about an hour. Likewise, we came up with an 8-ingredient version of Hungary's chicken paprikash that takes less than an hour.

Many braises start by searing the meat, but **we don't bother with browning** in the Instant Pot. Browning can start a flavor foundation, but we find using high-impact ingredients and cutting back on liquids more than compensates.

To keep flavors vibrant, **we add herbs at the end.** In our Georgian-style chicken stew, cilantro and dill are stirred in off-heat to preserve their fragrance and colors. Similarly, we use an aromatic puree in our Indian chicken stew, using half of the puree during the cooking, but keeping the other half to stir in at the end for a bright, green jolt of flavor.

We love a rich-tasting dish, but not a heavy one, so **we keep fats in check.** We often remove skins from bone-in thighs, as we do in Senegalese braised chicken, and we use pureed cashews, not heavy cream, to add richness to our Indian butter chicken.

To make our simplified ingredient lists work, we **use high-impact ingredients to punch up flavor.** Sichuan peppercorns spike our Sichuan steamed chicken; chipotle chilies bring heat to our pulled chicken as well as to our version of a classic Mexican meatball.

We find that chicken thighs can handle high-pressure cooking better in a braise than white meat chicken. Even so, since chicken is a relatively delicate meat, we **often use natural pressure release to avoid making the meat too soft.** When the steam is released suddenly, the very hot water inside chicken muscle fibers causes them to open up to release the steam. The result is mushy meat.

Chicken in the Instant Pot opens up a world of flavor, from the French favorite of chicken en cocotte to India's rich butter chicken. We use tangy ginger and other one-stroke flavor solutions to balance the mild meat and add delicate herbs at the end to preserve their freshness.

VIETNAMESE-STYLE CHICKEN AND GLASS NOODLE SOUP

Active time: 25 minutes

Fast start to finish:
1 hour

Slow start to finish:
3½ to 4 hours

Servings: 4

1 star anise pod

2 large shallots, root end intact, halved

1-inch piece fresh ginger, peeled and thinly sliced

5 dried shiitake mushrooms (about ½ ounce)

1 bunch fresh cilantro, stems and leaves reserved separately

2 boneless, skinless chicken breasts (8 to 10 ounces each)

7 cups low-sodium chicken broth

Kosher salt and ground black pepper

4 ounces glass noodles (see note)

1 tablespoon fish sauce, plus more if needed

Lime wedges, to serve

This light yet flavor-packed soup is our Instant Pot take on the Vietnamese dish called mien ga. Aromatics and whole chicken breasts are cooked in chicken broth; the solids are discarded before serving and the chicken is shredded into bite-size pieces. Glass noodles are also called cellophane or bean thread noodles. Dried, they are wiry and white; they turn translucent and bouncy when cooked. The noodles often are so long they're unwieldy to serve and eat, so we snip them with kitchen shears into shorter lengths directly in the pot after cooking. Some brands also are thicker than others; refer to the package for approximate cooking times. If you like, offer some thinly sliced fresh chilies for adding to individual bowls.

Don't trim off the root ends of the shallots. *Leaving the root end intact prevents the layers from separating so the shallots are easier to remove after cooking. When prepping the cilantro, don't worry about plucking the leaves from the stems. Instead, simply lop off the leafy top of the entire bunch; reserve the stems and leaves separately because they are used at different times.*

START: In a 6-quart Instant Pot, combine the star anise, shallots, ginger, mushrooms, cilantro stems, chicken breasts, broth and 1 teaspoon each salt and pepper.

FAST

Lock the lid in place and move the pressure valve to **Sealing**. Select **Pressure Cook** or **Manual**; make sure the pressure level is set to **High**. Set the cooking time for 5 minutes. When pressure cooking is complete, allow the pressure to reduce naturally for 5 minutes, then release the remaining steam by moving the pressure valve to **Venting**. Press **Cancel**, then carefully open the pot.

SLOW

Select **More/High Sauté** and bring to a boil. Press **Cancel**, lock the lid in place and move the pressure valve to **Venting**. Select **Slow Cook** and set the temperature to **More/Low**. Set the cooking time for 3 to 3½ hours; the chicken and broth are done when a skewer inserted into the breasts meets no resistance. Press **Cancel**, then carefully open the pot.

FINISH: Using tongs, transfer the chicken and mushrooms to a plate and set aside. Using a slotted spoon, scoop out and discard the remaining solids in the broth. Thinly slice the mushrooms, discarding any tough stems. Using two forks, shred the chicken into bite-size pieces. Select **More/High Sauté** and bring the broth to a boil. Stir in the noodles and fish sauce, then cook, stirring occasionally, until tender, 3 to 6 minutes. Press **Cancel** to turn off the pot. Using kitchen shears, snip the noodles a few times directly in the pot to cut them into shorter lengths. Stir in the sliced mushrooms and chicken, then taste and season with additional fish sauce, if needed, and pepper. Serve sprinkled with additional pepper and cilantro leaves and with lime wedges on the side.

CHICKEN, CHICKPEA AND YOGURT SOUP WITH TOASTED ORZO

Active time: 40 minutes

Fast start to finish:
1¼ hours

Slow start to finish:
4¾ to 5¾ hours

Servings: 4 to 6

2 tablespoons salted butter, cut into 3 pieces

1 cup orzo

1 medium leek, white and light green parts halved, thinly sliced, rinsed and dried

Kosher salt and ground black pepper

3 medium garlic cloves, finely chopped

1¼ teaspoons red pepper flakes

2 bone-in, skin-on chicken breasts (10 to 12 ounces each), skin removed

15½-ounce can chickpeas, rinsed and drained

2 cups (1½ ounces) lightly packed baby spinach, chopped

¾ cup plain whole-milk yogurt

¼ cup chopped fresh dill, plus more to serve

We learned about warm Persian chickpea and yogurt soup from cookbook author Yasmin Khan, who suggested preparing the dish as a simple weeknight meal. This version is made with butter-toasted orzo pasta, which replaces the rice that Khan uses, and shredded chicken makes the soup especially hearty. We use regular yogurt here, not Greek-style. It lends the broth a subtle creaminess and tang without making the soup heavy. The spinach and dill are added at the end, so prep these ingredients while the chicken is cooking.

Don't use low-fat or nonfat yogurt *as they lack richness and will curdle when stirred into the soup. Also, don't add the yogurt until you have removed the insert from the Instant Pot housing. This helps ensure that the yogurt won't separate from overheating.*

START: On a 6-quart Instant Pot, select **More/High Sauté**. Add the butter and orzo, then cook, stirring often, until golden brown, 6 to 8 minutes. Using a slotted spoon, transfer to a small bowl and set aside. Add the leek, 1½ teaspoons salt and ¼ teaspoon black pepper to the fat remaining in the pot. Cook, stirring occasionally, until the leek is softened, about 6 minutes. Add the garlic and pepper flakes, then cook, stirring, until fragrant, about 1 minute. Pour in 2 quarts water and place the chicken breasts in the pot in an even layer.

FAST

Press **Cancel**, lock the lid in place and move the pressure valve to **Sealing**. Select **Pressure Cook** or **Manual**; make sure the pressure level is set to **High**. Set the cooking time for 12 minutes. When pressure cooking is complete, allow the pressure to release naturally for 10 minutes, then release the remaining steam by moving the pressure valve to **Venting**. Press **Cancel**, then carefully open the pot.

SLOW

With the pot still on **More/High Sauté**, bring the mixture to a boil. Press **Cancel**, lock the lid in place and move the pressure valve to **Venting**. Select **Slow Cook** and set the temperature to **More/High**. Set the cooking time for 4 to 5 hours; the chicken is done when a skewer inserted into the thickest part of the breasts meets no resistance. Press **Cancel**, then carefully open the pot.

FINISH: Using tongs, transfer the chicken to a plate. Select **More/High Sauté** and bring the broth to a boil. Stir in the toasted orzo and cook, stirring occasionally, until al dente, 10 to 12 minutes. Meanwhile, using 2 forks, shred the chicken into bite-size pieces, discarding the bones. Press **Cancel** to turn off the pot. Stir in the shredded chicken, the chickpeas and spinach. Using potholders, carefully remove the insert from the housing. Let cool for about 2 minutes, then stir in the yogurt and dill. Taste and season with salt and pepper. Serve sprinkled with additional dill and black pepper.

CHICKEN SOUP WITH BOK CHOY AND GINGER

Active time: 30 minutes

Fast start to finish:
1¼ hours

Slow start to finish:
5½ to 6½ hours

Servings: 6

1 tablespoon grapeseed or other neutral oil

4-inch piece fresh ginger (about 3 ounces), peeled and cut into 4 pieces

5 medium garlic cloves, smashed and peeled

½ cup dry sherry

2 teaspoons white peppercorns

Kosher salt and ground white pepper

2 pounds bone-in, skin-on chicken thighs, skin removed

1 pound baby bok choy, trimmed and cut crosswise into ½-inch pieces

Kosher salt and ground white pepper

4 scallions, thinly sliced

1 cup chopped fresh cilantro

2 tablespoons unseasoned rice vinegar

Chili oil or toasted sesame oil, to serve

We got the idea for this light, clean-tasting yet aromatic chicken soup from classic Chinese poached chicken, sometimes referred to as "white-cooked" chicken. The addition of baby bok choy, simmered in the broth until the stems are tender, gives the soup verdant color and turns it into a meal in a bowl. The bok choy, scallions and cilantro are added at the end of cooking, so prep these while the chicken cooks. Fragrant steamed jasmine rice would be a welcome accompaniment, either spooned directly into the bowls or offered on the side.

Don't use cooking sherry for this recipe; it usually has added sodium and little, if any, actual sherry flavor. And don't use boneless, skinless chicken for this soup. Bones give the broth body as well as flavor.

START: On a 6-quart Instant Pot, select **More/High Sauté**. Add the oil and heat until shimmering. Add the ginger and garlic and cook, stirring, until fragrant, about 30 seconds. Pour in the sherry and bring to a boil. Stir in 6 cups water, the peppercorns and 2 teaspoons salt. Add the chicken thighs, arranging them in an even layer.

FAST

Press **Cancel**, lock the lid in place and move the pressure valve to **Sealing**. Select **Pressure Cook** or **Manual**; make sure the pressure level is set to **High**. Set the cooking time for 20 minutes. When pressure cooking is complete, let the pressure reduce naturally for 15 minutes, then release the remaining steam by moving the pressure valve to **Venting**. Press **Cancel**, then carefully open the pot.

SLOW

With the pot still on **More/High Sauté**, bring the mixture to a boil. Press **Cancel**, lock the lid in place and move the pressure valve to **Venting**. Select **Slow Cook** and set the temperature to **Less/Low**. Set the cooking time for 5 to 6 hours; the chicken is done when a skewer inserted into a piece meets no resistance. Press **Cancel**, then carefully open the pot.

FINISH: Using a slotted spoon, transfer the chicken to a plate and set aside. Pour the broth through a fine mesh strainer set over a large bowl; discard the solids in the strainer. Let the broth settle for about 5 minutes, then, using a large spoon, skim off and discard the fat from the surface. Return the broth to the pot. Remove and discard any bones from the chicken and shred or chop the meat into bite-size pieces.

Select **Normal/Medium Sauté** and bring the broth to a simmer. Stir in the bok choy and cook, stirring occasionally, until the stems are tender, about 3 minutes. Press **Cancel** to turn off the pot. Stir in the chicken, scallions, cilantro and vinegar. Taste and season with salt and ground white pepper. Serve drizzled with chili oil or sesame oil.

GEORGIAN-STYLE CHICKEN STEW WITH TOMATOES AND HERBS

Active time: 30 minutes

Fast start to finish:
1¼ hours

Slow start to finish:
4½ to 5½ hours

Servings: 4

2 tablespoons extra-virgin olive oil

8 medium garlic cloves, finely chopped

1 medium yellow onion, chopped

1½ teaspoons fennel seeds

Kosher salt and ground black pepper

1 pint grape or cherry tomatoes, halved

½ cup dry white wine

2 teaspoons dry mustard

1½ teaspoons ground coriander

2 pounds boneless, skinless chicken thighs, trimmed

½ cup lightly packed fresh cilantro, chopped

½ cup lightly packed fresh dill, chopped

This flavorful braised chicken is based on the Georgian dish chakhokbili, an aromatic stew that combines garlic, fresh tomatoes and a spice blend called khmeli-suneli, which includes blue fenugreek and coriander. We approximated the flavor of blue fenugreek by pairing dry ground mustard with fennel seeds. Though not a flawless imitation, the stew still tastes full and rich. To keep the herbs tasting fresh and bright, we add the cilantro and dill at the end, after cooking is complete. Prep the herbs while the chicken cooks. Serve the stew with rice, mashed potatoes or hunks of crusty bread.

Don't let the garlic brown too much. Caramelization adds deep, nutty flavor, but overcooked garlic will give the dish harsh, bitter notes. When the garlic is golden brown, add the onion and fennel seeds to help cool the pot, then stir often until the wine and tomatoes are added.

START: On a 6-quart Instant Pot, select **Normal/Medium Sauté**. Add the oil and garlic, then cook, stirring, until golden brown, about 4 minutes. Add the onion, fennel seeds and 2 teaspoons salt. Cook, stirring often, until the onion begins to soften, about 4 minutes. Stir in the tomatoes, wine, mustard and coriander, then bring to a simmer. Cook, stirring occasionally, until the liquid has thickened and the tomatoes begin to stick to the bottom of the pot, about 8 minutes. Nestle the chicken in an even layer, slightly overlapping the pieces, if needed.

FAST

Press **Cancel**, lock the lid in place and move the pressure valve to **Sealing**. Select **Pressure Cook** or **Manual**; make sure the pressure level is set to **High**. Set the cooking time for 8 minutes. When pressure cooking is complete, allow the pressure to reduce naturally for 15 minutes, then release any remaining steam by moving the pressure valve to **Venting**. Press **Cancel**, then carefully open the pot.

SLOW

Select **More/High Sauté** and bring the mixture to a boil. Press **Cancel**, lock the lid in place and move the pressure valve to **Venting**. Select **Slow Cook** and set the temperature to **Less/Low**. Set the cooking time for 4 to 5 hours; the chicken is done when a skewer inserted into the a piece meets no resistance. Press **Cancel**, then carefully open the pot.

FINISH: Stir in the cilantro and dill, then taste and season with salt and pepper.

INDIAN CHICKEN AND CILANTRO STEW

Active time: 30 minutes

Fast start to finish:
1 hour

Slow start to finish:
3¾ to 4¾ hours

Servings: 4

3 cups lightly packed fresh cilantro leaves and tender stems, roughly chopped, plus cilantro leaves, to serve

2-inch piece fresh ginger (about 1½ ounces), peeled and cut into 4 pieces

6 medium garlic cloves, smashed and peeled

2 jalapeño chilies, stemmed, halved and seeded

3 scallions, roughly chopped

1 teaspoon ground coriander

Kosher salt and ground black pepper

2 pounds boneless, skinless chicken thighs, trimmed

2 tablespoons packed brown sugar

1 cup coconut milk

2 tablespoons lime juice, plus lime wedges to serve

For this Instant Pot version of chicken cafreal, a spicy green curry from the coastal Indian state of Goa, we make an aromatic cilantro puree and use half of it as a marinade for boneless chicken thighs and add the remaining half after cooking is complete so the flavors and color remain fresh and vibrant. Coconut milk tempers the mild heat of the jalapeños and gives the sauce richness and body. If you're a fan of spiciness, leave the seeds in one or both of the chilies. We shred the chicken after cooking so each bite is deeply flavored. Serve the stew with basmati rice or warmed naan.

Don't use chicken breasts in place of the thighs. Breast meat will end up overcooked and dry, and the dish will not be as flavorful.

START: In a blender, combine the cilantro, ginger, garlic, jalapeños, scallions, coriander, 1 teaspoon salt, ½ teaspoon pepper and ½ cup water. Blend until smooth, about 30 seconds. Add the chicken and half the puree to a 6-quart Instant Pot. Toss to coat, then let stand for 15 minutes. Meanwhile, transfer the remaining puree to a small bowl; set aside at room temperature if pressure cooking or cover and refrigerate if slow cooking. Stir another ½ cup water and the sugar into the chicken mixture, then distribute in an even layer.

FAST

Lock the lid in place and move the pressure valve to **Sealing**. Select **Pressure Cook** or **Manual**; make sure the pressure level is set to **High**. Set the cooking time for 4 minutes. When pressure cooking is complete, let the pressure reduce naturally for 10 minutes, then release the remaining steam by moving the pressure valve to **Venting**. Press **Cancel**, then carefully open the pot.

SLOW

Select **More/High Sauté** and bring the mixture to a boil. Press **Cancel**, lock the lid in place and move the pressure valve to **Venting**. Select **Slow Cook** and set the temperature to **Less/Low**. Set the cooking time for 3 to 4 hours; the chicken is done when a skewer inserted into the largest thigh meets no resistance. Press **Cancel**, then carefully open the pot.

FINISH: Using a slotted spoon, transfer the chicken to a medium bowl and let cool for about 5 minutes. Using two forks, shred the meat. Return the chicken to the pot and stir in the coconut milk. Select **More/High Sauté** and bring to a simmer, then press **Cancel** to turn off the pot. Stir in the remaining puree and the lime juice. Taste and season with salt and pepper. Serve sprinkled with cilantro leaves, additional black pepper and lime wedges on the side.

CHICKEN IN GREEN MOLE

Active time: 40 minutes

Fast start to finish:
1½ hours

Slow start to finish:
4¾ to 5¾ hours

Servings: 4

4 medium tomatillos, husked and halved

1 small white onion, peeled, root end intact, quartered lengthwise

4-ounce can chopped green chilies

1 bunch cilantro, stems roughly chopped and leaves chopped, reserved separately

1 cup lightly packed fresh mint, chopped

1½ teaspoons fennel seeds

Kosher salt and ground black pepper

Five 6-inch corn tortillas, torn into quarters

2 pounds boneless, skinless chicken thighs, trimmed and halved crosswise

1 medium yellow summer squash, quartered lengthwise and thinly sliced

When most of us think of Mexican mole, mahogany-colored mole negro comes to mind. But mole comes in many varieties, each with a unique character. Mole verde—or green mole—gets its bright, fresh flavor from a blend of green chilies, tomatillos and herbs. This recipe starts by browning halved tomatillos and a quartered onion directly in the Instant Pot—it's a worthwhile step that builds deep flavor in the finished dish. But for ease, we use canned green chilies instead of fresh and corn tortillas instead of masa dough to thicken the broth. Serve the mole with rice and/or tortillas.

Don't forget to stir frequently after you've added the squash. The broth is lightly thickened and therefore requires stirring to prevent the bottom from scorching.

START: On a 6-quart Instant Pot, select **More/High Sauté**. Add the tomatillos and onion, then cook, turning occasionally, until the vegetables are charred all over, 5 to 7 minutes. Press **Cancel** to turn off the pot. Transfer the vegetables to a blender and let cool slightly, about 5 minutes. To the blender, add the green chilies with their liquid, the cilantro stems, half the mint, the fennel seeds and ½ cup water. Blend on high until smooth, about 1 minute. Pour the puree into the pot, select **More/High Sauté** and bring to a simmer, scraping up any browned bits. Stir in 2½ cups water, the tortillas, 2 teaspoons salt and ½ teaspoon pepper. Add the chicken, stir to combine and distribute in an even layer.

FAST

Press **Cancel**, lock the lid in place and move the pressure valve to **Sealing**. Select **Pressure Cook** or **Manual**; make sure the pressure level is set to **High**. Set the cooking time for 8 minutes. When pressure cooking is complete, let the pressure release naturally for 20 minutes, then release any remaining steam by moving the pressure valve to **Venting**. Press **Cancel**, then carefully open the pot.

SLOW

With the pot still on **More/High Sauté**, bring the mixture to a boil. Press **Cancel**, lock the lid in place and move the pressure valve to **Venting**. Select **Slow Cook** and set the temperature to **Less/Low**. Set the cooking time for 4 to 5 hours; the chicken is done when a skewer inserted into a piece meets no resistance. Press **Cancel**, then carefully open the pot.

FINISH: Select **More/High Sauté** and bring the mixture to a simmer. Add the squash and cook, stirring often, until the broth is slightly thickened and the squash is tender, 5 to 8 minutes. Press **Cancel** to turn off the pot, then taste and season with salt and pepper. Stir in the cilantro leaves and the remaining mint.

MISO AND BOURBON SMOTHERED CHICKEN

Active time: 35 minutes

**Fast start to finish:
1¼ hours**

Slow start to finish:
4½ to 5½ hours

Servings: 4

3 tablespoons soy sauce

2 tablespoons white miso

½ cup orange juice

2 tablespoons grapeseed
or other neutral oil

2 medium yellow onions,
halved and thinly sliced

8 ounces shiitake
mushrooms, stemmed,
caps thinly sliced

5 medium garlic cloves,
finely chopped

⅔ cup bourbon

3 pounds bone-in, skin-on
chicken thighs, skin removed
and discarded

2 tablespoons cornstarch

2 tablespoons tahini
(optional)

Kosher salt and ground
black pepper

3 scallions, thinly sliced
on the diagonal

This is our Instant Pot spin on a recipe in "Smoke and Pickles" by chef Edward Lee. Smothered dishes are all about the gravy. In this version, bone-in chicken thighs get sauced with a shiitake mushroom–laced combination of umami-rich soy sauce and miso, woodsy bourbon and sweet-tangy orange juice. Tahini is optional, but it makes a silky-smooth, lightly creamy sauce, and its nutty, slightly bitter flavor works well with the other ingredients. Serve with steamed Asian rice or light, fluffy biscuits.

Don't forget to trim the stems from the mushrooms. Shiitake stems are tough and fibrous. Extended pressure cooking can render them tender enough to eat, but the cooking time in this recipe is too brief.

START: In a small bowl, whisk the soy sauce and miso until smooth, then whisk in the orange juice; set aside. On a 6-quart Instant Pot, select **More/High Sauté**. Add the oil and heat until shimmering. Add the onions and cook, stirring occasionally, until softened, 5 to 8 minutes. Add the mushrooms and garlic, then continue to cook, stirring occasionally, until the vegetables are lightly browned, about 5 minutes. Add the bourbon and cook, scraping up any browned bits, until most of the liquid has evaporated, 1 to 2 minutes. Stir in the miso mixture and 1 cup water, then nestle the chicken, skin side down, in an even layer, slightly overlapping the pieces if needed.

FAST

Press **Cancel**, lock the lid in place and move the pressure valve to **Sealing**. Select **Pressure Cook** or **Manual**; make sure the pressure level is set to **High**. Set the cooking time for 15 minutes. When pressure cooking is complete, allow the pressure to release naturally for 10 minutes, then release the remaining steam by moving the pressure valve to **Venting**. Press **Cancel**, then carefully open the pot.

SLOW

With the pot still on **More/High Sauté**, bring the mixture to a boil. Press **Cancel**, lock the lid in place and move the pressure valve to **Venting**. Select **Slow Cook** and set the temperature to **More/High**. Set the cooking time for 4 to 5 hours; the chicken is done when a skewer inserted into the largest thigh meets no resistance. Press **Cancel**, then carefully open the pot.

FINISH: Using tongs, transfer the chicken to a serving dish and tent with foil. In a small bowl, whisk the cornstarch and about ⅓ cup of the cooking liquid until smooth, then stir the mixture into the pot. Select **More/High Sauté** and bring to a simmer, stirring constantly, then cook until the sauce is thickened, 2 to 3 minutes. Press **Cancel** to turn off the pot. Using potholders, carefully remove the insert from the housing. Stir in the tahini, if using. Taste and season with salt and pepper. Pour the sauce over the chicken and top with the scallions.

CHICKEN PAPRIKASH

Active time: 25 minutes

**Fast start to finish:
55 minutes**

Slow start to finish:
3½ to 4½ hours

Servings: 4

2 tablespoons salted butter

1 large yellow onion,
finely chopped

Kosher salt and ground
black pepper

2 tablespoons sweet paprika

1 tablespoon tomato paste

3 pounds bone-in, skin-on
chicken thighs, skin removed
and discarded

1 cup sour cream

1 tablespoon cornstarch

4 tablespoons chopped
fresh dill, divided

Pressure cooked in the Instant Pot, this Hungarian classic can be on the table in an hour, and with fewer than 10 ingredients. To streamline the process even more, prep the dill while the chicken cooks, as it's not used until the end of cooking to finish the sauce and as a garnish. Paprika is a key ingredient in this dish, so make sure yours is fresh and fragrant; paprika that has gone stale and lost its flavor and color will result in a bland, lackluster stew. Buttered egg noodles are the perfect accompaniment.

Don't use low-fat sour cream. It lacks richness and body and will make a lean, watery chicken paprikash.

START: On a 6-quart Instant Pot, select **More/High Sauté**. Add the butter and let melt. Add the onion, ½ teaspoon salt and ¼ teaspoon pepper, then cook, stirring occasionally, until the onion is golden brown, about 6 minutes. Add the paprika and tomato paste and cook, stirring, until fragrant, about 1 minute. Stir in ½ cup water, scraping up the browned bits. Nestle the chicken in an even layer, skin side down, slightly overlapping the pieces if needed.

FAST

Press **Cancel**, lock the lid in place and move the pressure valve to **Sealing**. Select **Pressure Cook** or **Manual**; make sure the pressure level is set to **High**. Set the cooking time for 10 minutes. When pressure cooking is complete, allow the pressure to reduce naturally for 10 minutes, then release the remaining steam by moving the pressure valve to **Venting**. Press **Cancel**, then carefully open the pot.

SLOW

With the pot still on **More/High Sauté**, bring the mixture to a boil. Press **Cancel**, lock the lid in place and move the pressure valve to **Venting**. Select **Slow Cook** and set the temperature to **More/High**. Set the cooking time for 3 to 4 hours; the chicken is done when a skewer inserted into the largest thigh meets no resistance. Press **Cancel**, then carefully open the pot.

FINISH: Using tongs, transfer the chicken to a dish and tent with foil. In a small bowl, whisk together the sour cream and cornstarch. Whisk the mixture into the pot, then select **More/High Sauté** and cook, whisking constantly, until the sauce begins to simmer and is lightly thickened. Press **Cancel** to turn off the pot, then taste and season with salt and pepper. Stir in 2 tablespoons of dill. Using potholders, carefully remove the insert from the housing and pour the sauce over the chicken. Sprinkle with the remaining 2 tablespoons dill.

CHICKEN ROGAN JOSH

Active time: 40 minutes

**Fast start to finish:
1¼ hours**

Slow start to finish:
4¾ to 5¾ hours

Servings: 4

2 tablespoons salted butter

2 medium yellow onions,
finely chopped

4 medium garlic cloves,
smashed and peeled

6 whole cardamom pods,
lightly crushed

2 cinnamon sticks

2 tablespoons finely
grated fresh ginger

2 tablespoons tomato paste

1½ teaspoons cumin seeds

1 teaspoon sweet paprika

¼ teaspoon ground allspice

¼ teaspoon cayenne pepper

Kosher salt and ground
black pepper

3 pounds bone-in, skin-on
chicken thighs, skin removed
and discarded

½ cup whole-milk Greek
yogurt

Chopped fresh cilantro,
to serve

The rich, highly aromatic Kashmiri dish known as rogan josh typically is made with lamb. We use bone-in chicken thighs that have had their skin removed before cooking to prevent the sauce from becoming too greasy. Butter and warm spices flavor the dish, and yogurt stirred in at the end adds creaminess. We use cinnamon sticks, whole cardamom pods and cumin seeds instead of ground spices so the sauce is velvety. Serve with basmati rice or warm naan.

Don't use regular yogurt in place of the Greek yogurt. Its thinner consistency will make the sauce watery. We preferred the richness of whole-milk Greek yogurt, but low-fat will work, too. Don't use nonfat, which lacks flavor.

START: On a 6-quart Instant Pot, select **Normal/Medium Sauté**. Add the butter and let melt, then add the onions, garlic, cardamom, cinnamon and ½ teaspoon salt. Cook, stirring often, until the onions have softened, about 5 minutes. Add the ginger, tomato paste, cumin, paprika, allspice, cayenne, and 1 teaspoon each salt and black pepper, then cook, stirring, until fragrant, about 30 seconds. Stir in 1 cup water, scraping up any browned bits. Nestle the chicken in an even layer, slightly overlapping the pieces if needed.

FAST

Press **Cancel**, lock the lid in place and move the pressure release valve to **Sealing**. Select **Pressure Cook** or **Manual**; make sure the pressure level is set to **High**. Set the cooking time for 10 minutes. When pressure cooking is complete, let the pressure reduce naturally for 15 minutes, then release any remaining steam by moving the pressure valve to **Venting**. Press **Cancel**, then carefully open the pot.

SLOW

Select **More/High Sauté** and bring the mixture to a boil. Press **Cancel**, lock the lid in place and move the pressure valve to **Venting**. Select **Slow Cook** and set the temperature to **Less/Low**. Set the cooking time for 4 to 5 hours; the chicken is done when a skewer inserted into the largest thigh meets no resistance. Press **Cancel**, then carefully open the pot.

FINISH: Remove and discard the cinnamon and cardamom pods. Using a slotted spoon, transfer the chicken to a serving dish and tent with foil. Select **More/High Sauté**. Bring the cooking liquid to a boil and cook, stirring occasionally, until a spatula drawn though the mixture leaves a very brief trail, about 15 minutes. Press **Cancel** to turn off the pot, then whisk in the yogurt. Taste and season with salt and black pepper. Using potholders, carefully remove the insert from the housing and pour the sauce over the chicken and sprinkle with cilantro.

CHICKEN TAGINE WITH BUTTERNUT SQUASH AND SPINACH

Active time: 35 minutes

**Fast start to finish:
1 hour**

Slow start to finish:
4 to 4½ hours

Servings: 4

4 tablespoons extra-virgin olive oil, divided

Kosher salt and ground black pepper

2 teaspoons ground cinnamon

2 teaspoons ground cumin

2 teaspoons sweet paprika

1 teaspoon ground coriander

1½ pounds boneless, skinless chicken thighs, trimmed and cut into 1½-inch pieces

1 large yellow onion, thinly sliced lengthwise

4 medium garlic cloves, peeled and smashed

4 teaspoons finely grated fresh ginger

14½-ounce can diced tomatoes

8 ounces peeled butternut squash, cut into ¾-inch cubes (about 2 cups)

5-ounce container baby spinach

2 teaspoons grated lemon zest, plus 3 tablespoons lemon juice

A tagine is a North African stew cooked in a shallow, conical clay pot that goes by the same name. This richly aromatic dish features the warm spices and sweet-briny flavor profile common in Moroccan cooking. To simplify prep, look for already peeled and seeded butternut squash in the produce section of the supermarket. If you like, serve the tagine with chopped green olives and couscous, rice or warmed flatbread.

Don't drain the diced tomatoes. Their liquid adds sweetness and acidity to the stew.

START: In a small bowl, stir together 2 tablespoons of oil, 2½ teaspoons salt, ½ teaspoon pepper, the cinnamon, cumin, paprika and coriander. In a medium bowl, toss the chicken with 1 tablespoon of the spice paste.

On a 6-quart Instant Pot, select **More/High Sauté**. Add the remaining 2 tablespoons oil and heat until shimmering. Add the onion and 1 teaspoon salt, then cook, stirring occasionally, until softened, about 6 minutes. Add the garlic, ginger and the remaining spice paste. Cook, stirring constantly, until fragrant, 30 to 60 seconds. Stir in 2½ cups water, scraping up any browned bits. Add the tomatoes with their juices, the squash and chicken; stir to combine, then distribute the ingredients in an even layer.

FAST

Press **Cancel**, lock the lid in place and move the pressure valve to **Sealing**. Select **Pressure Cook** or **Manual**; make sure the pressure level is set to **High**. Set the cooking time for 3 minutes. When pressure cooking is complete, let the pressure reduce naturally for 10 minutes, then release the remaining steam by moving the pressure valve to **Venting**. Press **Cancel**, then carefully open the pot.

SLOW

With the pot still on **More/High Sauté**, bring the mixture to a boil. Press **Cancel**, lock the lid in place and move the pressure valve to **Venting**. Select **Slow Cook** and set the temperature to **Less/Low**. Set the cooking time for 3 to 3½ hours; the tagine is done when a skewer inserted into the chicken and squash meets no resistance. Press **Cancel**, then carefully open the pot.

FINISH: Stir in the spinach, then re-cover the pot without locking the lid in place. Let stand until the spinach wilts, about 3 minutes. Stir in the lemon zest and juice, then taste and season with salt and pepper.

SPICY BRAISED CHICKEN WITH COCONUT MILK, TURMERIC AND CASHEWS

Active time: 35 minutes

Fast start to finish:
1 hour

Slow start to finish:
4½ to 5½ hours

Servings: 4

3 tablespoons grapeseed or other neutral oil

1 medium yellow onion, halved and thinly sliced

Kosher salt

2 tablespoons tomato paste

1 tablespoon ground ginger

2 teaspoons ground turmeric

14½-ounce can diced tomatoes

⅓ cup coconut milk

⅓ cup roasted cashews, finely chopped

2 habanero chilies

3 pounds bone-in, skin-on chicken thighs, skin removed and discarded

Chopped fresh cilantro or flat-leaf parsley, to serve

Lime wedges, to serve

This curry-like chicken braise is our adaptation of a recipe in "Buttermilk Graffiti" by chef Edward Lee, who featured the dish in a chapter on Houston's Nigerian-American community. The combination of coconut milk and cashews gives the sauce a delicious richness. Whole habanero chilies add a backdrop of spiciness but not searing heat. If you want to turn up the dial, cut one or both of the chilies in half, keeping the seeds, but make sure to remove the halves before serving. Steamed rice is the perfect accompaniment to soak up all the creamy sauce.

Don't drain the tomatoes; their juices are needed for proper cooking and so that the finished sauce has the correct consistency. Also, make sure to press Cancel after the tomato paste and spices have cooked for about 30 seconds. This minimizes the amount of evaporation that occurs when the liquids are added.

START: On a 6-quart Instant Pot, select **Normal/Medium Sauté**. Add the oil and heat until shimmering. Add the onion and 1½ teaspoons salt, then cook, stirring occasionally, until lightly browned, 7 to 10 minutes. Add the tomato paste, ginger and turmeric, then cook, stirring, until fragrant, about 30 seconds. Press **Cancel**, then stir in the tomatoes with their juices, the coconut milk, cashews, habanero chilies and ⅓ cup water, scraping up any browned bits. Nestle the chicken in an even layer, skin side down, slightly overlapping the pieces if needed.

FAST

Lock the lid in place and move the pressure valve to **Sealing**. Select **Pressure Cook** or **Manual**; make sure the pressure level is set to **High**. Set the cooking time for 10 minutes. When pressure cooking is complete, allow the pressure to reduce naturally, then release any remaining steam by moving the pressure valve to **Venting**. Press **Cancel**, then carefully open the pot.

SLOW

Select **More/High Sauté** and bring the mixture to a boil. Press **Cancel**, lock the lid in place and move the pressure valve to **Venting**. Select **Slow Cook** and set the temperature to **Less/Low**. Set the cooking time for 4 to 5 hours; the chicken is done when a skewer inserted into the largest thigh meets no resistance. Press **Cancel**, then carefully open the pot.

FINISH: Using tongs, transfer the chicken to a serving dish and tent with foil. Remove and discard the chilies. Select **Normal/Medium Sauté**. Bring the cooking liquid to a simmer and cook, stirring often to prevent scorching, until the sauce is thick and creamy, about 15 minutes. Press **Cancel** to turn off the pot. Taste and season with salt. Using potholders, carefully remove the insert from the housing and pour the sauce over the chicken. Sprinkle with cilantro and serve with lime wedges.

BRAISED GINGER CHICKEN

Active time: 20 minutes

**Fast start to finish:
1 hour 10 minutes**

Slow start to finish:
4¼ to 5¼ hours

Servings: 4

1 tablespoon grapeseed
or other neutral oil

5 medium garlic cloves,
finely chopped

3-inch piece fresh ginger
(about 2 ounces), peeled
and sliced into thin coins

4 teaspoons fish sauce

½ cup sake

3 pounds bone-in, skin-on
chicken thighs, skin removed
and discarded, trimmed

1 tablespoon cornstarch

5 scallions, thinly sliced
on the diagonal, white and
green parts reserved
separately

1 Fresno or serrano chili,
halved, seeded and thinly
sliced

1 teaspoon unseasoned
rice vinegar

This simple chicken braise was inspired by a recipe in "The Slanted Door" by Charles Phan, chef/owner of the San Francisco restaurant by the same name. A generous amount of ginger and garlic, cooked only with sake, a splash of fish sauce and the chicken's natural juices, creates a meaty, aromatic broth that's made into a sauce to finish the dish. A mandoline makes quick work of slicing the ginger, but a chef's knife works, too. Fragrant jasmine rice is the perfect accompaniment, along with coarsely cracked white or black pepper.

Don't forget to remove the skin *from the chicken thighs. This prevents the cooking liquid, which is made into a sauce to finish the dish, from becoming too greasy. Don't worry about removing the ginger slices after cooking. Pressure-cooking tenderizes the ginger's fibrousness and mellows its fire.*

START: On a 6-quart Instant Pot, select **Normal/Medium Sauté**. Add the oil and heat until shimmering. Add the garlic and ginger, then cook, stirring, until fragrant, about 30 seconds. Add the fish sauce and sake, then bring to a gentle simmer. Nestle the chicken in an even layer, slightly overlapping the pieces, if needed.

FAST

Press **Cancel**, lock the lid in place and move the pressure valve to **Sealing**. Select **Pressure Cook** or **Manual**; make sure the pressure level is set to **High**. Set the cooking time for 10 minutes. When pressure cooking is complete, allow the pressure to reduce naturally, then release any remaining steam by moving the pressure valve to **Venting**. Press **Cancel**, then carefully open the pot.

SLOW

Select **More/High Sauté** and bring the mixture to a boil. Press **Cancel**, lock the lid in place and move the pressure valve to **Venting**. Select **Slow Cook** and set the temperature to **Less/Low**. Set the cooking time for 4 to 5 hours; the chicken is done when a skewer inserted into the largest thigh meets no resistance. Press **Cancel**, then carefully open the pot.

FINISH: Using tongs, transfer the chicken to a serving dish and tent with foil. In a small bowl, whisk together the cornstarch and ¼ cup of the cooking liquid until combined, then stir the mixture into the pot along with the scallion whites and half of the scallion greens. Select **Normal/Medium Sauté**. Bring to a simmer and cook, stirring constantly, until the sauce is lightly thickened, about 1 minute. Stir in the chilies and vinegar. Press **Cancel** to turn off the pot. Using potholders, carefully remove the insert from the housing and pour the sauce over the chicken, then sprinkle with the remaining scallion greens.

SENEGALESE BRAISED CHICKEN WITH ONIONS AND LIME

Active time: 35 minutes

Fast start to finish:
1¼ hours

Slow start to finish:
4½ to 5½ hours

Servings: 4

2 tablespoons grated lime zest, plus ¼ cup lime juice

1 habanero chili, stemmed, seeded and minced

3 tablespoons grapeseed or other neutral oil, divided

Kosher salt and ground black pepper

2 medium yellow onions, halved and thinly sliced

3 pounds bone-in, skin on chicken thighs, skin removed and discarded

1 tablespoon cornstarch

Chopped fresh chives, to serve

A riff on a recipe in "Yolele!" by Pierre Thiam, this dish gets big, bold flavor from just eight easy-to-find ingredients. Lightly caramelized onions deliver savory-sweet notes, lime zest adds fruitiness and lime juice gives the braising liquid bracing tartness. We use bone-in, skin-on chicken thighs but remove the skins before cooking so they don't render fat and make the sauce greasy and slick. Serve the braise with steamed rice.

Don't omit the habanero chili, as it adds subtle spiciness and unique fruity notes to the dish. But don't leave in the seeds, which contain the bulk of the heat; make sure to remove them before mincing (if you have rubber gloves, wear them to protect your hands from the heat-containing capsaicin).

START: In a small bowl, mix together the lime zest, habanero, 1 tablespoon oil, 1 tablespoon salt and 1 teaspoon pepper. Measure out 1 tablespoon of the mixture into another small bowl and set aside.

On a 6-quart Instant Pot, select Medium/Normal Sauté. Heat the remaining 2 tablespoons oil until shimmering. Add the onions and cook without stirring until golden brown on the bottom, about 7 minutes. Stir and continue to cook, stirring only occasionally, until the onions are evenly golden brown, another 7 to 10 minutes. Press **Cancel**. Add the lime juice, 2 tablespoons water and remaining zest-habanero mixture, scraping up any browned bits. Nestle the chicken in an even layer, skin side down, slightly overlapping the pieces if needed.

FAST

Lock the lid in place and move the pressure release valve to **Sealing**. Select **Pressure Cook** or **Manual**; make sure the pressure level is set to **High**. Set the cooking time for 10 minutes. When pressure cooking is complete, allow the pressure to release naturally for 15 minutes, then release any remaining steam by moving the pressure valve to **Venting**. Press **Cancel**, then carefully open the pot.

SLOW

Select **More/High Sauté** and bring the mixture to a boil. Press **Cancel**, lock the lid in place and move the pressure valve to **Venting**. Select **Slow Cook** and set the temperature to **Less/Low**. Set the cooking time for 4 to 5 hours; the chicken is done when a skewer inserted into the largest thigh meets no resistance. Press **Cancel**, then carefully open the pot.

FINISH: Using tongs, transfer the chicken to a serving dish and tent with foil. In a small bowl, whisk together the cornstarch and ¼ cup of the cooking liquid until combined, then stir into the pot. Select **Normal/Medium Sauté** and bring to a simmer, stirring constantly, then cook until lightly thickened, about 1 minute. Stir in the reserved zest-habanero mixture, then taste and season with salt and pepper. Using potholders, carefully remove the insert from the housing and pour the sauce over the chicken, then sprinkle with chives.

VERMOUTH-BRAISED CHICKEN AND POTATOES WITH FENNEL

Active time: 15 minutes

Fast start to finish:
40 minutes

Slow start to finish:
4¼ to 5 hours

Servings: 4

½ cup white vermouth

6 medium garlic cloves, smashed and peeled

1 tablespoon fennel seeds

Kosher salt and ground black pepper

2 pounds boneless, skinless chicken thighs, trimmed

8 ounces small Yukon Gold potatoes (1 to 1½ inches in diameter), halved

1 medium fennel bulb, trimmed, halved, cored and thinly sliced

1 tablespoon all-purpose flour

2 cups (about 1 ounce) lightly packed baby arugula, roughly chopped

1 tablespoon lemon juice

This one-pot meal with classic Italian flavors couldn't be easier. The ingredients are combined in the Instant Pot, then pressure cooked or slow cooked until the chicken is fork-tender. To finish the dish and create a flavorful sauce, we thicken the cooking liquid with 1 tablespoon of flour—just enough for clingability but without any heft. A little lemon juice adds acidity and brightness. Serve over polenta or with hunks of crusty bread.

Don't worry that ½ cup vermouth is too little liquid. The chicken and vegetables release flavorful juices as they cook that, combined with the vermouth, form the base for the sauce.

START: In a 6-quart Instant Pot, stir together the vermouth, garlic, fennel seeds, 1 teaspoon salt and ¼ teaspoon pepper. Add the chicken, potatoes and fennel; stir to combine, then distribute in an even layer.

FAST

Lock the lid in place and move the pressure valve to **Sealing**. Select **Pressure Cook** or **Manual**; make sure the pressure level is set to **High**. Set the cooking time for 8 minutes. When pressure cooking is complete, let the pressure release naturally, then release any remaining steam by moving the pressure valve to **Venting**. Press **Cancel**, then carefully open the pot.

SLOW

Select **More/High Sauté**, add ½ cup water and bring to a boil. Press **Cancel**, lock the lid in place and move the pressure valve to **Venting**. Select **Slow Cook** and set the temperature to **Less/Low**. Set the cooking time for 4 to 5 hours; the braise is done when a skewer inserted into the chicken meets no resistance. Press **Cancel**, then carefully open the pot.

FINISH: Using a slotted spoon, transfer the chicken and potatoes to a serving dish, then tent with foil. In a small bowl, whisk the flour with 2 tablespoons of the cooking liquid until smooth, then stir into the pot. Select **Normal/Medium Sauté** and bring the liquid to a simmer. Cook, stirring often, until lightly thickened, 2 to 5 minutes. Off heat, stir in the arugula and lemon juice, then taste and season with salt and pepper. Using potholders, carefully remove the insert from the housing and pour the sauce over the chicken and potatoes.

SPICY KOREAN BRAISED CHICKEN AND VEGETABLES

Active time: 10 minutes

**Fast start to finish:
55 minutes**

Slow start to finish:
4½ to 5½ hours

Servings: 4

3 tablespoons gochujang

2 tablespoons unseasoned rice vinegar

2 tablespoons soy sauce

1 tablespoon packed brown sugar

1 tablespoon toasted sesame oil, plus more to serve

2-inch piece fresh ginger (about 1½ ounces), peeled, cut into 3 pieces and smashed

5 medium garlic cloves, finely chopped

1 bunch scallions, whites chopped, greens cut into 1-inch lengths, reserved separately

2 pounds boneless, skinless chicken thighs, trimmed and halved

10 ounces Yukon Gold potatoes, peeled and cut into 1-inch chunks

2 medium carrots, peeled and cut into 1-inch pieces

Sesame seeds, toasted, to serve

This flavor-packed stew, called dakbokkeumtang, counts gochujang, or Korean fermented chili paste, as one of its primary seasonings. The thick, bright-red paste usually is sold in plastic tubs or bottles in Asian markets or in the international aisle of regular supermarkets. Soy sauce and a dose of brown sugar add salty-sweet flavor to balance the dish, while sesame oil and seeds add nutty notes. The potatoes and carrots absorb the seasonings so the pieces are flavored throughout. Make sure to cut the vegetables into 1-inch pieces, not smaller, so they don't end up overdone. Serve with steamed rice.

Don't use chicken breasts instead of thighs. *Sturdy dark meat does well when braised, but more delicate white meat dries out and turns tough. Dark meat also lends the finished dish richer, meatier flavor.*

START: In a 6-quart Instant Pot, whisk together the gochujang, vinegar, soy sauce, sugar, sesame oil, ginger, garlic and scallion whites. Add the chicken and toss to coat. Let stand for 15 minutes. Stir in the potatoes, carrots and ½ cup water, then distribute in an even layer.

FAST

Lock the lid in place and move the pressure valve to **Sealing**. Select **Pressure Cook** or **Manual**; make sure the pressure level is set to **High**. Set the cooking time for 8 minutes. When pressure cooking is complete, let the pressure reduce naturally for 10 minutes, then release the remaining steam by moving the pressure valve to **Venting**. Press **Cancel**, then carefully open the pot.

SLOW

Select **More/High Sauté** and bring the mixture to a boil. Press **Cancel**, lock the lid in place and move the pressure valve to **Venting**. Select **Slow Cook** and set the temperature to **Less/Low**. Set the cooking time for 4 to 5 hours; the stew is done when a skewer inserted into the chicken meets no resistance. Press **Cancel**, then carefully open the pot.

FINISH: Remove and discard the ginger, then stir in the scallion greens. Transfer to a serving bowl, drizzle with additional sesame oil and sprinkle with sesame seeds.

CHICKEN EN COCOTTE WITH WHITE WINE, GRAINY MUSTARD AND TARRAGON

Active time: 35 minutes
Start to finish: 1¼ hours
Servings: 4

3½-pound whole chicken, patted dry, wings tucked

Kosher salt and ground black pepper

5 tablespoons salted butter, cut into 1-tablespoon pieces, divided

1 medium yellow onion, halved and thinly sliced

8 medium garlic cloves, peeled and halved

1 cup dry white wine

2 thyme sprigs or 1 teaspoon dried thyme

3 tablespoons lemon juice

3 tablespoons whole-grain mustard

½ cup finely chopped fresh tarragon

In the classic French dish chicken en cocotte, a whole chicken is gently cooked in a covered pot (cocotte) until tender and moist, then carved for serving. The technique requires little prep and much of the cooking is hands-off and fuss-free. Using the Instant Pot makes the dish even easier by shaving off cooking time. To make this recipe, you will need the steam rack with handles included with the Instant Pot. The tarragon is added to the sauce just before serving so it remains vibrant and fresh; a good time to prep it is during the natural pressure release. We came up with two variations (see following pages), one with cherry tomatoes and green olives and another with shallots and apples. Roasted potatoes are an excellent accompaniment.

Don't use a chicken larger than 3½ pounds or it will be too large to allow heat to circulate and will cook unevenly. Don't worry if the chicken isn't completely done after 16 minutes of pressure cooking and a 20-minute natural pressure release. Simply reseal the pot and pressure cook for a few minutes more following the directions in the recipe.

START: Season the chicken on all sides with salt and pepper. Place the chicken breast side up on the steam rack with handles; set aside. On a 6-quart Instant Pot, select **More/High Sauté**. Add 1 tablespoon of butter and let melt. Add the onion and cook, stirring occasionally, until beginning to brown, about 8 minutes. Add the garlic and cook, stirring, until fragrant, about 30 seconds. Stir in the wine and thyme and bring to a simmer. Press **Cancel**, then lower the rack with the chicken into the pot.

FAST

Lock the lid in place and move the pressure valve to **Sealing**. Select **Pressure Cook** or **Manual**; make sure the pressure level is set to **High**. Set the cooking time for 16 minutes. When pressure cooking is complete, allow the pressure to reduce naturally for 20 minutes, then release the remaining steam by moving the pressure valve to **Venting**. Press **Cancel**, then carefully open the pot. The center of the thickest part of the breast should register about 160°F and the thickest part of the thighs about 175°F. If they do not, lock the lid back in place and move the pressure valve to **Sealing**. Select **Pressure**

Cook or **Manual**; make sure the pressure level is set to **High**. Set the cooking time for 3 or 4 minutes. When pressure cooking is complete, quick-release the steam by moving the pressure valve to **Venting**. Press **Cancel**, then carefully open the pot. Recheck the internal temperature; if the chicken is still not done, repeat the process and pressure cook for another 3 to 4 minutes. Using a kitchen towel or 2 pairs of tongs, carefully grab the handles of the rack, lift out the chicken and set the rack on a cutting board. Let rest while you make the sauce.

FINISH: If you used thyme sprigs, remove and discard them. Using a large spoon, skim off and discard the fat from the surface of the cooking liquid. Select **More/High Sauté**, bring to a simmer and cook, stirring occasionally, until slightly thickened and reduced to about 1 cup with solids, about 5 minutes. Press **Cancel** to turn off the pot. Using potholders, carefully remove the insert from the housing. Whisk in the remaining 4 tablespoons butter, the lemon juice and mustard, then taste and season with salt and pepper. Transfer the chicken from the rack directly to the board. Remove the legs by cutting through the hip joints. Remove and discard the skin from the legs, then separate the thighs from the drumsticks. Remove the breast meat from the bone, remove and discard the skin, then cut each crosswise into thin slices. Arrange the chicken on a platter. Transfer the sauce to a bowl, stir in the tarragon and serve with the chicken.

CHICKEN EN COCOTTE WITH CHERRY TOMATOES, GREEN OLIVES AND OREGANO

Active time: 40 minutes

Start to finish: 1¼ hours

Servings: 4

3½-pound whole chicken, patted dry, wings tucked

Kosher salt and ground black pepper

2 tablespoons extra-virgin olive oil

1 medium yellow onion, halved and thinly sliced

1 teaspoon smoked paprika

1 pint grape or cherry tomatoes

½ cup pimiento-stuffed green olives, halved

2 teaspoons grated orange zest, plus 1 cup orange juice

1 teaspoon dried oregano

2 teaspoons cornstarch

¼ cup finely chopped fresh oregano

In this version of chicken en cocotte, the mildness of the bird is accented with robust Mediterranean flavors. We use fresh orange juice as the cooking liquid and stir in grated zest at the end to infuse the sauce with citrus. It's easiest to grate the zest when the fruit is whole, so be sure to zest before halving and juicing. Oregano in two forms, dried and fresh, gives the dish layered herbal flavor. Serve with warm crusty bread.

Don't use a chicken larger than 3½ pounds or it will be too large to allow heat to circulate and will cook unevenly. Don't worry if the chicken isn't completely done after 16 minutes of pressure cooking and a 20-minute natural pressure release. Simply reseal the pot and pressure cook for a few minutes more following the directions in the recipe.

START: Season the chicken on all sides with salt and pepper. Place the chicken breast side up on the steam rack with handles; set aside. On a 6-quart Instant Pot, select **More/High Sauté**. Add the oil and heat until shimmering. Add the onion and cook, stirring occasionally, until beginning to brown, about 8 minutes. Add the paprika and cook, stirring, until fragrant, about 30 seconds. Stir in the tomatoes, olives, orange juice and dried oregano, then bring to a simmer. Press **Cancel**, then lower the rack with the chicken into the pot.

FAST

Lock the lid in place and move the pressure valve to **Sealing**. Select **Pressure Cook** or **Manual**; make sure the pressure level is set to **High**. Set the cooking time for 16 minutes. When pressure cooking is complete, allow the pressure to reduce naturally for 20 minutes, then release the remaining steam by moving the pressure valve to **Venting**. Press **Cancel**, then carefully open the pot. The center of the thickest part of the breast should register about 160°F and the thickest part of the thighs about 175°F. If they do not, lock the lid back in place and move the pressure valve to **Sealing**. Select **Pressure**

Cook or **Manual**; make sure the pressure level is set to **High**. Set the cooking time for 3 or 4 minutes. When pressure cooking is complete, quick-release the steam by moving the pressure valve to **Venting**. Press **Cancel**, then carefully open the pot. Recheck the internal temperature; if the chicken is still not done, repeat the process to pressure cook for another 3 to 4 minutes. Using a kitchen towel or two pairs of tongs, carefully grab the handles of the rack, lift out the chicken and set the rack on a cutting board. Let rest while you make the sauce.

FINISH: Using a large spoon, skim off and discard the fat from the surface of the cooking liquid. Select **More/High Sauté** and bring to a simmer. Cook, stirring occasionally, until the tomatoes burst, about 5 minutes. In a small bowl, stir together the cornstarch and 2 tablespoons water, then stir into the tomato-olive mixture. Cook, stirring constantly, until the sauce is slightly thickened, about 1 minute. Press **Cancel** to turn off the pot. Using potholders, carefully remove the insert from the housing, then stir in the orange zest and the fresh oregano. Taste and season with salt and pepper. Transfer the chicken from the rack directly to the cutting board. Remove the legs from the chicken by cutting through the hip joints. Remove and discard the skin from the legs, then separate the thighs from the drumsticks. Remove the breast meat from the bone, remove and discard the skin, then cut each crosswise into thin slices. Arrange the chicken on a platter. Transfer the sauce to a bowl and serve with the chicken.

CHICKEN EN COCOTTE WITH SHALLOTS, APPLES AND PARSLEY

Active time: 40 minutes
Start to finish: 1¼ hours
Servings: 4

2 crisp, red-skinned apples, unpeeled, quartered lengthwise, cored and thinly sliced

2 tablespoons cider vinegar

Kosher salt and ground black pepper

3½-pound whole chicken, patted dry, wings tucked

2 tablespoons salted butter

3 large shallots, halved and thinly sliced

1 cup unfiltered apple juice or apple cider

2 sprigs thyme or 1 teaspoon dried thyme

2 teaspoons cornstarch

¼ cup finely chopped fresh flat-leaf parsley

Tangy-sweet sliced apples and savory shallots add depth to a cider-based sauce in this version of chicken en cocotte. A crisp, red-skinned apple such as Honeycrisp or Fuji works best; we leave the skins on for color. The chicken is cooked on the steam rack with handles included with the Instant Pot; the long handles make it easy to lower the bird into the pot and to remove it when done.

Don't use a chicken larger than 3½ pounds or it will be too large to allow heat to circulate and will cook unevenly. Don't worry if the chicken isn't completely done after 16 minutes of pressure cooking and a 20-minute natural pressure release. Simply reseal the pot and pressure cook for a few minutes more following the directions in the recipe.

START: In a small bowl, stir together the apples, vinegar and ½ teaspoon salt; set aside. Season the chicken on all sides with salt and pepper. Place the chicken breast side up on a steam rack with handles; set aside. On a 6-quart Instant Pot, select **More/High Sauté**. Add the butter and let melt. Add the shallots and cook, stirring occasionally, until beginning to brown, about 8 minutes. Stir in the cider and thyme and bring to a simmer. Press **Cancel**, then lower the rack with the chicken into the pot.

FAST

Lock the lid in place and move the pressure valve to **Sealing**. Select **Pressure Cook** or **Manual**; make sure the pressure level is set to **High**. Set the cooking time for 16 minutes. When pressure cooking is complete, allow the pressure to reduce naturally for 20 minutes, then release the remaining steam by moving the pressure valve to **Venting**. Press **Cancel**, then carefully open the pot. The center of the thickest part of the breast should register about 160°F and the thickest part of the thighs about 175°F. If they do not, lock the lid back in place and move the pressure valve to **Sealing**. Select **Pressure**

Cook or **Manual**; make sure the pressure level is set to **High**. Set the cooking time for 3 or 4 minutes. When pressure cooking is complete, quick-release the steam by moving the pressure valve to **Venting**. Press **Cancel**, then carefully open the pot. Recheck the internal temperature; if the chicken is still not done, repeat the process to pressure cook for another 3 to 4 minutes. Using a kitchen towel or two pairs of tongs, carefully grab the handles of the rack, lift out the chicken and set the rack on a cutting board. Let rest while you make the sauce.

FINISH: If you used thyme sprigs, remove and discard them. Using a large spoon, skim off and discard the fat from the surface of the cooking liquid. Select **More/High Sauté** and bring to a simmer. Stir in the apples along with their liquid and cook, stirring occasionally, until tender, about 5 minutes. In a small bowl, stir together the cornstarch and 2 tablespoons water, then stir into the apple mixture. Cook, stirring constantly, until the sauce is lightly thickened, about 1 minute. Press **Cancel** to turn off the pot. Using potholders, carefully remove the insert from the housing. Taste and season with salt and pepper. Transfer the chicken from the rack directly to the cutting board. Remove the legs from the chicken by cutting through the hip joints. Remove and discard the skin from the legs, then separate the thighs from the drumsticks. Remove the breast meat from the bone, remove and discard the skin, then cut each crosswise into thin slices. Arrange the chicken on a platter. Transfer the sauce to a bowl, stir in the parsley and serve with the chicken.

PULLED CHICKEN WITH CHIPOTLE CHILIES

Active time: 30 minutes

Fast start to finish:
1½ hours

Slow start to finish:
4½ to 5½ hours

Servings: 4

3 or 4 chipotle chilies in adobo sauce, minced, plus 2 tablespoons adobo sauce

Kosher salt and ground black pepper

2½ pounds boneless, skinless chicken thighs, patted dry and halved crosswise

1 tablespoon extra-virgin olive oil

1 large white onion, halved and thinly sliced

6 medium garlic cloves, finely chopped

1 tablespoon ground cumin

Two 6-inch corn tortillas, torn into rough 2-inch pieces

28-ounce can crushed tomatoes

½ cup finely chopped fresh cilantro

This is a version of classic tinga from the Mexican state of Puebla. We skipped the typical pork and chorizo sausage in favor of leaner, faster-cooking chicken thighs. And we took a cue from our recipe for chicken in green mole and thickened the sauce by cooking tortillas right in the pot with the other ingredients. The shredded chicken can be tucked into tacos or wrapped up with other fillings to make a burrito, or serve it simply with rice or tortillas alongside. Diced white onion, shredded cabbage, sliced avocado and/or crumbled queso fresco are excellent additions that add color, flavor and texture.

Don't use flour tortillas or tortillas made from a corn-flour blend; neither will break down properly to thicken the sauce. After pouring the tomatoes into the pot, don't stir them because they have a tendency to stick and burn on the bottom of the pot.

START: In a large bowl, combine the adobo sauce and 1 teaspoon salt, then add the chicken and stir to coat. On a 6-quart Instant Pot, select **More/High Sauté**. Add the oil and heat until shimmering. Add the onion and cook, stirring occasionally, until softened, about 5 minutes. Stir in the garlic, cumin and chipotle chilies, then cook, stirring, until fragrant, about 1 minute. Add ½ cup water, scraping up any browned bits. Add the chicken, stir to combine, then distribute in an even layer. Scatter the tortilla pieces evenly over the chicken. Pour the tomatoes over the top but do not stir.

FAST

Press **Cancel**, lock the lid in place and move the pressure valve to **Sealing**. Select **Pressure Cook** or **Manual**; make sure the pressure level is set to **High**. Set the cooking time for 8 minutes. When pressure cooking is complete, allow the pressure to reduce naturally for 15 minutes, then release the remaining steam by moving the pressure valve to **Venting**. Press **Cancel**, then carefully open the pot.

SLOW

With the pot still on **More/High Sauté**, bring the mixture to a boil. Press **Cancel**, lock the lid in place and move the pressure valve to **Venting**. Select **Slow Cook** and set the temperature to **Less/Low**. Set the cooking time for 4 to 5 hours; the chicken is done when a skewer inserted into the largest piece meets no resistance. Press **Cancel**, then carefully open the pot.

FINISH: Using a slotted spoon, transfer the chicken to a large bowl and let cool for about 5 minutes. Using two forks, shred the meat. Select **More/High Sauté** and bring the sauce to a simmer. Cook, stirring often and scraping the bottom of the pot, until slightly thickened, 5 to 8 minutes. Press **Cancel** to turn off the pot. Return the chicken to the pot, add the cilantro and stir to combine. Taste and season with salt and pepper.

SPICY SICHUAN STEAMED CHICKEN

Active time: 20 minutes
Start to finish: 1 hour
Servings: 4

¼ cup chili oil

1-inch piece fresh ginger, peeled and thinly sliced

1 bunch cilantro, stems minced, leaves chopped, reserved separately

2 teaspoons Sichuan peppercorns (see note)

3 tablespoons soy sauce

2 tablespoons unseasoned rice vinegar

2 teaspoons white sugar

3 bone-in, skin-on chicken breasts (10 to 12 ounces each), skin removed and discarded

1 tablespoon cornstarch

¼ cup roasted peanuts, chopped

This Sichuan chicken dish, called kou shui ji, usually is a poached whole chicken that's sliced, then drenched in an aromatic chili oil sauce. Here we use only chicken breasts, cooking them in a chili oil infusion; the resulting cooking liquid becomes a spicy, flavorful sauce that's drizzled over the sliced meat. Sichuan peppercorns, which have a unique tongue-tingling flavor, are unrelated to black or white peppercorns; they are reddish-brown and resemble tiny dried berries. Look for them in Asian supermarkets; if not available, use 1 teaspoon black peppercorns instead. The flavor will be different, but still good. The chicken can be served warm, room temperature or cold. Wrap the slices in lettuce leaves or serve over steamed jasmine rice with an extra drizzle of chili oil, if desired.

Don't forget to remove the skin from the chicken. This helps the seasonings penetrate the meat and prevents the cooking liquid from becoming greasy with rendered fat.

START: On a 6-quart Instant Pot, select **Normal/Medium Sauté**. Add the chili oil, ginger, cilantro stems and Sichuan peppercorns. Cook, stirring, until sizzling and fragrant, 2 to 3 minutes. Press **Cancel** and let the mixture cool until the sizzling stops, about 5 minutes. Whisk in the soy sauce, vinegar, sugar and ¼ cup water. Place the chicken breasts flesh side down in the liquid.

FAST

Lock the lid in place and move the pressure valve to **Sealing**. Select **Pressure Cook** or **Manual**; adjust the pressure level to **Low**. Set the cooking time for 8 minutes. When pressure cooking is complete, allow the pressure to reduce naturally, then release any remaining steam by moving the pressure valve to **Venting**. Press **Cancel**, then carefully open the pot.

FINISH: Transfer the chicken to a deep serving platter. Set a fine mesh strainer over a medium bowl. Using potholders, carefully remove the insert from the housing and pour the cooking liquid through the strainer; return the insert to the housing. Press on the solids in the strainer to remove as much liquid as possible; discard the solids. Add the cornstarch to the strained liquid and whisk to combine. Return the liquid to the insert and add the peanuts, then select **Normal/Medium Sauté**. Bring to a simmer, stirring constantly, until lightly thickened, 2 to 3 minutes. Press **Cancel** to turn off the pot. Carve the chicken off the bones, slicing the breasts crosswise into ¼-inch slices, and return to the platter. Sprinkle with the cilantro leaves, then pour the sauce over. Let stand for about 10 minutes before serving.

BUTTER CHICKEN

Active time: 25 minutes
Start to finish: 1 hour
Slow 3½ to 4½ hours
Servings: 4 to 6

28-ounce can whole peeled tomatoes

1 cup roasted salted cashews

¼ cup garam masala

5 teaspoons ground cumin

2 tablespoons finely grated fresh ginger

Kosher salt and ground black pepper

2½ pounds boneless, skinless chicken thighs, cut into 1½-inch pieces

2 tablespoons salted butter, cut into 2 pieces

1 medium yellow onion, chopped

6 medium garlic cloves, finely chopped

4 tablespoons finely chopped fresh cilantro, divided

2 tablespoons lime juice

2 tablespoons honey

Our Instant Pot version of classic Indian butter chicken is rich and flavorful, but its creaminess is supplied by just 2 tablespoons of butter along with pureed cashews, not by glugs of heavy cream, as often is the case. For best flavor, use roasted salted cashews rather than raw. The cilantro is used at the very end, so to save time and ensure it remains fresh and fragrant, prep it while the chicken cooks. Serve with basmati rice or warm naan.

Don't bother washing out the blender between pureeing the tomatoes and cashews; you can leave the cashew puree in the blender jar until ready to use to avoid dirtying another bowl.

START: In a blender, puree the tomatoes with their juices until smooth, about 1 minute; transfer to a medium bowl and set aside. Add the cashews and ¾ cup water to the blender, then puree until smooth, about 1 minute; set aside if pressure cooking or transfer to a small bowl, cover and refrigerate if slow cooking. In a large bowl, whisk together the garam masala, cumin, ginger and 2 teaspoons salt. Add the chicken and toss to coat; set aside. On a 6-quart Instant Pot, select **More/High Sauté**. Add the butter and let melt. Add the onion and cook, stirring occasionally, until softened, 3 to 5 minutes. Add the garlic and cook, stirring, until fragrant, about 30 seconds. Stir in the chicken and tomatoes, then distribute in an even layer.

FAST

Press **Cancel**, lock the lid in place and move the pressure valve to **Sealing**. Select **Pressure Cook** or **Manual**; make sure the pressure level is set to **High**. Set the cooking time for 10 minutes. When pressure cooking is complete, quick-release the steam by moving the pressure valve to **Venting**. Press **Cancel**, then carefully open the pot.

SLOW

With the pot still on **More/High Sauté**, bring the mixture to a boil. Press **Cancel**, lock the lid in place and move the pressure valve to **Venting**. Select **Slow Cook** and set the temperature to **Less/Low**. Set the cooking time for 3 to 4 hours; the chicken is done when a skewer inserted into a large piece meets no resistance. Press **Cancel**, then carefully open the pot.

FINISH: Stir the cashew puree into the chicken mixture, scraping the bottom of the pot. Select **Less/Low Sauté** and cook, stirring often, until the sauce has thickened and coats the chicken, 4 to 5 minutes. Using potholders, carefully remove the insert from the housing. Let cool for about 5 minutes. Stir in 3 tablespoons of cilantro, the lime juice and honey, then taste and season with salt and pepper. Serve sprinkled with the remaining 1 tablespoon cilantro.

CHICKEN BIRYANI

Active time: 30 minutes

**Start to finish:
1 hour 10 minutes**

Servings: 4

2 teaspoons garam masala

1½ teaspoons ground turmeric

1 teaspoon ground cardamom

6 medium garlic cloves, finely chopped

1 tablespoon finely grated fresh ginger

1 jalapeño chili, stemmed and sliced into thin rounds

⅓ cup chopped fresh cilantro

2 pounds boneless, skinless chicken thighs, trimmed and cut into 3-inch pieces

2 tablespoons grapeseed or other neutral oil

2 medium yellow onions, chopped

1 cinnamon stick

Kosher salt

2 bay leaves

1 cup basmati rice, rinsed and drained

Lemon wedges, to serve

Made the traditional way, this classic Indian and Pakistani chicken and rice dish requires a long list of ingredients and time-intensive prep. Our simplified Instant Pot version can be on the table with only about 30 minutes active work. And because we've pared back the ingredients, the flavors are lighter and brighter, yet still complex and balanced. If you like, offer yogurt on the side; its cooling qualities perfectly complement the spice-rich biryani.

Don't mix the rice into the chicken mixture after sprinkling the grains into the pot. Sitting on top of the layer of chicken, the rice steams gently so the grains cook up light and fluffy, not dense and sodden. Also, after opening the pot before allowing the rice to rest, don't forget to cover it with a kitchen towel. The towel absorbs moisture while preventing the rice from cooling too quickly.

START: In a medium bowl, stir together the garam masala, turmeric, cardamom, garlic, ginger and 3 tablespoons water to form a paste. Add the jalapeño, half the cilantro and the chicken, then toss until well combined.

On a 6-quart Instant Pot, select **Normal/Medium Sauté**. Add the oil and heat until shimmering. Add the onions and cinnamon, then cook, stirring often, until the onions are golden brown, 10 to 12 minutes. Pour in 1 cup water, scraping up any browned bits. Stir in 2 teaspoons salt and the bay. Add the chicken with its marinade; stir to combine, then distribute in an even layer. Sprinkle the rice evenly into the pot; do not stir.

FAST

Press **Cancel**, lock the lid in place and move the pressure valve to **Sealing**. Select **Pressure Cook** or **Manual**; adjust the pressure level to **Low**. Set the cooking time for 10 minutes. When pressure cooking is complete, quick-release the steam by moving the pressure valve to **Venting**. Press **Cancel**, then carefully open the pot.

FINISH: Drape a clean kitchen towel across the pot and let stand for 10 minutes. Transfer the biryani to a serving dish, removing and discarding the cinnamon and bay. Sprinkle with the remaining cilantro and serve with lemon wedges.

TURKEY MEATBALLS
IN TOMATO-CHIPOTLE SAUCE

Active time: 30 minutes
Start to finish: 1 hour
Servings: 4

¾ cup fine dry breadcrumbs

4 teaspoons ground cumin

½ cup finely chopped fresh cilantro, divided

2 or 3 chipotle chilies in adobo, minced, plus 1 tablespoon adobo sauce

4 ounces pepper jack cheese, 2 ounces finely shredded (½ cup), 2 ounces shredded (½ cup)

Kosher salt and ground black pepper

1 pound ground turkey (preferably dark meat)

2 tablespoons salted butter

28-ounce can crushed tomatoes

14½-ounce can diced tomatoes

Finely chopped white onion, to serve

Lime wedges, to serve

Albóndigas en chipotle, or meatballs in chipotle sauce, is a Mexican classic. We use ground turkey (dark meat is best for flavor and texture, but white meat works, too), and we bind it with both breadcrumbs and pepper jack cheese. Additional cheese goes on after cooking for richness. Make sure to grate the pepper jack that goes into the meatballs on the small holes of a box grater so it integrates easily with the other ingredients; the cheese that goes on as garnish can be shredded on the large holes. If you're sensitive to chili heat, start by adding only two chipotle chilies when making the sauce, then when adjusting the salt and pepper at the end, stir in additional minced chipotle if you'd like more kick. Serve with rice or warmed tortillas.

Don't add the meatballs to the pot without first refrigerating them. *Chilling firms them up so they better retain their shape when pressure-cooked.*

START: In a large bowl, stir together the breadcrumbs, cumin, ¼ cup of cilantro, the adobo sauce, the finely shredded cheese, 1½ teaspoons salt and ½ cup water until well combined. Add the turkey and mix with your hands until homogenous. Divide into 10 portions (about ⅓ cup each), then form into balls about 2 inches in diameter and place on a large plate. Refrigerate uncovered for 15 minutes.

FAST

On a 6-quart Instant Pot, select **More/High Sauté**. Add the butter and let melt. Add the crushed tomatoes, diced tomatoes with juices and minced chipotle chilies, then bring to a simmer, stirring occasionally. Place the chilled meatballs in an even layer in the tomato mixture, gently pressing to submerge them. Press **Cancel**, lock the lid in place and move the pressure valve to

Sealing. Select **Pressure Cook** or **Manual**; make sure the pressure level is set to **High**. Set the cooking time for 10 minutes. When pressure cooking is complete, allow the pressure to reduce naturally for 10 minutes, then release the remaining steam by moving the pressure valve to **Venting**. Press **Cancel**, then carefully open the pot.

FINISH: Using a slotted spoon, transfer the meatballs to a serving dish. Sprinkle with the shredded cheese, dividing it evenly, then tent with foil. Select **More/High Sauté**. Bring the tomato mixture to a simmer and cook, stirring often, until the sauce has thickened, about 10 minutes (you should have about 4 cups). Press **Cancel** to turn off the pot. Taste and season with salt and pepper. Stir in the remaining ¼ cup cilantro, then spoon about half of the sauce over the meatballs. Sprinkle with chopped onion and serve with the remaining sauce and lime wedges on the side.

PORK

CONTENTS

PORK

We **balance the sweetness of pork with spicy and savory flavors.** White miso adds savory notes to our pork and tofu soup. Gochujang, a Korean fermented chili paste, brings spicy warmth to our glazed baby back ribs and our miso-gochujang pork. In a pairing borrowed from Portugal, we combine braised pork with steamed clams; the mild meat and briny shellfish are stellar together. Spicy, tangy ginger is another great match for pork. For maximum impact that keeps flavors fresh, we add it both during and after the cooking in our braised pork with ginger and star anise.

To keep the fat factor down, **we rigorously trim the fat from pork shoulder.** We also skim surface fat from dishes such as our pork, corn and butternut squash stew to make sure the flavors aren't dulled. For lean pork loin, on the other hand, we leave the fat to keep the cut juicy. And we **use acid to complement rich roasts and braises.** Pickled red onions add a piquant contrast to our carnitas; red wine and lemon juice bring balance to our coriander-braised pork, a take on afelia, a pork stew from Cyprus.

Pork in the Instant Pot doesn't always need to be a chunky stew or a sliceable roast. We sometimes shred the pork after cooking, as we do for our Cuban-inspired mojo and for our Mexican carnitas. And we call for ground pork to make a spicy, umami-packed sauce for Chinese dan dan noodles.

The Instant Pot moves slower-cooking cuts of pork into everyday territory. We use boneless shoulder in our version of Filipino adobo and baby back ribs for an Asian-inspired dish rich with a sticky, spicy-sweet glaze. Even lean pork loin roast turns out tender and moist, with about 30 minutes hands-on time.

PORK AND TOFU SOUP WITH MISO AND CABBAGE

Active time: 20 minutes

Fast cook time:
1 hour 10 minutes

Slow cook time:
4½ to 5½ hours

Servings: 4

½ cup white miso

6 medium garlic cloves, smashed and peeled

3-inch piece fresh ginger (about 2 ounces), peeled and thinly sliced

2 tablespoons grapeseed or other neutral oil

⅔ cup sake

1 pound boneless pork shoulder, trimmed and cut across the grain into ½-inch slabs

Kosher salt and ground white pepper

½ medium head napa cabbage (1 to 1½ pounds), halved lengthwise, then cut crosswise into 1-inch pieces

14-ounce container firm tofu, drained and cut into 1-inch cubes

3 tablespoons soy sauce

4 scallions, thinly sliced on the diagonal

Toasted sesame oil, to serve

White miso already is packed with umami, but browning it as we do to make this soup builds even more flavor. Just a small amount of pork is enough to create a rich, flavorful broth; firm tofu gives the dish substance without making it heavy. Make sure to use napa cabbage, not regular green cabbage; the frilly leaves of napa are more delicate and become tender and silky after just a few minutes of simmering, but the stems will remain crisp-tender. The cabbage, tofu and scallions aren't needed until near the end of cooking, so prep these ingredients while the soup cooks. If you like, garnish with toasted sesame seeds and serve with Japanese short-grain rice.

Don't fret when the miso begins to stick to the bottom of the pot. Just keep stirring to create an even coating of caramelized miso. Also, be sure to stir and scrape up the browned bottom before turning on the pressure cooker function in order to avoid getting a "burn" error message.

START: On a 6-quart Instant Pot, select **Normal/Medium Sauté**. Add the miso, garlic, ginger and oil. Cook, stirring constantly, until the miso sticks to the bottom of the pot and browns evenly, 3 to 4 minutes. Add the sake and 4 cups water, scraping up the browned bits. Add the pork and 1 teaspoon white pepper; stir, then distribute in an even layer.

FAST

Press **Cancel**, lock the lid in place and move the pressure valve to **Sealing**. Select **Pressure Cook** or **Manual**; make sure the pressure level is set to **High**. Set the cooking time for 27 minutes. When pressure cooking is complete, let the pressure reduce naturally for 15 minutes, then release the remaining steam by moving the pressure valve to **Venting**. Press **Cancel**, then carefully open the pot.

SLOW

With the pot still on **Normal/Medium Sauté**, bring the mixture to a boil. Press **Cancel**, lock the lid in place and move the pressure valve to **Venting**. Select **Slow Cook** and set the temperature to **More/High**. Set the cooking time for 4 to 5 hours; the soup is done when a skewer inserted into a piece of pork meets no resistance. Press **Cancel**, then carefully open the pot.

FINISH: Using a large spoon, skim off and discard the fat from the surface. Select **Normal/Medium Sauté** and bring to a simmer. Add the cabbage and tofu, then cook, stirring gently, until the leaves are wilted and the stems are crisp-tender, 2 to 4 minutes. Press **Cancel** to turn off the pot. Stir in the soy sauce, then taste and season with salt and pepper. Serve sprinkled with the scallions and drizzled with sesame oil.

PORK AND HOMINY STEW WITH CILANTRO AND LIME

Active time: 30 minutes

Fast start to finish:
1½ hours

Slow start to finish:
5½ to 6½ hours

Servings: 6

1 tablespoon grapeseed or other neutral oil

1 large yellow onion, chopped

Kosher salt and ground black pepper

3 jalapeño chilies, stemmed, seeded and thinly sliced

8 medium garlic cloves, finely chopped

2 teaspoons ground cumin

2 cups low-sodium chicken broth

29-ounce can hominy, rinsed and drained

3 pounds boneless pork shoulder, trimmed and cut into 1-inch chunks

1 cup finely chopped fresh cilantro

¼ cup lime juice, plus lime wedges to serve

Hominy is made by drying corn kernels, treating them with alkali, then cooking them until chewy-tender. This recipe pairs canned hominy with chunks of pork shoulder—a classic match in Mexican cooking—to create a simple, hearty and flavorful stew. The mild sweetness and earthy, nutty notes of the hominy balance the richness of the pork. Be sure to trim off as much fat as possible from the pork to prevent a greasy stew. Serve with shredded cabbage, sliced radishes and warmed tortillas.

Don't be shy about trimming the pork. *Pork shoulder is a fatty cut; to prevent the finished stew from being greasy, remove as much fat as possible before cooking.*

START: On a 6-quart Instant Pot, select **More/High Sauté**. Add the oil and heat until shimmering. Add the onion and ½ teaspoon salt, then cook, stirring occasionally, until the onion is golden brown, about 5 minutes. Add half of the jalapeños, the garlic and cumin, then cook, stirring, until fragrant, about 30 seconds. Pour in the broth, scraping up any browned bits. Add the hominy, pork and ½ teaspoon each salt and pepper; stir to combine, then distribute in an even layer.

FAST

Press **Cancel**, lock the lid in place and move the pressure valve to **Sealing**. Select **Pressure Cook** or **Manual**; make sure the pressure level is set to **High**. Set the cooking time for 25 minutes. When pressure cooking is complete, allow the pressure to reduce naturally for 15 minutes, then release the remaining steam by moving the pressure valve to **Venting**. Press **Cancel**, then carefully open the pot.

SLOW

With the pot still on **More/High Sauté**, bring the mixture to a boil. Press **Cancel**, lock the lid in place and move the pressure valve to **Venting**. Select **Slow Cook** and set the temperature to **More/High**. Set the cooking time for 5 to 6 hours; the stew is done when a skewer inserted into a chunk of pork meets no resistance. Press **Cancel**, then carefully open the pot.

FINISH: Using a large spoon, skim off and discard the fat from the surface. Stir in the cilantro and lime juice, then taste and season with salt and pepper. Serve with the remaining jalapeños.

PORK, CORN AND BUTTERNUT SQUASH STEW

Active time: 30 minutes

Fast start to finish:
1½ hours

Slow start to finish:
4½ to 5½ hours

Servings: 4 to 6

2 ears fresh corn, husks and silk removed

3 tablespoons extra-virgin olive oil

2 medium yellow onions, halved and thinly sliced

4 medium garlic cloves, finely chopped

1 tablespoon sweet paprika

1 tablespoon cumin seeds

¼ teaspoon cayenne pepper

2 pounds boneless pork shoulder, trimmed and cut into 1-inch chunks

8 ounces peeled and seeded butternut squash, cut into 1-inch chunks (about 2 cups)

1 cup grape or cherry tomatoes, halved

Kosher salt

¼ cup lightly packed fresh cilantro, chopped

Lemon wedges, to serve

This colorful stew is loosely based on Argentinian locro, a stick-to-your-ribs dish that traditionally includes multiple cuts of fresh and cured meats, hominy, legumes and winter squash. The flavors here skew sweet from the corn, tomatoes and butternut squash, but the cumin, garlic and pork balance with their savoriness. We prefer this stew made with fresh corn kernels cut from cobs, as this leaves us with stripped cobs to infuse even more corn flavor into the mix. But when fresh corn is not in season, frozen corn is a fine substitute. Use 2 cups frozen corn kernels; no need to thaw before use.

Don't cut the butternut squash into pieces smaller than 1 inch, *or they will become too soft and begin to break down.*

START: One at a time, stand each ear of corn in a bowl and use a chef's knife to cut off the kernels; you should have about 2 cups. Then use the back of the knife to scrape from top to bottom all around each cob, allowing the liquid to fall into the bowl. Add the kernels to the bowl, then cut each cob in half and reserve separately. On a 6-quart Instant Pot, select **More/High Sauté**. Add the oil and heat until shimmering. Add the onions and cook, stirring occasionally, until beginning to brown, 5 to 7 minutes. Stir in the garlic, paprika, cumin and cayenne, then cook until fragrant, about 30 seconds. Stir in the pork, squash, corn kernels and liquid, tomatoes, 2 cups water and 1 teaspoon salt, then distribute in an even layer. Add the corn cobs to the pot.

FAST

Press **Cancel**, lock the lid in place and move the pressure valve to **Sealing**. Select **Pressure Cook** or **Manual**; make sure the pressure level is set to **High**. Set the cooking time for 25 minutes. When pressure cooking is complete, allow the pressure to reduce naturally for 15 minutes, then release the remaining steam by moving the pressure valve to **Venting**. Press **Cancel**, then carefully open the pot.

SLOW

With the pot still on **More/High Sauté**, bring the mixture to a boil. Press **Cancel**, lock the lid in place and move the pressure valve to **Venting**. Select **Slow Cook** and set the temperature to **More/High**. Set the cooking time for 4 to 5 hours; the pork is done when a skewer inserted into the largest piece meets no resistance. Press **Cancel**, then carefully open the pot.

FINISH: Remove and discard the corn cobs. Using a large spoon, skim off and discard the fat from the surface. Taste and season with salt and pepper. Serve sprinkled with the cilantro and with lemon wedges on the side.

DAN DAN NOODLES

Active time: 50 minutes

Fast start to finish: 1½ hours

Servings: 4

10 ounces dried Asian wheat noodles, cooked, drained and rinsed

2 tablespoons plus 2 teaspoons toasted sesame oil

4 baby bok choy, roughly chopped

Kosher salt

2 tablespoons unseasoned rice vinegar

¼ cup sesame seeds

4 medium shallots, halved and thinly sliced

12 ounces ground pork

4 medium garlic cloves, finely chopped

¾ cup low-sodium beef broth or water

¼ cup oyster sauce

3 tablespoons hoisin sauce

1 tablespoon chili-garlic sauce, plus more as needed

1 tablespoon finely grated fresh ginger

Chili oil, to serve (optional)

Sichuan dan dan mian is a spicy ground pork and sesame sauce served over a tangle of wheat noodles. We use a few Chinese staple ingredients—oyster sauce, hoisin and chili-garlic sauce—to build big flavor. Preserved mustard greens are a common addition to dan dan noodles; for ease, we instead make a quick pickle with bok choy and stir it in at the end. You can use just about any variety of dried Asian wheat noodles as long as they're sturdy enough to stand up to the sauce.

Don't forget to rinse the noodles after cooking and draining so their excess starch doesn't make them overly sticky. Tossing them with a couple teaspoons of sesame oil will help prevent them from clinging together so that they're easier to portion.

START: Drizzle the rinsed noodles with the 2 teaspoons sesame oil, then toss until evenly coated; transfer to a serving bowl and set aside. In a medium bowl, combine the bok choy and 1 teaspoon salt. Massage the salt into the bok choy, then stir in the vinegar; set aside.

On a 6-quart Instant Pot, select **More/High Sauté**. Add the sesame seeds and toast, stirring often, until golden brown and fragrant, about 5 minutes. Press **Cancel** to turn off the pot. Using potholders, carefully remove the insert from the housing and pour the seeds into a small bowl; return the insert to the housing.

Select **More/High Sauté**. Add the remaining 2 tablespoons oil and shallots, then cook, stirring often, until the shallots are golden brown, 3 to 5 minutes. Add the pork and cook, stirring occasionally, until it begins to brown, 3 to 5 minutes. Stir in the garlic and cook until fragrant, about 30 seconds. Stir in the broth, oyster sauce, hoisin, 1 tablespoon of chili-garlic sauce and the sesame seeds, scraping the bottom of the pot; distribute the mixture in an even layer.

FAST

Press **Cancel**, lock the lid in place and move the pressure valve to **Sealing**. Select **Pressure Cook** or **Manual**; make sure the pressure level is set to **High**. Set the cooking time for 12 minutes. When pressure cooking is complete, allow the pressure to reduce naturally for 15 minutes, then release the remaining steam by moving the pressure valve to **Venting**. Press **Cancel**, then carefully open the pot.

FINISH: Using a large spoon, skim off and discard the fat from the surface. Select **More/High Sauté** and bring the mixture to a boil. Cook, stirring often and breaking up the meat, until the mixture begins to sizzle, about 5 minutes. Stir in the ginger and cook until fragrant, about 30 seconds. Using potholders, carefully remove the insert from the housing. Add the bok choy mixture and stir to combine. Let stand for 5 minutes. Taste and season with additional chili-garlic sauce, if desired. Pour the sauce onto the noodles and drizzle with chili oil, if using.

PORK RAGU WITH
GREEN OLIVES AND WARM SPICES

Active time: 30 minutes

**Fast start to finish:
1½ hours**

Slow start to finish:
5½ to 6½ hours

Servings: 4 to 6

2 tablespoons extra-virgin olive oil

8 ounces cremini mushrooms, trimmed and roughly chopped

3 bay leaves

Kosher salt and ground black pepper

¾ cup dry red wine

4 medium garlic cloves, smashed and peeled

1 teaspoon ground cinnamon

¼ teaspoon ground allspice

14½-ounce can crushed tomatoes

3 medium carrots, halved and cut into ½-inch pieces

2 medium celery stalks, sliced ½ inch thick

½ cup chopped pitted green olives (see note)

2 pounds boneless pork shoulder, trimmed and cut into 1-inch chunks

This hearty ragu straddles the line between sauce and stew. All the ingredients—from the cremini mushrooms to the warm spices to the crushed tomatoes—combine for an amazing depth of flavor in the braise. Green olives, added both at the beginning and end of cooking, add a wonderful briny undertone that balances the ragu's richness. Look for Castelvetrano olives, which are firm and meaty; they are sold in jars, or check the olive bar in the deli department. If not available, use any large jarred green olive; avoid canned olives, which tend to be soft and taste metallic. Toss the ragu with a chunky pasta shape such as ziti, spoon it over polenta or simply offer warm, crusty bread alongside. However you serve it, offer grated Parmesan cheese for sprinkling at the table.

Don't chop the carrots too finely. *Aim for ½-inch pieces to ensure they cook through fully yet retain their shape.*

START: On a 6-quart Instant Pot, select **More/High Sauté**. Add the oil and heat until shimmering. Add the mushrooms, bay and 1 teaspoon salt, then cook, stirring occasionally, until the liquid released by the mushrooms has evaporated, about 7 minutes. Stir in the wine, garlic, cinnamon and allspice, scraping up any browned bits, then bring to a simmer. Cook, stirring occasionally, until the wine has reduced to a syrup, 5 to 7 minutes. Press **Cancel**, then stir in the tomatoes, carrots, celery, half of the olives and ½ teaspoon pepper. Add the pork and stir to combine, then distribute in an even layer.

FAST

Lock the lid in place and move the pressure valve to **Sealing**. Select **Pressure Cook** or **Manual**; make sure the pressure level is set to **High**. Set the cooking time for 25 minutes. When pressure cooking is complete, allow the pressure to reduce naturally for 15 minutes, then release the remaining steam by moving the pressure valve to **Venting**. Press **Cancel**, then carefully open the pot.

SLOW

Select **More/High Sauté** and bring the mixture to a boil. Press **Cancel**, lock the lid in place and move the pressure valve to **Venting**. Select **Slow Cook** and set the temperature to More/Normal. Set the cooking time for 5 to 6 hours; the pork is done when a skewer inserted into a chunk meets no resistance. Press **Cancel**, then carefully open the pot.

FINISH: Remove and discard the bay. Using a large spoon, skim off and discard the fat from the surface. Stir in the remaining olives, slightly breaking up the meat and carrots to lightly thicken the sauce. Taste and season with salt and pepper.

PORTUGUESE PORK AND CLAMS

Active time: 30 minutes

Fast start to finish:
1½ hours

Slow start to finish:
5½ to 6½ hours

Servings: 6

2 pounds boneless pork shoulder, trimmed and cut into 1½-inch chunks

1 cup roasted red peppers, patted dry and thinly sliced

½ cup dry white wine

6 medium garlic cloves, finely chopped

4 teaspoons sweet paprika

3 bay leaves

2 tablespoons extra-virgin olive oil, plus more to serve

Kosher salt and ground black pepper

2 pounds hard-shell clams (about 1½ inches diameter), such as littleneck, scrubbed

2 cups lightly packed fresh cilantro, roughly chopped

Lemon wedges, to serve

This recipe is an Instant Pot take on traditional Portuguese carne de porco à Alentejana, or braised pork with steamed clams. It may seem like an unusual pairing, but the mild pork combined with briny clams, garlic, wine and olive oil is a winning combination. Massa de pimentão, a red pepper paste, traditionally is used to season the dish; we approximated its flavor by adding jarred roasted red peppers and sweet paprika. The clams and cilantro are added at the end of cooking. Scrub the clams and prep the cilantro while the pork cooks. The classic accompaniment for this dish is crisp fried potatoes, but roasted potatoes or warm crusty bread are excellent, too. We also like hot sauce on the side.

Don't use clams that are larger than 2 inches across. *They are too large to cook through with the pot's residual heat.*

START: To a 6-quart Instant Pot, add the pork, roasted peppers, wine, garlic, paprika, bay, oil, 1 teaspoon each salt and pepper, and ¼ cup water. Stir to combine, then distribute in an even layer.

FAST

Lock the lid in place and move the pressure valve to **Sealing**. Select **Pressure Cook** or **Manual**; make sure the pressure level is set to **High**. Set the cooking time for 25 minutes. When pressure cooking is complete, allow the pressure to reduce naturally for 15 minutes, then release the remaining steam by moving the pressure valve to **Venting**. Press **Cancel**, then carefully open the pot.

SLOW

Select **More/High Sauté** and bring the mixture to a boil. Press **Cancel**, lock the lid in place and move the pressure valve to **Venting**. Select **Slow Cook** and set the temperature to **More/High**. Set the cooking time for 5 to 6 hours; the pork is done when a skewer inserted into a chunk meets no resistance. Press **Cancel**, then carefully open the pot.

FINISH: Select **More/High Sauté** and bring the pork mixture to a simmer. Add the clams and stir, breaking the pork into slightly smaller pieces. Cook, stirring often, until the clams just begin to open, 2 to 5 minutes. Press **Cancel** to turn off the pot. Re-cover without locking the lid in place and let stand until the clams are fully opened, 5 to 7 minutes. Remove and discard any that do not open. Stir in the cilantro, then taste and season with salt and pepper. Serve drizzled with additional oil and with lemon wedges on the side.

FILIPINO PORK ADOBO

Active time: 25 minutes

**Fast start to finish:
1 hour 20 minutes**

Slow start to finish:
4½ to 5½ hours

Servings: 4 to 6

2 tablespoons grapeseed or other neutral oil

2 bunches scallions, white and light green parts cut into 1-inch pieces, green parts thinly sliced, reserved separately

8 medium garlic cloves, smashed and peeled

3 bay leaves

½ cup low-sodium soy sauce

¼ cup white vinegar

2 tablespoons honey

2 serrano chilies, stemmed and halved

Ground black pepper

3 pounds boneless pork shoulder, trimmed and cut into 2-inch chunks

1 tablespoon cornstarch

Adobo may well be the national dish of the Philippines, and each household has its own version. The defining flavors are vinegar, garlic, black pepper, bay and salt in some form (often soy sauce). For this version of pork adobo, instead of the more typical pork belly, we opted for boneless shoulder because it is easier to find in supermarkets but still is rich and flavorful. Honey, or any type of sweetener, is an unconventional ingredient in adobo, but we liked the way it balanced the salty and sour flavors in the dish. The serranos give the braise a gentle spiciness; if you prefer, use just one chili or keep both whole. Serve this over rice to soak up the sauce.

*Don't use regular soy sauce or the adobo will end up too salty. When cooking the scallion whites, garlic and bay, don't overstir; the goal is to develop deep browning, which builds flavor. And don't forget to press **Cancel** to turn off the pot before adding the soy and vinegar. This prevents the liquids from evaporating too quickly.*

START: On a 6-quart Instant Pot, select **More/High Sauté**. Add the oil and heat until shimmering. Add the scallion whites, garlic and bay, then cook without stirring until golden brown on the bottom, about 4 minutes. Stir and continue to cook, stirring only once or twice, until deeply browned, about another 2 minutes. Press **Cancel**, then stir in the soy, vinegar, honey, serranos and 1 teaspoon pepper, scraping up any browned bits. Add the pork; stir to combine, then distribute in an even layer.

FAST

Lock the lid in place and move the pressure valve to **Sealing**. Select **Pressure Cook** or **Manual**; make sure the pressure level is set to **High**. Set the cooking time for 30 minutes. When pressure cooking is complete, allow the pressure to release naturally for 15 minutes, then release the remaining steam by moving the pressure valve to **Venting**. Press **Cancel**, then carefully open the pot.

SLOW

Select **More/High Sauté** and bring the mixture to a boil. Press **Cancel**, lock the lid in place and move the pressure valve to **Venting**. Select **Slow Cook** and set the temperature to **More/High**. Set the cooking time for 4 to 5 hours; the pork is done when a skewer inserted into a piece meets no resistance. Press **Cancel**, then carefully open the pot.

FINISH: Using a large spoon, skim off and discard the fat from the surface. Remove and discard the chilies and bay. In a small bowl, whisk the cornstarch with 3 tablespoons of the cooking liquid, then stir into the pot. Select **Normal/Medium Sauté** and bring to a simmer, stirring constantly, and cook, stirring, until lightly thickened, about 1 minute. Press **Cancel** to turn off the pot. Taste and season with salt and pepper. Serve sprinkled generously with the scallion greens.

AGRODOLCE PORK LOIN WITH GRAPES, PARSLEY AND HAZELNUTS

Active time: 35 minutes

Fast start to finish:
1 hour 10 minutes

Servings: 4 to 6

2- to 2½-pound boneless pork loin

Kosher salt and ground black pepper

1 teaspoon grapeseed or other neutral oil

3 medium shallots, chopped

2 tablespoons honey

1 cup balsamic vinegar

3 tablespoons salted butter, cut into ½-inch pieces

1 cup lightly packed fresh flat-leaf parsley, chopped

½ cup seedless red grapes, halved

⅓ cup hazelnuts, toasted and finely chopped

Agrodolce is the Italian term for sweet and sour. In this recipe, honey provides the sweet while balsamic vinegar adds the sour. We sear only one side—the fat side—of a pork loin roast, then pressure cook it on a rack above the liquid that later becomes the sauce. Make sure your pork loin will fit comfortably in the pot and don't trim off the fat, as it adds richness to an otherwise lean cut. A simple salad of fresh parsley, red grapes and toasted hazelnuts makes this roast an elegant meal. To save time, prep the salad ingredients while the pork cooks.

Don't opt out of using the rack. If the pork sits directly in the liquid, the texture of the submerged areas will be affected by the vinegar's acidity. When making the sauce, don't add all the butter at once and make sure to reduce the sauce until glossy and full-bodied. If the sauce breaks and the butter separates, whisk in droplets of water until the sauce is once again shiny and emulsified.

START: Season the pork on all sides with salt and pepper. On a 6-quart Instant Pot, select **More/High Sauté**. Add the oil and heat until shimmering. Add the pork fat side down and cook until golden brown, about 10 minutes. Using tongs, transfer to a plate. Add the shallots to the pot and cook, stirring occasionally, until browned and slightly softened, about 4 minutes. Add the honey and continue to cook, stirring, until slightly darker in color, 1 to 2 minutes. Stir in the vinegar, bring to a simmer and cook, stirring occasionally, until slightly reduced, about 2 minutes. Press **Cancel** then set the pork fat side up on the rack with handles. Place in the pot and pour in any accumulated juices.

FAST

Lock the lid in place and move the pressure valve to **Sealing**. Select **Pressure Cook** or **Manual**; adjust the pressure level to **Low**. Set the cooking time for 25 minutes. When pressure cooking is complete, allow the pressure to reduce naturally, then release any remaining steam by moving the pressure valve to **Venting**. Press **Cancel**, then carefully open the pot. The center of the pork loin should register 135°F.

FINISH: Using a kitchen towel or tongs, carefully grab the handles of the rack and lift it out with the pork loin. Set on a large plate or cutting board. Select **More/High Sauté** and bring the liquid to a simmer. Whisk in the butter one piece at a time until fully incorporated. After all the butter has been added, cook until the sauce is glossy and a spoon drawn through it leaves a trail, 10 to 12 minutes. Meanwhile, in a small bowl, stir together the parsley, grapes, hazelnuts and ¼ teaspoon each salt and pepper; set aside. When the sauce is done, press **Cancel** to turn off the pot. Taste and season with salt and pepper. Transfer the pork from the rack directly to the cutting board. Thinly slice the pork and transfer to a platter, then spoon the sauce on and around the meat. Serve with the parsley-grape mixture.

BRAISED PORK WITH GINGER AND STAR ANISE

Active time: 25 minutes

Fast start to finish:
1¼ hours

Slow start to finish:
5½ to 6½ hours

Servings: 4

2 tablespoons grapeseed or other neutral oil

4 medium shallots, halved and thinly sliced

Ground white pepper

3-inch piece fresh ginger (about 2 ounces), peeled, 1 teaspoon finely grated, the remainder cut into 3 pieces and smashed

8 medium garlic cloves, smashed and peeled

3 star anise pods

3 tablespoons packed brown sugar

⅓ cup low-sodium soy sauce

3 pounds boneless pork shoulder, trimmed and cut into 1-inch chunks

1 tablespoon cornstarch

Roughly chopped fresh cilantro, to serve

This aromatic dish draws flavors from various Asian and Southeast Asian cuisines. Star anise lends the braise spicy warmth and complexity, while browned shallots and white pepper add depth and earthiness. We use fresh ginger two ways: cooked with the pork so its flavor mellows while its aroma perfumes the braising liquid, and stirred in at the very end to add sharpness to balance the richness of the pork. To complete the meal, serve with jasmine rice along with a steamed vegetable, such as baby bok choy.

Don't use regular soy sauce; it will overwhelm the braise with saltiness. Low-sodium soy sauce provides ample salinity, deep color and plenty of umami.

START: On a 6-quart Instant Pot, select **Normal/Medium Sauté**. Add the oil and heat until shimmering. Add the shallots and ½ teaspoon white pepper, then cook, stirring occasionally, until the shallots are golden brown, about 5 minutes. Add the smashed ginger, garlic, star anise and sugar, then cook, stirring, until fragrant, about 30 seconds. Pour in the soy sauce and ⅓ cup water, scraping up any browned bits. Add the pork; stir to combine, then distribute in an even layer.

FAST

Press **Cancel**, lock the lid in place and move the pressure valve to **Sealing**. Select **Pressure Cook** or **Manual**; make sure the pressure level is set to **High**. Set the cooking time for 25 minutes. When pressure cooking is complete, allow the pressure to reduce naturally for 15 minutes, then release the remaining steam by moving the pressure valve to **Venting**. Press **Cancel**, then carefully open the pot.

SLOW

Select **More/High Sauté** and bring the mixture to a boil. Press **Cancel**, lock the lid in place and move the pressure valve to **Venting**. Select **Slow Cook** and set the temperature to **More/High**. Set the cooking time for 5 to 6 hours; the braise is done when a skewer inserted into a chunk of pork meets no resistance. Press **Cancel**, then carefully open the pot.

FINISH: Using a large spoon, skim off and discard the fat from the surface, then remove and discard the star anise and ginger. In a small bowl, whisk the cornstarch with ¼ cup of the cooking liquid until combined, then stir into the pot. Select **Normal/Medium Sauté** and bring the mixture to a simmer, stirring constantly, then cook, stirring, until lightly thickened, about 1 minute. Press **Cancel** to turn off the pot, then stir in the grated ginger. Taste and season with white pepper. Serve sprinkled with cilantro.

CORIANDER-BRAISED PORK WITH OREGANO AND FETA

Active time: 40 minutes

Fast start to finish:
1½ hours

Slow start to finish:
4¾ to 5¾ hours

Servings: 4 to 6

3 tablespoons extra-virgin olive oil, plus more to serve

1 medium yellow onion, halved and thinly sliced

3 tablespoons ground coriander

1 cup dry red wine

3 pounds boneless pork shoulder, trimmed and cut into 1-inch chunks

Kosher salt and ground black pepper

6 bay leaves

1 tablespoon cornstarch

3 tablespoons minced fresh oregano

1 tablespoon lemon juice

2 ounces feta cheese, crumbled (½ cup)

¼ cup finely chopped fresh flat-leaf parsley

This simple, rustic braise is based on the pork stew called afelia from the Mediterranean island-country of Cyprus. The red wine, reduced to concentrate its flavor, lends depth, but the citrusy notes of ground coriander and a spoonful of lemon juice added at the end balance the richness of the pork. The oregano and parsley aren't needed until it's time to finish the sauce, so you can prep the herbs while the pork cooks. Serve the stew with crusty bread, simply prepared potatoes or a hearty grain such as bulgur.

Don't use coriander that has gone stale. *This dish relies on the spice for its unique flavor, so it's important to use coriander that is fresh and fragrant.*

START: On a 6-quart Instant Pot, select **More/High Sauté**. Add the oil and heat until shimmering. Add the onion and cook, stirring occasionally, until beginning to brown, about 7 minutes. Add the coriander and cook, stirring, until fragrant, about 1 minute. Pour in the wine and cook, stirring occasionally, until most of the moisture has evaporated, 2 to 3 minutes. Add the pork, 1 teaspoon salt, ½ teaspoon pepper and the bay; stir to combine, then distribute in an even layer.

FAST

Press **Cancel**, lock the lid in place and move the pressure valve to **Sealing**. Select **Pressure Cook** or **Manual**; make sure the pressure level is set to **High**. Set the cooking time for 25 minutes. When pressure cooking is complete, allow the pressure to reduce naturally for 15 minutes, then release the remaining steam by moving the pressure valve to **Venting**. Press **Cancel**, then carefully open the pot.

SLOW

With the pot still on **More/High Sauté**, bring the mixture to a boil. Press **Cancel**, lock the lid in place and move the pressure valve to **Venting**. Select **Slow Cook** and set the temperature to **More/High**. Set the cooking time for 4 to 5 hours; the pork is done when a skewer inserted into a piece meets no resistance. Press **Cancel**, then carefully open the pot.

FINISH: Using a slotted spoon, transfer the pork to a medium bowl. Using a large spoon, skim off and discard the fat from the surface of the cooking liquid. Remove and discard the bay leaves. Select **More/High Sauté** and bring to a boil. Cook, stirring occasionally, until the liquid is reduced to about 1 cup (or ½-inch depth in the pot), about 10 minutes. In a small bowl, whisk the cornstarch and 2 tablespoons water, then stir into the pot. Cook, stirring constantly, until lightly thickened, about 1 minute. Press **Cancel** to turn off the pot. Stir in the pork, oregano and lemon juice. Taste and season with salt and pepper. Transfer to a serving dish and sprinkle with feta and parsley, then drizzle with additional oil.

HOISIN-GLAZED BABY BACK RIBS

Active time: 25 minutes

Fast start to finish:
1 hour 40 minutes

Slow start to finish:
8½ to 9½ hours

Servings: 4 to 6

1 cup hoisin sauce

½ cup honey

1 tablespoon Chinese five-spice powder

5 tablespoons gochujang, divided

2 tablespoons minced fresh ginger

Two 2½- to 3-pound racks baby back pork ribs, each cut in half if pressure cooking or cut into 3- or 4-rib sections if slow cooking

2 tablespoons finely chopped fresh cilantro

2 tablespoons sesame seeds, toasted

3 scallions, thinly sliced

These addictive ribs balance sweet and heat. A thick, flavorful paste made with honey and a handful of basic Asian ingredients acts as both a wet rub and a glaze. Gochujang is a Korean fermented chili paste; look for it in the international aisle of the supermarket or in Asian grocery stores. Racks of baby back ribs, cut so they fit in the pot, are cooked until tender, then glazed and broiled until burnished before being separated into individual ribs. Serve them as a main course with rice and steamed or stir-fried vegetables or offer as an appetizer.

Don't use pork spareribs. They're larger than baby backs and won't fit in the pot; they also require a slightly longer cooking time. Don't prep the cilantro and scallions at the same time as you prep the ribs; use the half hour or so that it takes the ribs to pressure cook to chop and slice them. This saves some up-front time and ensures the herbs are fresh and flavorful for serving.

START: In a large bowl, whisk together the hoisin, honey, five-spice powder and 2 table-spoons gochujang. Measure ¾ cup of the mixture into a small bowl and stir in the remaining 3 tablespoons gochujang and the ginger; set aside at room temperature if pressure cooking or cover and refrigerate if slow cooking. Add the rib sections to the remaining hoisin mixture in the large bowl and turn to coat. Place the steam rack in a 6-quart Instant Pot, then pour in 1 cup water. Arrange the ribs upright in a circle, with the meaty sides facing the walls of the pot.

FAST

Lock the lid in place and move the pressure valve to **Sealing**. Select **Pressure Cook** or **Manual**; make sure the pressure level is set to **High**. Set the cooking time for 25 minutes. When pressure cooking is complete, allow the pressure to reduce naturally for 15 minutes, then release the remaining steam by moving the pressure valve to **Venting**. Press **Cancel**, then carefully open the pot. Let cool for 5 minutes.

SLOW

Select **More/High Sauté** and bring the water to a boil. Press **Cancel**, lock the lid in place and move the pressure valve to **Venting**. Select **Slow Cook** and set the temperature to **More/High**. Set the cooking time for 8 to 9 hours; the ribs are done when a skewer inserted into the meat between the bones meets no resistance. Press **Cancel**, then carefully open the pot. Let cool for 5 minutes.

FINISH: While the ribs cool, heat the broiler with a rack about 6 inches from the element. Line a rimmed baking sheet with foil. Using tongs, carefully transfer the ribs meat side up to the prepared baking sheet. Generously brush with half of the reserved hoisin mixture and broil until the glaze begins to bubble, 2 to 3 minutes. Remove from the broiler, brush with the remaining mixture and continue to broil until bubbling, another 2 to 3 minutes. Cool for 5 minutes, then cut between the bones to separate into individual ribs. Transfer to a platter, then sprinkle with the cilantro, sesame seeds and scallions.

MOJO SHREDDED PORK

Active time: 30 minutes

Fast start to finish:
1½ hours

Slow start to finish:
5½ to 6½ hours

Servings: 4

1 tablespoon ground cumin

1 tablespoon smoked paprika

1 teaspoon dried oregano

Kosher salt and ground black pepper

2 pounds boneless pork butt, trimmed and cut into 1-inch chunks

1 tablespoon grapeseed or other neutral oil

1 large yellow onion, finely chopped

8 medium garlic cloves, finely chopped

2 chipotle chilies in adobo sauce, minced, plus 2 tablespoons adobo sauce

1 teaspoon grated orange zest, plus 1¼ cups orange juice, divided

1 teaspoon grated lime zest, plus 3 tablespoons lime juice

1 cup finely chopped fresh cilantro

Cuban mojo, a tangy garlic-citrus mixture that's often used as a marinade for pork roasts as well as a sauce, was the inspiration for this delicious shredded pork. Sour Seville oranges are used in authentic mojo. To mimic their flavor, we combined regular orange juice and lime juice, and used their zests for fragrance. We also added smoked paprika and chipotle chilies in adobo for a touch of earthy, smoky complexity. We like the pork tucked into warmed corn tortillas for tacos, but it's also excellent with rice and beans and slices of avocado.

Don't forget to grate the zest from the oranges and limes before juicing them. The zest is easier to remove when the fruits are whole. Grate off only the colored portion of the skin; the white pith beneath is bitter.

START: In a medium bowl, stir together the cumin, paprika, oregano, 1 teaspoon salt and ½ teaspoon pepper. Add the pork and toss until evenly coated; set aside. On a 6-quart Instant Pot, select **More/High Sauté**. Add the oil and heat until shimmering. Add the onion and cook, stirring occasionally, until softened, about 3 minutes. Stir in the garlic and cook until fragrant, about 30 seconds, then stir in the chipotle chilies and adobo sauce. Add the pork and 1 cup of the orange juice; stir to combine, then distribute in an even layer.

FAST

Press **Cancel**, lock the lid in place and move the pressure valve to **Sealing**. Select **Pressure Cook** or **Manual**; make sure the pressure level is set to **High**. Set the cooking time for 25 minutes. When pressure cooking is complete, allow the pressure to reduce naturally for 15 minutes, then release the remaining steam by moving the pressure valve to **Venting**. Press **Cancel**, then carefully open the pot.

SLOW

With the pot still on **More/High Sauté**, bring the mixture to a boil. Press **Cancel**, lock the lid in place and move the pressure valve to **Venting**. Select **Slow Cook** and set the temperature to **More/High**. Set the cooking time for 5 to 6 hours; the meat is done when a skewer inserted into a chunk meets no resistance. Press **Cancel**, then carefully open the pot.

FINISH: Using a slotted spoon, transfer the pork to a medium bowl. Let cool for about 5 minutes, then use two forks to shred the meat into bite-size pieces. Using a large spoon, skim off and discard the fat from the surface of the cooking liquid. Select **More/High Sauté**, bring the liquid to a boil and cook, stirring occasionally, until reduced to ¾ cup (or scant ½-inch depth in the pot), about 15 minutes. Stir in the remaining ¼ cup orange juice, the lime juice and the cilantro. Press **Cancel** to turn off the pot. Add the pork and both zests, then stir until the pork is heated through, 2 to 3 minutes. Taste and season with salt and pepper.

CARNITAS WITH PICKLED RED ONIONS

Active time: 35 minutes

Fast start to finish:
1¾ hours

Slow start to finish:
5½ to 6½ hours

Servings: 4 to 6

2 tablespoons grapeseed or other neutral oil

1 large yellow onion, halved and thinly sliced

10 medium garlic cloves, smashed and peeled

3 pounds boneless pork butt, untrimmed, cut into 1-inch chunks

2 tablespoons ground cumin

2 tablespoons ground coriander

2 teaspoons dried oregano

½ teaspoon dried thyme

1 teaspoon red pepper flakes

Kosher salt and ground black pepper

Carnitas, or shredded pork that typically is fried to create delicious browned, crisp bits, is a Mexican classic. For our version, we cook cubes of pork shoulder with spices, aromatics and a little water until the meat is fork-tender. We then break the pork into smaller pieces and moisten it with its own juices. You can stop there and serve the pork as is or you can crisp it in a hot skillet in its own rendered fat. To do so, in a 12-inch nonstick skillet over medium-high, heat 1 teaspoon of the reserved pork fat until barely smoking. Add the pork in an even layer and cook without stirring, pressing the meat against the skillet with a spatula, until the bottom is browned and crisp, 3 to 5 minutes. Serve carnitas with rice and beans or make tacos with warmed tortillas. Either way, pickled red onions (recipe follows) are a must—their acidity balances the rich pork.

Don't trim the fat from the pork. The fat rendered during cooking is essential for flavoring the carnitas. And if you plan to fry the pork after shredding, make sure to reserve the fat you skim off the cooking liquid—it's ideal for crisping the meat.

START: On a 6-quart Instant Pot, select **More/High Sauté**. Add the oil and heat until shimmering. Add the onion and cook, stirring occasionally, until softened, about 3 minutes. Stir in the garlic and cook until fragrant, about 30 seconds. Add the pork, cumin, coriander, oregano, thyme, pepper flakes and 1 teaspoon salt and 1 cup water; stir to combine, then distribute in an even layer.

FAST

Press **Cancel**, lock the lid in place and move the pressure valve to **Sealing**. Select **Pressure Cook** or **Manual**; make sure the pressure level is set to **High**. Set the cooking time for 25 minutes. When pressure cooking is complete, allow the pressure to reduce naturally for 15 minutes, then release the remaining steam by moving the pressure valve to **Venting**. Press **Cancel**, then carefully open the pot.

SLOW

With the pot still on **More/High Sauté**, bring the mixture to a boil. Press **Cancel**, lock the lid in place and move the pressure valve to **Venting**. Select **Slow Cook** and set the temperature to **More/High**. Set the cooking time for 5 to 6 hours; the meat is done when a skewer inserted into a chunk meets no resistance. Press **Cancel**, then carefully open the pot.

FINISH: Using a slotted spoon, transfer the meat to a large bowl and cool for 5 minutes. Using two forks, shred the meat into bite-size pieces. Using a large spoon, skim off the fat from the surface of the cooking liquid (reserve the fat if you plan to fry the pork before serving; see note). Select **More/High Sauté**. Bring the liquid to a boil and cook, stirring occasionally, until reduced to about 1 cup (or ½-inch depth in the pot), 10 to 15 minutes. Press **Cancel** to turn off the pot. Add the pork and stir until heated through, about 2 minutes. Taste and season with salt and pepper.

PICKLED RED ONIONS

Start to finish: 10 minutes, plus chilling
Makes about 2 cups

1 cup white vinegar

2 teaspoons white sugar

Kosher salt

2 medium red onions, halved
and thinly sliced

1 jalapeño chili, stemmed, halved
lengthwise and seeded

In a medium bowl, stir together the vinegar,
sugar and 2 teaspoons salt until dissolved.
Stir in the onions and jalapeño. Cover and
refrigerate for at least 1 hour or up to
24 hours.

BEEF

CONTENTS

Braised Beef with Pancetta, Mushrooms and Red Wine (p. 266)

BEEF

Our inspiration for beef Instant Pot dishes took us to multiple continents. We came up with a dish based on Vietnamese bò kho, a soup fragrant with cinnamon and star anise, and another inspired by Austrian Tafelspitz, a pot roast with braised root vegetables. We also offer a spin on French boeuf bourguignon, and our stellar line up of stews includes one drawn from Pakistan's nihari. For a change of pace, we tucked in a few lamb recipes, but they'll work just as well with beef if you prefer. We also found that ground beef can shine in the pressure cooker, as in our fennel-infused meatballs and tangy, sweet and salty picadillo.

When prepping beef for the Instant Pot, we **thoroughly trim the meat before cooking.** Cheaper cuts often are fattier cuts and it's important to remove the fat to prevent greasiness. And we **keep liquid levels low for concentrated flavors** in a rich, meaty braise. The meat and any vegetables will produce their own moisture. If a dish calls for cooking large hunks of meat and then slicing for serving, we **divide larger cuts into smaller, evenly sized pieces and tie them to keep them compact.** They cook quicker and more evenly and don't fall apart in the process.

We **don't bother browning beef before cooking it in the Instant Pot;** we get plenty of flavor from layers of spices and other seasonings. In our chili con carne, we use ancho chili powder to get the flavor of dried chilies without having to toast, soak and puree whole dried chilies. This dish taught us it's important to **scrape the bottom of the pot to avoid scorching.** This applies as a general rule when using a pressure cooker, but it's particularly useful for dishes where, as in our chili, the sautéed ingredients that form the sauce need to be thoroughly scraped up before pressure cooking. Otherwise they can burn, which triggers the burn sensor and automatic shut-off.

We **add fresh and tangy ingredients at the end of cooking to keep flavors bright.** So fruity tomatillos go in at the end of our version of the Mexican stew entomatado de res. And red wine vinegar and a garnish of feta cheese bring sharp contrast to our lighter version of the Greek dish moshari stifado.

The Instant Pot takes the investment out of beef. No need to lay out cash on quick-cooking but pricey steak or tenderloin; no need to spend hours coaxing cheaper (but flavorful) chuck roast and shanks to tenderness. Even all-day pot roast becomes Tuesday night-friendly with less than 30-minutes hands-on effort.

VIETNAMESE-STYLE BEEF SOUP

Active time: 30 minutes

Fast start to finish:
1 hour 50 minutes

Slow start to finish:
7½ to 8½ hours

Servings: 4

1 tablespoon grapeseed
or other neutral oil

3 tablespoons tomato paste

5 medium garlic cloves,
smashed and peeled

4 star anise pods

2 cinnamon sticks

3-inch piece fresh ginger
(about 2 ounces), peeled and
sliced into 6 coins

3 stalks lemon grass,
trimmed to the bottom
6 inches, dry outer layers
removed, bruised and halved

¼ cup fish sauce

2 tablespoons white sugar

2 teaspoons chili powder

Kosher salt and ground
black pepper

2½ pounds boneless beef
chuck roast, trimmed and
cut into 1-inch chunks

4 medium carrots (about
1 pound), peeled and cut into
1- to 1½-inch chunks

1 tablespoon lime juice,
plus lime wedges to serve

Fresh mint and/or cilantro,
to serve

This flavorful soup, a simplified version of traditional Vietnamese bò kho, is perfumed with cinnamon and star anise as well as ginger and lemon grass. The broth is not thickened and individual bowlfuls are finished with fresh herbs, so despite the dish's meaty underpinnings, it's a light, refreshing meal. For added substance, you could serve a warm, crusty baguette on the side, or supplement with cooked rice or rice noodles; prepare the noodles according to package instructions, then divide among bowls before ladling in the soup. Garnish with shaved onion and drizzle with chili oil for spicy heat.

Don't use double-concentrated tomato paste, which often is sold in a tube. Its potent flavor will overwhelm the other ingredients in the soup. Also, don't cut the carrots too small. Large chunks cook in the same time as the beef and won't end up mushy and overdone.

START: On a 6-quart Instant Pot, select **Normal/Medium Sauté**. Heat the oil until shimmering, then add the tomato paste and garlic and cook, stirring often, until the paste is slightly darker, 2 to 3 minutes. Add the star anise, cinnamon sticks, ginger and lemon grass, then cook, stirring, until fragrant, about 30 seconds. Stir in 5 cups water, the fish sauce, sugar, chili powder and 1 teaspoon pepper, scraping up any browned bits. Add the beef and carrots, then distribute in an even layer.

FAST

Press **Cancel**, lock the lid in place and move the pressure valve to **Sealing**. Select **Pressure Cook** or **Manual**; make sure the pressure level is set to **High**. Set the cooking time for 25 minutes. When pressure cooking is complete, let the pressure reduce naturally for 15 minutes, then release the remaining steam by moving the pressure valve to **Venting**. Press **Cancel**, then carefully open the pot.

SLOW

Select **More/High Sauté** and bring the mixture to a boil. Press **Cancel**, lock the lid in place and move the pressure valve to **Venting**. Select **Slow Cook** and set the temperature to **More/High**. Set the cooking time for 7 to 8 hours; the soup is done when a skewer inserted into a piece of beef meets no resistance. Press **Cancel**, then carefully open the pot.

FINISH: Using a large spoon, skim off and discard the fat from the surface of the broth. Remove and discard the star anise, cinnamon sticks, ginger and lemon grass. Stir in the lime juice, then taste and adjust the seasoning with salt. Ladle into bowls and top with mint and/or cilantro, then serve with lime wedges.

CINNAMON-SPICED BEEF NOODLE SOUP WITH SPINACH

Active time: 30 minutes

**Fast start to finish:
50 minutes**

Slow start to finish:
8½ to 9½ hours

Servings: 4

6 cinnamon sticks

2 teaspoons aniseed (optional)

½ cup soy sauce

½ cup sake

1 bunch scallions, white and green parts separated, green parts thinly sliced

4-inch piece fresh ginger (3 ounces), peeled, thinly sliced and smashed

1 bunch cilantro

2½ pounds beef shanks (each about 1 inch thick), trimmed

5-ounce container baby spinach

Ground white pepper

8 ounces dried wheat noodles (see note), cooked, drained and briefly rinsed

This meal in a bowl is hearty and satisfying, yet the flavors are light and clean. We use beef shanks, as the bones lend the broth both meaty flavor and rich body. They also yield enough meat to give the soup substance. Thick dried Asian wheat noodles such as udon or lo mein are ideal, but even Italian linguine will work. If you can't find anise seed, the broth still is delicious without it. You can prepare the broth and meat up to three days ahead; refrigerate both until needed, then discard the solid fat from the surface of the broth and proceed. For some spiciness, offer chili-garlic sauce on the side.

Don't cook the noodles in advance. Wait until the soup is nearly done before boiling them. And make sure to rinse them briefly after draining to wash off excess starch, then immediately portion them into individual serving bowls.

START: On a 6-quart Instant Pot, select **More/High Sauté**. Add the cinnamon sticks and aniseed (if using), then toast, stirring often, until fragrant, 2 to 3 minutes. Add 5 cups water, the soy sauce, sake, scallion whites and ginger. Set aside ½ cup loosely packed cilantro sprigs and add the remainder to the pot. Bring to a simmer, then add the beef, arranging the pieces in an even layer; they should be mostly submerged.

FAST

Press **Cancel**, lock the lid in place and move the pressure valve to **Sealing**. Select **Pressure Cook** or **Manual**; make sure the pressure level is set to **High**. Set the cooking time for 45 minutes. When pressure cooking is complete, quick-release the steam by moving the pressure valve to **Venting**. Press **Cancel**, then carefully open the pot.

SLOW

With the pot still on **More/High Sauté**, bring the mixture to a boil. Press **Cancel**, lock the lid in place and move the pressure valve to **Venting**. Select **Slow Cook** and set the temperature to **More/High**. Set the cooking time for 8 to 9 hours; the shanks are done when a skewer inserted into the meat meets no resistance. Press **Cancel**, then carefully open the pot.

FINISH: Using a slotted spoon, transfer the shanks to a large plate and let cool slightly. Pour the broth through a fine mesh strainer set over a large bowl. Discard the solids and return the broth to the pot. Cut the meat into ½-inch chunks, discarding the fat and bones, then return the meat to the broth. Select **Normal/Medium Sauté** and bring to a simmer. Stir in the spinach and cook just until wilted, about 1 minute. Press **Cancel** to turn off the pot. Taste and season with white pepper. Divide the noodles among serving bowls and ladle the soup over. Top with scallion greens, the reserved cilantro and additional white pepper.

MOROCCAN BEEF OR LAMB SOUP WITH CHICKPEAS AND LENTILS

Active time: 25 minutes

Fast start to finish: 1 hour 10 minutes

Slow start to finish: 7½ to 8½ hours

Servings: 4

Kosher salt and ground black pepper

2 tablespoons extra-virgin olive oil, plus more to serve

6 medium celery stalks, sliced ½ to ¾ inch thick

1 medium yellow onion, roughly chopped

6 medium garlic cloves, smashed and peeled

3 tablespoons finely chopped fresh ginger

¾ teaspoon ground cinnamon

½ teaspoon sweet paprika

14½-ounce can whole peeled tomatoes, crushed by hand

2 pounds boneless lamb shoulder or beef chuck roast, trimmed and cut into ¾- to 1-inch chunks

⅓ cup lentils du Puy

15½-ounce can chickpeas, drained and rinsed

1 cup lightly packed fresh cilantro, flat-leaf parsley or a mixture, chopped, plus more to serve

Harira, an aromatic Moroccan dish, traditionally is served during Ramadan to break the daily fast. It's sometimes vegetarian, other times meaty. And, depending on the cook, its consistency may be thick and hearty or light and brothy. Our recipe calls for either lamb or boneless beef chuck. Serve with lemon wedges and a drizzle of extra-virgin olive oil, and offer crusty bread for soaking up the broth.

Don't use brown or regular green lentils in place of the lentils du Puy. Though those varieties do hold their shape, they cook up with a softer, more yielding texture than Puy lentils, which stay quite firm and offer textural contrast to the stew.

START: On a 6-quart Instant Pot, select **Normal/Medium Sauté**. Add the oil and heat until shimmering. Add the celery, onion, garlic, ginger and 2½ teaspoons salt. Cook, stirring occasionally, until the vegetables are softened, about 5 minutes. Add the cinnamon, paprika and 1½ teaspoons pepper, then cook, stirring, until fragrant, about 10 seconds. Stir in the tomatoes with their juices and 4 cups water, scraping up browned bits. Add the lamb or beef and lentils and stir to combine, then distribute in an even layer.

FAST

Press **Cancel**, lock the lid in place and move the pressure valve to **Sealing**. Select **Pressure Cook** or **Manual**; make sure the pressure level is set to **High**. Set the cooking time for 15 minutes. When pressure cooking is complete, let the pressure reduce naturally for 15 minutes, then release the remaining steam by moving the pressure valve to **Venting**. Press **Cancel**, then carefully open the pot.

SLOW

Select **More/High Sauté**, bring the mixture to a boil. Press **Cancel**, lock the lid in place and move the pressure valve to **Venting**. Select **Slow Cook** and set the temperature to **More/High**. Set the cooking time for 7 to 8 hours; the stew is done when a skewer inserted into a piece of meat meets no resistance. Press **Cancel**, then carefully open the pot.

FINISH: Stir in the chickpeas. Taste and season with salt and pepper, then stir in the parsley and/or cilantro. Serve sprinkled with additional herbs and drizzled with oil.

PERSIAN BEEF, HERB AND KIDNEY BEAN STEW

Active time: 20 minutes

Fast start to finish:
1¼ hours

Slow start to finish:
7¼ to 8¼ hours

Servings: 4

Leaves and tender stems from 1 bunch cilantro (4 cups lightly packed)

Leaves and tender stems from ½ bunch flat-leaf parsley (2 cups lightly packed)

1 bunch scallions, sliced, white and green parts reserved separately

¼ cup extra-virgin olive oil

2 tablespoons grated lime zest, plus ¼ cup lime juice, plus lime wedges to serve

2 teaspoons ground turmeric

2½ to 3 pounds boneless beef chuck roast, trimmed and cut into 1½- to 2-inch chunks

Kosher salt and ground black pepper

Two 14½-ounce cans kidney beans or small red beans, drained but not rinsed, liquid reserved

This classic Persian stew, called ghormeh sabzi, often is regarded as Iran's national dish. Dried limes and an assortment of fresh herbs that are fried give the sauce a unique flavor and an unusual deep-green hue. In our simplified version, we streamlined the method and used easier-to-source ingredients, including opting for canned beans. If you prefer, use an equal amount of boneless lamb shoulder in place of the beef. Serve with plenty of steamed basmati rice and a cucumber-tomato salad.

Don't discard the bean liquid when draining the cans. Using it instead of water or broth adds both body and depth of flavor. If you accidentally throw it out, substitute an equal amount of chicken broth or vegetable broth, or even water, though the stew will have a thinner consistency.

START: In a food processor, combine the cilantro, parsley and scallion greens. Pulse until finely chopped, about 10 pulses; transfer to a small bowl and set aside. On a 6-quart Instant Pot, select **Normal/Medium Sauté**. Add the oil and heat until shimmering. Add the scallion whites and cook, stirring, until golden brown, 3 to 5 minutes. Stir in half the chopped herbs and cook, stirring, until wilted and the color is no longer vibrant green, about 2 minutes. If slow cooking, cover and refrigerate the remaining herb mixture. Add the lime zest and juice, turmeric, beef, 1 teaspoon salt and ½ cup of the reserved bean liquid if pressure cooking or 1 cup if slow cooking. Stir, loosening any bits stuck to the bottom of the pot, then distribute in an even layer.

FAST

Press **Cancel**, lock the lid in place and move the pressure valve to **Sealing**. Select **Pressure Cook** or **Manual**; make sure the pressure level is set to **High**. Set the cooking time for 25 minutes. When pressure cooking is complete, let the pressure reduce naturally for 15 minutes, then release the remaining steam by moving the pressure valve to **Venting**. Press **Cancel**, then carefully open the pot.

SLOW

Select **More/High Sauté**, bring the mixture to a boil. Press **Cancel**, lock the lid in place and move the pressure valve to **Venting**. Select **Slow Cook** and set the temperature to **More/High**. Set the cooking time for 7 to 8 hours; the stew is done when a skewer inserted into a piece of beef meets no resistance. Press **Cancel**, then carefully open the pot.

FINISH: Stir in the beans and remaining chopped herbs, then taste and season with salt and pepper. Serve with lime wedges.

TUSCAN BEEF AND BLACK PEPPER STEW

Active time: 35 minutes

Fast start to finish:
1 hour 40 minutes

Slow start to finish:
7½ to 8½ hours

Servings: 6

2 tablespoons extra-virgin olive oil

1 large yellow onion, halved and thinly sliced

12 medium garlic cloves, smashed and peeled

2 cups dry red wine

3 tablespoons tomato paste

2 sprigs fresh rosemary, plus 1½ teaspoons minced

4 pounds boneless beef chuck roast, trimmed and cut into 1½-inch chunks

Kosher salt and coarsely ground black pepper

3 tablespoons all-purpose flour

The simple, generously peppered beef stew known as peposo alla fornacina is said to have been created by 15th century kiln (fornacina) workers in Tuscany, Italy. Chianti is the best-known wine produced in that region and is the traditional choice for peposo, but any dry, medium-bodied red wine works. The stew keeps well, so it can be made up to three days ahead and reheated in the microwave or in a saucepan over low. It's especially delicious with soft polenta (p. 40) or buttery mashed potatoes.

Don't use finely ground black pepper. *Coarsely ground pepper has more presence in this braise and gives it character. For best flavor and aroma, it's best to start with whole peppercorns and pulse them in an electric spice grinder until coarsely cracked.*

START: On a 6-quart Instant Pot, select **More/High Sauté**. Add the oil and heat until shimmering. Add the onion and garlic, then cook, stirring occasionally, until the onion is lightly browned, 7 to 9 minutes. Add the wine and cook, scraping up any browned bits, until reduced to about ½ cup, about 15 minutes. Stir in the tomato paste, rosemary sprigs and 1 tablespoon pepper. Stir in the beef and 2 teaspoons salt, then distribute in an even layer.

FAST

Press **Cancel**, lock the lid in place and move the pressure valve to **Sealing**. Select **Pressure Cook** or **Manual**; make sure the pressure level is set to **High**. Set the cooking time for 25 minutes. When pressure cooking is complete, let the pressure reduce naturally for 15 minutes, then release the remaining steam by moving the pressure valve to **Venting**. Press **Cancel**, then carefully open the pot.

SLOW

With the pot still on **More/High Sauté**, bring the mixture to a boil. Press **Cancel**, lock the lid in place and move the pressure valve to **Venting**. Select **Slow Cook** and set the temperature to **More/High**. Set the cooking time for 7 to 8 hours; the stew is done when a skewer inserted into a piece of beef meets no resistance. Press **Cancel**, then carefully open the pot.

FINISH: Using a large spoon, skim off and discard the fat from the surface of the cooking liquid. In a small bowl, whisk the flour with 6 tablespoons of the cooking liquid until smooth, then whisk into the pot. Select **Normal/Medium Sauté**. Bring to a simmer, stirring, and cook until lightly thickened, 6 to 8 minutes. Press **Cancel** to turn off the pot, then stir in the minced rosemary and 1 to 1½ tablespoons pepper. Taste and season with salt.

CUMIN-SPICED BEEF AND SWEET POTATO STEW

Active time: 35 minutes

**Fast start to finish:
1 hour 20 minutes**

Slow start to finish:
7½ to 8½ hours

Servings: 6

1 tablespoon grapeseed
or other neutral oil

1 large yellow onion, finely
chopped

10 medium garlic cloves,
smashed and peeled

2 tablespoons tomato paste

1 tablespoon ground cumin

1 jalapeño chili, stemmed,
seeded and minced

2½ pounds boneless beef
chuck roast, trimmed and
cut into ¾-inch chunks

28-ounce can whole peeled
tomatoes, crushed by hand

Kosher salt and ground
black pepper

12 ounces sweet potatoes,
peeled and cut into ½-inch
chunks

3 tablespoons lime juice

½ cup finely chopped fresh
cilantro

Sour cream, to serve

Pickled jalapeños, to serve
(optional)

This hearty stew is all about flavor balance. The natural sugars in the tomatoes and sweet potatoes counter the meatiness of beef chuck. Alliums and cumin tie together the sweet and savory flavors, while lime juice adds brightness. Sour cream is a cooling garnish and if you'd like a little tangy heat, offer some pickled jalapeños. This doesn't need any sides for serving, but warmed tortillas or cilantro rice would be great accompaniments.

Don't cut the beef any larger than ¾-inch chunks. If the pieces are larger, the meat may not tenderize in the time specified.

START: On a 6-quart Instant Pot, select **More/High Sauté**. Add the oil and heat until shimmering, then add the onion and cook, stirring occasionally, until softened, about 5 minutes. Stir in the garlic, tomato paste, cumin and jalapeño, then cook until fragrant, about 30 seconds. Add the beef, tomatoes with their juices and 1½ teaspoons salt; stir to combine, then distribute in an even layer.

FAST

Press **Cancel**, lock the lid in place and move the pressure valve to **Sealing**. Select **Pressure Cook** or **Manual**; make sure the pressure level is set to **High**. Set the cooking time for 30 minutes. When pressure cooking is complete, allow the pressure to release naturally for 15 minutes, then release the remaining steam by moving the pressure valve to **Venting**. Press **Cancel**, then carefully open the pot.

SLOW

With the pot still on **More/High Sauté**, bring the mixture to a boil. Press **Cancel**, lock the lid in place and move the pressure valve to **Venting**. Select **Slow Cook** and set the temperature to **More/High**. Set the cooking time for 7 to 8 hours; the stew is done when a skewer inserted into a piece of beef meets no resistance. Press **Cancel**, then carefully open the pot.

FINISH: Select **Normal/Medium Sauté** and add the sweet potatoes. Cook, stirring occasionally, until a skewer inserted into the potatoes meets no resistance, 10 to 15 minutes. Press **Cancel** to turn off the pot. Stir in the lime juice and cilantro, then taste and season with salt and pepper. Serve with sour cream and pickled jalapeños (if desired).

MEXICAN BEEF AND TOMATILLO STEW

Active time: 40 minutes
Fast start to finish: 2 hours
Servings: 4

1 tablespoon grapeseed or other neutral oil

1 medium yellow onion, cut into 1-inch chunks

5 medium garlic cloves, smashed and peeled

1 jalapeño chili, stemmed, seeded and roughly chopped

3 bay leaves

Kosher salt and ground black pepper

1 teaspoon dried oregano

½ teaspoon ground cumin

2½ pounds boneless beef chuck roast, trimmed and cut into 1½-inch chunks

1 pound Yukon Gold potatoes, cut into 1½-inch chunks

8 small tomatillos (about 12 ounces), husked, cored and quartered

Fresh cilantro, to serve

Mexican entomatado de res slow-simmers tangy, fruity tomatillos with chunks of beef. This is our easy, Instant Pot version. We add the tomatillos at the end to keep their flavors bright and fresh. Yukon Gold potatoes simmered with the beef make the stew more substantial; the potatoes become infused with the flavors of the braise while lending the broth light body. If you like, serve the stew with pickled or fresh jalapeños or toasted pumpkin seeds for a little crunch. Warmed tortillas are a great accompaniment, too.

Don't leave any browned bits stuck to the pot before pressure cooking. After adding the water, thoroughly scrape the bottom of the pot to loosen any clinging food before adding the beef and potatoes. This will prevent a "burn" error message from occurring after pressure cooking starts.

START: On a 6-quart Instant Pot, select **Normal/Medium Sauté**. Add the oil and heat until shimmering, then stir in the onion, garlic, jalapeño, bay and 1 teaspoon salt. Cook, stirring often, until the onion is soft and golden brown around the edges, 5 to 7 minutes. Add 1 teaspoon pepper, the oregano and the cumin, then cook, stirring, until fragrant, about 30 seconds. Stir in 2 tablespoons water, scraping up any browned bits. Add the beef and potatoes; stir to combine, then distribute in an even layer.

FAST

Press **Cancel**, lock the lid in place and move the pressure valve to **Sealing**. Select **Pressure Cook** or **Manual**; make sure the pressure level is set to **High**. Set the cooking time for 25 minutes. When pressure cooking is complete, allow the pressure to reduce naturally for 15 minutes, then release the remaining steam by moving the pressure valve to **Venting**. Press **Cancel**, then carefully open the pot.

FINISH: Using a slotted spoon, transfer the meat and potatoes to a medium bowl and set aside. Add the tomatillos to the pot and select **Normal/Medium Sauté**. Bring the mixture to a boil and cook, stirring occasionally and crushing the tomatillos, until the cooking liquid has thickened and the tomatillos are fully softened, about 15 minutes. Stir in ½ teaspoon salt, then return the meat and potatoes to the pot. Return to a simmer and cook, stirring just once or twice, until heated through, 1 to 2 minutes. Press **Cancel** to turn off the pot. Taste and season with salt and pepper, then serve topped with cilantro.

PAKISTANI-STYLE SPICED BEEF STEW

Active time: 40 minutes

Fast start to finish: 1¾ hours

Slow start to finish: 7¾ to 8¾ hours

Servings: 4

4 tablespoons (½ stick) salted butter

2 medium yellow onions, halved and sliced ½ inch thick

4 medium garlic cloves, smashed and peeled

3-inch piece fresh ginger (about 2 ounces), peeled and cut into 6 coins

2 cinnamon sticks

Kosher salt and ground black pepper

2 teaspoons sweet paprika

1½ teaspoons fennel seeds

1½ teaspoons ground coriander

1 teaspoon curry powder

½ teaspoon garam masala

2½-pound boneless beef chuck roast, trimmed and cut into 1½-inch chunks

2 tablespoons all-purpose flour

2 tablespoons lemon juice, plus lemon wedges to serve

Chopped fresh cilantro, to serve

The rich, aromatic stew, called nihari, traditionally is made with a special seasoning blend known as nihari masala, a mixture that might contain more than a dozen spices. To create similar complexity with far fewer ingredients, we rely on curry powder (for color and savory notes) and garam masala (for its spicy warmth). Lemon juice stirred in at the end adds brightness that balances the stew's richness. Serve with basmati rice or warmed flatbread and, if you desire a little spice, garnish with sliced jalapeño or serrano chilies.

Don't slice the onions too thinly. *A ½-inch thickness or so ensures the pieces won't turn to mush during pressure cooking. Make sure to cook the onions until browned, as this builds flavor.*

START: On a 6-quart Instant Pot, select **Normal/Medium Sauté**. Add the butter and melt, then cook, stirring, until it is golden brown and has a nutty aroma, 2 to 3 minutes. Add the onions, garlic, ginger, cinnamon and ½ teaspoon salt. Cook, stirring, until the onions are soft and golden brown at the edges, 10 to 12 minutes. Stir in the paprika, fennel seeds, coriander, curry powder, garam masala, 2 teaspoons salt and 1½ teaspoons pepper, then cook until fragrant, about 30 seconds. Add 1 cup water and scrape up any browned bits. Add the beef and stir to combine, then distribute in an even layer.

FAST

Press **Cancel**, lock the lid in place and move the pressure valve to **Sealing**. Select **Pressure Cook** or **Manual**; make sure the pressure level is set to **High**. Set the cooking time for 25 minutes. When pressure cooking is complete, let the pressure reduce naturally for 15 minutes, then release the remaining steam by moving the pressure valve to **Venting**. Press **Cancel**, then carefully open the pot.

SLOW

Select **More/High Sauté** and bring the mixture to a boil. Press **Cancel**, lock the lid in place and move the pressure valve to **Venting**. Select **Slow Cook** and set the temperature to **More/High**. Set the cooking time for 7 to 8 hours; the stew is done when a skewer inserted into a piece of beef meets no resistance. Press **Cancel**, then carefully open the pot.

FINISH: Using a large spoon, skim off and discard the fat from the surface of the cooking liquid. Remove and discard the cinnamon sticks and ginger coins. In a small bowl, whisk the flour with 6 tablespoons of the cooking liquid until smooth, then stir into the pot. Select **Normal/Medium Sauté**. Bring the stew to a simmer, stirring often, and cook until lightly thickened, 2 to 3 minutes. Press **Cancel** to turn off the pot. Stir in the lemon juice, then taste and season with salt and pepper.

SPANISH BEEF, RED PEPPER AND PAPRIKA STEW

Active time: 30 minutes

**Fast start to finish:
1 hour 50 minutes**

Slow start to finish:
9½ to 10½ hours

Servings: 4

1 tablespoon extra-virgin olive oil

10 medium garlic cloves, smashed and peeled

1 large shallot, halved and thickly sliced

1 plum tomato, cored, seeded and chopped

½ cup jarred roasted red peppers, patted dry and finely chopped

4 ounces prosciutto or pancetta, chopped

4 teaspoons finely chopped fresh rosemary, divided

1 tablespoon sweet paprika

3 pounds boneless beef chuck roast, trimmed and cut into 2-inch chunks

2 tablespoons all-purpose flour

1 teaspoon lemon juice

Kosher salt and ground black pepper

Chilindrón, a hearty stew from Aragon in northeastern Spain, gets savory, meaty flavor from jamón serrano (dry-cured Spanish ham) balanced by subtly sweet tomato and red bell peppers. Paprika adds earthy flavor as well as a rich, brick-red color. Chicken, lamb or game sometimes is used, but we particularly liked the succulence of a beef chuck roast cut into chunks. In place of jamón serrano, we opted to use easier-to-find Italian prosciutto, which has a similar texture and salty, nutty flavor. Pancetta, a fattier cut, works in a pinch, though it lacks some complexity. Serve the stew with roasted or mashed potatoes or warm, crusty bread.

Don't use bacon in place of the prosciutto or pancetta. Its sweetness and intense smokiness will overpower the other ingredients. Similarly, don't use deli ham, which is wet-cured and typically has an overly assertive artificial smoke flavor.

START: On a 6-quart Instant Pot, select **More/High Sauté**. Add the oil and heat until shimmering. Add the garlic, shallot, tomato, roasted peppers and prosciutto. Cook, stirring occasionally, until the shallot is very soft and the tomato has broken down, about 5 minutes. Stir in 3 teaspoons of rosemary and the paprika. Add the beef and stir to combine, then distribute in an even layer.

FAST

Press **Cancel**, lock the lid in place and move the pressure valve to **Sealing**. Select **Pressure Cook** or **Manual**; make sure the pressure level is set to **High**. Set the cooking time for 35 minutes. When pressure cooking is complete, let the pressure reduce naturally for 15 minutes, then release the remaining steam by moving the pressure valve to **Venting**. Press **Cancel**, then carefully open the pot.

SLOW

With the pot still on **More/High Sauté**, bring the mixture to a boil. Press **Cancel**, lock the lid in place and move the pressure valve to **Venting**. Select **Slow Cook** and set the temperature to **More/High**. Set the cooking time for 9 to 10 hours; the stew is done when a skewer inserted into a piece of beef meets no resistance. Press **Cancel**, then carefully open the pot.

FINISH: Using a large spoon, skim off and discard the fat from the surface of the cooking liquid. In a small bowl, whisk the flour with 6 tablespoons of the cooking liquid until smooth, then stir the mixture into the pot along with the remaining 1 teaspoon rosemary. Select **Less/Low Sauté**. Bring the stew to a simmer and cook, stirring often, until thickened, 2 to 3 minutes. Press **Cancel** to turn off the pot. Stir in the lemon juice, then taste and season with salt and pepper.

Active time: 30 minutes

Fast start to finish:
1¾ hours

Slow start to finish:
7½ to 8½ hours

Servings: 4

SPICY SOUTH AFRICAN BEEF STEW WITH OLIVES

2½ pounds boneless beef short ribs, trimmed and cut into 1-inch chunks

⅓ cup Worcestershire sauce

Kosher salt and ground black pepper

2 tablespoons salted butter

2 medium yellow onions, chopped

4 medium garlic cloves, smashed and peeled

3 or 4 Fresno or serrano chilies, stemmed, seeded and thinly sliced, divided

½ cup brandy

4 bay leaves

½ cup pitted Kalamata olives, halved lengthwise

3 tablespoons all-purpose flour

Chopped fresh flat-leaf parsley, to serve

The South African stew called trinchado likely originates with the Portuguese in neighboring Mozambique and Angola. Worcestershire sauce—though neither South African nor Portuguese—is a common ingredient for the dish. It adds its characteristic savory-sweetness, while brandy brings a touch of fruitiness, fresh chilies spice things up and olives offer brininess. The result is a hearty stew with layers of bold flavor. Serve with warm crusty bread, or do as they do in South Africa and offer french fries alongside.

Don't discard the beef marinade. Add it to the pot along with the beef—it's essential for seasoning the stew.

START: In a large bowl, stir together the beef, Worcestershire sauce, 1½ teaspoons salt and 1 teaspoon pepper. Set aside. On a 6-quart Instant Pot, select **Normal/Medium Sauté**. Add the butter and let melt, then add the onions and garlic and cook, stirring occasionally, until the onions are browned, 8 to 10 minutes. Add half of the chilies and cook, stirring, until fragrant, about 1 minute. Pour in the brandy and cook, scraping up any browned bits. Add the bay and beef with its marinade; stir to combine, then distribute in an even layer.

FAST

Press **Cancel**, lock the lid in place and move the pressure valve to **Sealing**. Select **Pressure Cook** or **Manual**; make sure the pressure level is set to **High**. Set the cooking time for 25 minutes. When pressure cooking is complete, let the pressure reduce naturally for 15 minutes, then release the remaining steam by moving the pressure valve to **Venting**. Press **Cancel**, then carefully open the pot.

SLOW

Select **More/High Sauté** and bring the mixture to a boil. Press **Cancel**, lock the lid in place and move the pressure valve to **Venting**. Select **Slow Cook** and set the temperature to **More/High**. Set the cooking time for 7 to 8 hours; the stew is done when a skewer inserted into a piece of beef meets no resistance. Press **Cancel**, then carefully open the pot.

FINISH: Using a large spoon, skim off and discard any fat from the surface of the cooking liquid. Remove and discard the bay, then stir in the olives and remaining chilies. In a small bowl, whisk the flour with 6 tablespoons of the cooking liquid until smooth, then stir into the pot. Select **Normal/Medium Sauté**. Bring the stew to a simmer, stirring often, and cook until lightly thickened, 2 to 3 minutes. Press **Cancel** to turn off the pot. Taste and season with salt and pepper. Serve sprinkled with parsley.

BEEF STEW WITH PAPRIKA AND CARAWAY

Active time: 30 minutes

**Fast start to finish:
1½ hours**

Slow start to finish:
7½ to 8½ hours

Servings: 6

4 pounds boneless beef chuck roast, trimmed and cut into 1½-inch chunks

6 tablespoons sweet paprika, divided

4 tablespoons (½ stick) salted butter

1 large yellow onion, finely chopped

Kosher salt and ground black pepper

2 tablespoons caraway seeds, lightly crushed

1 tablespoon hot paprika

2 cups low-sodium beef broth

¼ cup tomato paste

3 bay leaves

6 tablespoons all-purpose flour

¼ cup finely chopped fresh dill, plus dill sprigs to serve

1 tablespoon cider vinegar

Sour cream, to serve

Our Instant Pot version of Austrian goulash, derives much of its bold flavor and rich color from sweet and hot paprika, so make sure the paprika you use is fresh and fragrant. For the deepest, earthiest flavor, we recommend seeking out true Hungarian paprika. Serve with egg noodles, Spätzle or mashed potatoes.

Don't forget to crush the caraway seeds *so they release their full flavor into the cooking liquid. Use either a mortar and pestle or pulse them in an electric spice grinder. But don't pulverize the seeds to a powder; they should still have a good amount of texture.*

START: In a large bowl, toss the beef with 2 tablespoons sweet paprika until evenly coated. On a 6-quart Instant Pot, select **More/High Sauté**. Add the butter and let melt. Add the onion and 1 teaspoon salt, then cook, stirring occasionally, until the onion is lightly browned, about 8 minutes. Add the caraway and cook, stirring, until fragrant, about 30 seconds. Add the remaining 4 tablespoons sweet paprika and the hot paprika, then cook, stirring, until fragrant, about 30 seconds. Whisk in the broth and tomato paste, scraping up any browned bits. Add the bay and beef; stir to combine, then distribute in an even layer.

FAST

Press **Cancel**, lock the lid in place and move the pressure valve to **Sealing**. Select **Pressure Cook** or **Manual**; make sure the pressure level is set to **High**. Set the cooking time for 25 minutes. When pressure cooking is complete, let the pressure release naturally for 15 minutes, then release the remaining steam by moving the pressure valve to **Venting**. Press **Cancel**, then carefully open the pot.

SLOW

With the pot still on **More/High Sauté**, bring the mixture to a boil. Press **Cancel**, lock the lid in place and move the pressure valve to **Venting**. Select **Slow Cook** and set the temperature to **More/High**. Set the cooking time for 7 to 8 hours; the stew is done when a skewer inserted into a piece of beef meets no resistance. Press **Cancel**, then carefully open the pot.

FINISH: Using a large spoon, skim off and discard the fat from the surface of the cooking liquid. In a medium bowl, whisk the flour with 1 cup of the cooking liquid until smooth, then whisk the mixture into the pot. Select **Normal/Medium Sauté**. Bring the stew to a simmer and cook, stirring often, until thickened, about 2 minutes. Press **Cancel** to turn off the pot. Stir in the dill and vinegar, then taste and season with salt and pepper. Serve garnished with dill sprigs and with sour cream on the side.

BEEF AND WHITE BEAN STEW WITH TOMATOES AND DILL

Active time: 25 minutes

Fast start to finish: 2¼ hours

Slow start to finish: 8½ to 9½ hours

Servings: 6

2 tablespoons extra-virgin olive oil, plus more to serve

1 large yellow onion, chopped

8 medium garlic cloves, smashed and peeled

3 tablespoons tomato paste

1 tablespoon sweet paprika

1 teaspoon red pepper flakes

1 quart low-sodium chicken broth

Kosher salt and ground black pepper

2¾ to 3 pounds beef shanks (each about 1 inch thick), trimmed

2½ cups (1 pound) dried navy beans

14½-ounce can diced tomatoes, drained

½ cup finely chopped fresh dill, plus more to serve

2 tablespoons pomegranate molasses, plus more to serve (see note)

This hearty one-pot dinner combines dried navy beans and beef shanks, which cook at the same rate. Pomegranate molasses adds a bright, tangy, slightly fruity finish that perks up the other flavors. Look for it in bottles in the international section of the supermarket or in Middle Eastern grocery stores. If you can't find pomegranate molasses, stir 1 tablespoon lemon juice into the stew at the end and serve with lemon wedges.

Don't soak the dried white beans. If soaked before cooking, they will cook more quickly than the beef shanks and will wind up soft and overdone. Also, don't forget to drain the tomatoes before use, otherwise their juice will thin the stew.

START: On a 6-quart Instant Pot, select **More/High Sauté**. Add the oil and heat until shimmering. Add the onion and cook, stirring, until lightly browned, about 8 minutes. Stir in the garlic, tomato paste, paprika and pepper flakes, then cook until fragrant, about 30 seconds. Add the broth and 1 tablespoon salt, then stir in the beans and distribute in an even layer. Place the shanks in the pot in a single layer, submerging them in the liquid.

FAST

Lock the lid in place and move the pressure valve to **Sealing**. Select **Pressure Cook** or **Manual**; make sure the pressure level is set to **High**. Set the cooking time for 45 minutes. When pressure cooking is complete, allow the pressure to reduce naturally, about 40 minutes, then move the pressure valve to **Venting** to release any remaining steam. Press **Cancel**, then carefully open the pot.

SLOW

With the pot still on **More/High Sauté**, bring the mixture to a boil. Press **Cancel**, lock the lid in place and move the pressure valve to **Venting**. Select **Slow Cook** and set the temperature to **More/High**. Set the cooking time for 8 to 9 hours; the shanks are done when a skewer inserted into the meat meets no resistance. Press **Cancel**, then carefully open the pot. Taste a few beans; they should be creamy and tender. If too firm, select **Normal/Medium Sauté** and cook, stirring often, until tender, 6 to 10 minutes. Press **Cancel** to turn off the pot.

FINISH: Remove and discard the shank bones; the meat should easily fall away from the bones. Stir in the tomatoes, dill and pomegranate molasses, breaking the meat into large bite-size pieces. Taste and season with salt and black pepper. Serve sprinkled with additional dill and drizzled with additional oil and pomegranate molasses.

Active time: 30 minutes

Fast start to finish:
1¾ hours

Slow start to finish:
7¾ to 8¾ hours

Servings: 6

BEEF AND CHICKPEA STEW WITH CILANTRO AND WARM SPICES

Kosher salt and ground black pepper

2 tablespoons salted butter

1 large yellow onion, chopped

2 medium carrots (about 8 ounces), peeled and shredded

8 medium garlic cloves, smashed and peeled

⅓ cup tomato paste

1 tablespoon sweet paprika

1 tablespoon ground cumin

1 teaspoon ground cardamom

1 teaspoon ground cinnamon

2 pounds boneless beef chuck roast, trimmed and cut into ¾-inch chunks

Two 15½-ounce cans chickpeas, rinsed and drained

2 cups lightly packed fresh cilantro, chopped

3 tablespoons lemon juice

For this hearty stew, rather than cut the carrots into chunks, we shred them on the large holes of a box grater. As they cook, the carrots break down slightly, lending the broth some body while balancing the spices with their natural sweetness. This is a one-pot meal, but if you're craving a starchy accompaniment, serve it with warmed flatbread or couscous. A dollop of plain yogurt is a nice finishing touch that adds a tangy flavor as well as a little creaminess. Harissa is excellent if you desire a little spice.

Don't prep the cilantro too far in advance or it will lose its freshness. If you're pressure cooking, a good time to wash and chop the cilantro is during the natural pressure release. If you're slow cooking, do so during the last 15 minutes or so of cooking.

START: On a 6-quart Instant Pot, select **Normal/Medium Sauté**. Add the butter and melt. Add the onion and carrots, then cook, stirring occasionally, until the vegetables are softened, about 5 minutes. Stir in the garlic, tomato paste, paprika, cumin, cardamom, cinnamon and 1 teaspoon salt, then cook, stirring, until fragrant, about 1 minute. Add 1 quart water and scrape up any browned bits. Stir in the beef, then distribute in an even layer.

FAST

Press **Cancel**, lock the lid in place and move the pressure valve to **Sealing**. Select **Pressure Cook** or **Manual**; make sure the pressure level is set to **High**. Set the cooking time for 30 minutes. When pressure cooking is complete, let the pressure reduce naturally for 15 minutes, then release the remaining steam by moving the pressure valve to **Venting**. Press **Cancel**, then carefully open the pot.

SLOW

With the pot still on **More/High Sauté**, bring the mixture to a boil. Press **Cancel**, lock the lid in place and move the pressure valve to **Venting**. Select **Slow Cook** and set the temperature to **More/High**. Set the cooking time for 7 to 8 hours; the stew is done when a skewer inserted into a piece of beef meets no resistance. Press **Cancel**, then carefully open the pot.

FINISH: Stir in the chickpeas, cilantro and lemon juice, then taste and season with salt and pepper.

FRENCH BEEF OR LAMB AND VEGETABLE STEW WITH TARRAGON

Active time: 30 minutes

Fast start to finish:
1 hour 20 minutes

Slow start to finish:
7½ to 8½ hours

Servings: 4

2 tablespoons salted butter

8 ounces (about 2 cups) peeled pearl onions (see note)

8 medium garlic cloves, peeled and smashed

1 tablespoon fennel seeds

1 cup dry white wine

Kosher salt and ground black pepper

2½ pounds boneless lamb shoulder or boneless beef chuck, trimmed and cut into 1½-inch chunks

6 ounces green beans, trimmed and cut into 1-inch pieces

1 cup cherry or grape tomatoes, halved

2 tablespoons lemon juice

½ cup lightly packed fresh tarragon, roughly chopped

The French stew known as navarin d'agneau is satisfying yet light thanks to the vegetables that counter the richness of the meat and the white wine that adds bright acidity. Fennel seed and tarragon bring licorice notes that accentuate the fresh, grassy flavor of the green beans. Lamb is classic here but boneless beef chuck also is great; the cooking time remains the same. Look for already peeled fresh pearl onions in the refrigerator case of your supermarket's produce section, near the pre-prepped fresh vegetables; if you cannot find them, use frozen instead, but make sure to thaw the onions first, then pat them dry to remove excess moisture. Serve the stew with warm, crusty bread.

Don't stir the tarragon directly into the stew. *The heat causes it to discolor and it loses its freshness. Add at the table for the brightest color and flavor.*

START: On a 6-quart Instant Pot, select **Normal/Medium Sauté**. Add the butter and melt. Add the onions, garlic and fennel seeds, then cook, stirring occasionally, until the onions are lightly browned, 3 to 4 minutes. Add the wine, ½ cup water, 2 teaspoons salt and ½ teaspoon pepper, then bring to a simmer. Add the lamb or beef and stir to combine, then distribute in an even layer.

FAST

Press **Cancel**, lock the lid in place and move the pressure valve to **Sealing**. Select **Pressure Cook** or **Manual**; make sure the pressure level is set to **High**. Set the cooking time for 25 minutes. When pressure cooking is complete, let the pressure reduce naturally for 15 minutes, then release the remaining steam by moving the pressure valve to **Venting**. Press **Cancel**, then carefully open the pot.

SLOW

Select **More/High Sauté** and bring the mixture to a boil. Press **Cancel**, lock the lid in place and move the pressure valve to **Venting**. Select **Slow Cook** and set the temperature to **More/High**. Set the cooking time for 7 to 8 hours; the stew is done when a skewer inserted into a piece of meat meets no resistance. Press **Cancel**, then carefully open the pot.

FINISH: Using a large spoon, skim off and discard the fat from the surface of the cooking liquid. Select **Normal/Medium Sauté** and bring to a simmer. Add the green beans and tomatoes, then cook, stirring occasionally, until the beans are tender, 7 to 10 minutes. Press **Cancel** to turn off the pot. Stir in the lemon juice, then taste and season with salt and pepper. Serve sprinkled with the tarragon.

GREEK BEEF STEW WITH TOMATOES, ONIONS AND ALLSPICE

Active time: 20 minutes

Fast start to finish:
1½ hours

Slow start to finish:
7¼ to 8¼ hours

Servings: 4

2 tablespoons extra-virgin olive oil, plus more to serve

2 medium tomatoes (about 10 ounces), cored and chopped

2 cinnamon sticks

1 teaspoon ground allspice

1 teaspoon white sugar

½ cup dry red wine

2 pounds boneless beef short ribs, trimmed and cut into 1½-inch chunks

8 ounces (about 2 cups) peeled pearl onions (see note)

Kosher salt and ground black pepper

1 tablespoon red wine vinegar, plus more to serve

Feta cheese, crumbled, to serve

Chopped fresh flat-leaf parsley, to serve

This recipe is a simpler, lighter version of the rustic Greek stew known as moshari stifado, which gets its unique character from a combination of tomatoes, onions and spices, namely allspice and cinnamon. The flavors are savory-sweet, warm and comforting. Red wine vinegar and a garnish of feta cheese add a sharpness that balances the dish's meatiness. Look for already peeled fresh pearl onions in the produce section of your supermarket, or use frozen pearl onions, but make sure to thaw them first, then pat dry to remove excess moisture. Serve the stew with crusty bread or roasted or mashed potatoes.

Don't seed the tomatoes; simply core and chop them. Make sure to include their juices when adding the tomatoes to the pot, as they help build flavor.

START: On a 6-quart Instant Pot, select **More/High Sauté**. Add the oil and heat until shimmering. Add the tomatoes and their juices, the cinnamon, allspice and sugar, then cook, stirring occasionally, until the juices evaporate and the tomatoes begin to brown, about 5 minutes. Add the wine and scrape up any browned bits. Add the beef, onions, 2 teaspoons salt and 1 teaspoon pepper; stir to combine, then distribute in an even layer.

FAST

Press **Cancel**, lock the lid in place and move the pressure valve to **Sealing**. Select **Pressure Cook** or **Manual**; make sure the pressure level is set to **High**. Set the cooking time for 30 minutes. When pressure cooking is complete, let the pressure reduce naturally for 15 minutes, then release the remaining steam by moving the pressure valve to **Venting**. Press **Cancel**, then carefully open the pot.

SLOW

With the pot still on **More/High Sauté**, bring the mixture to a boil. Press **Cancel**, lock the lid in place and move the pressure valve to **Venting**. Select **Slow Cook** and set the temperature to **More/High**. Set the cooking time for 7 to 8 hours; the stew is done when a skewer inserted into a piece of beef meets no resistance. Press **Cancel**, then carefully open the pot.

FINISH: Using a large spoon, skim off and discard the fat from the surface of the cooking liquid. Remove and discard the cinnamon sticks. Select **Normal/Medium Sauté**. Bring the stew to a simmer, stir in the vinegar and cook, stirring occasionally, until slightly thickened, about 5 minutes. Press **Cancel** to turn off the pot. Taste and season with salt and pepper. Serve sprinkled with feta cheese and parsley and drizzled with oil; offer additional vinegar at the table.

MEATBALLS IN SPICY TOMATO-BASIL SAUCE

Active time: 20 minutes

Fast start to finish: 1 hour 10 minutes, plus chilling and standing time

Servings: 4

½ cup fine dry breadcrumbs

Two 28-ounce cans whole peeled tomatoes, drained, juices reserved

2 teaspoons dried oregano

2 teaspoons fennel seeds, finely ground

1 teaspoon granulated garlic

1 pound 85 percent lean ground beef

Kosher salt and ground black pepper

4 tablespoons (½ stick) salted butter

¾ teaspoon red pepper flakes

3 tablespoons tomato paste

3 tablespoons finely chopped fresh basil

Grated Parmesan or pecorino Romano cheese, to serve

Ground fennel seeds lend these meatballs a subtle licorice-like sweetness, making them reminiscent of Italian sausage. Use a spice grinder or mortar and pestle to grind the whole seeds to a powder, or if you're able to find preground fennel seed at the store use an equal amount. You can, of course, serve the meatballs and sauce over pasta, or you can tuck the meatballs into toasted sub rolls lined with slices of provolone cheese, spoon some sauce over the top and finish with a sprinkle of grated Parmesan or pecorino Romano cheese.

Don't use ground beef that's leaner than 85 percent or the meatballs will be dry and bland. When shaping the meat mixture, form it into firm, compact meatballs, not loosely packed orbs; this helps them hold together when pressure cooked. And don't forget to refrigerate the meatballs for at least 15 minutes before cooking, as this helps them retain their shape.

START: In a large bowl, mix together the breadcrumbs, ½ cup tomato juices, the oregano, fennel seeds and garlic. Add the beef, 1½ teaspoons salt and 1 teaspoon black pepper. Mix with your hands until no streaks of breadcrumbs remain. Divide into 10 portions and form each into a compact ball about 2 inches in diameter, placing the meatballs on a large plate. Refrigerate for 15 minutes.

FAST

On a 6-quart Instant Pot, select **More/High Sauté**. Add the tomatoes and their remaining juices, the butter and pepper flakes, then bring to a boil, stirring. Set the meatballs on top of the tomatoes in an even layer, gently pressing to submerge them. Lock the lid in place and move the pressure valve to **Sealing**. Press **Cancel**, then select **Pressure Cook** or **Manual**; make sure the pressure level is set to **High**. Set the cooking time for 3 minutes. When pressure cooking is complete, allow the pressure to reduce naturally for 10 minutes, then release the remaining steam by moving the pressure valve to **Venting**. Press **Cancel**, then carefully open the pot.

FINISH: Using a slotted spoon, transfer the meatballs to a clean plate. Select **More/High Sauté**. Bring the tomato mixture to a boil, mashing with a potato masher to break up the tomatoes. Whisk in the tomato paste and cook, stirring occasionally, until slightly thickened, about 8 minutes. Taste and season with salt and black pepper. Add the basil and return the meatballs to the pot, then gently stir. Press **Cancel** to turn off the pot. Let stand until the meatballs are heated through, about 10 minutes. Serve sprinkled with Parmesan.

BEEF PICADILLO

Active time: 20 minutes
Fast start to finish: 1 hour
Servings: 4

2 tablespoons salted butter

1 large red onion, halved and thinly sliced

Kosher salt and ground black pepper

1 tablespoon ground cumin

2 teaspoons dried oregano

2 medium garlic cloves, finely chopped

3 tablespoons tomato paste

1½ pounds 85 percent lean ground beef

1 cup low-sodium beef broth

¾ cup golden raisins, divided

¾ cup pimiento-stuffed green olives, chopped

¼ cup chopped fresh cilantro

Picadillo—a ground beef dish popular in Cuba, the Caribbean and Latin America—combines tangy, sweet and salty flavors. There are many variations, but the essentials are a stew of ground meat and tomato with raisins for sweetness and chopped olives for a balancing touch of brine. Prep the olives and cilantro while the beef cooks. Serve with beans, rice and, if you like, chopped fresh tomatoes and hot sauce.

Don't use double-concentrated tomato paste, often sold in a tube. Its potent flavor will overwhelm the other ingredients. Also, don't use ground beef that's leaner than 85 percent or the meat in the finished dish will have a dry, pebbly texture.

START: On a 6-quart Instant Pot, select **More/High Sauté**. Add the butter and let melt. Add the onion and 1 teaspoon salt, then cook, stirring often, until golden brown at the edges, 5 to 7 minutes. Stir in the cumin, oregano and garlic, then cook until fragrant, about 30 seconds. Stir in the tomato paste and cook until the paste begins to brown, about 1 minute. Stir in the beef and broth, scraping up any browned bits and breaking the meat into smaller pieces. Stir in ¼ cup of raisins, then distribute the mixture in an even layer.

FAST

Press **Cancel**, lock the lid in place and move the pressure valve to **Sealing**. Select **Pressure Cook** or **Manual**; make sure the pressure level is set to **High**. Set the cooking time for 12 minutes. When pressure cooking is complete, allow the pressure to reduce naturally for 10 minutes, then release the remaining steam by moving the pressure valve to **Venting**. Press **Cancel**, then carefully open the pot.

FINISH: Using a large spoon, skim off and discard the fat from the surface. Select **Normal/Medium Sauté**. Stir in the olives and the remaining ½ cup raisins, then cook, breaking up large clumps of beef with a wooden spoon, until most of the liquid has evaporated and the mixture begins to sizzle, 5 to 7 minutes. Press **Cancel** to turn off the pot. Taste and season with salt and pepper, then stir in the cilantro.

CHILI CON CARNE

Active time: 40 minutes

Fast start to finish:
2 hours

Slow start to finish:
8¾ to 9¾ hours

Servings: 6

3 tablespoons ancho
chili powder

2 tablespoons chili powder

2 tablespoons packed light
or dark brown sugar

2 tablespoons ground cumin

1 tablespoon dried oregano

Kosher salt

4 pounds boneless beef
chuck roast, trimmed and
cut into 1- to 1½-inch chunks

3 tablespoons grapeseed
or other neutral oil

1 large yellow onion, finely
chopped

6 medium garlic cloves,
finely chopped

3 tablespoons tomato paste

14½-ounce can diced
fire-roasted tomatoes

4 chipotle chilies in adobo
sauce, finely chopped, plus
3 tablespoons adobo sauce

3 ounces (2 cups) tortilla
chips, finely crushed (about
1 cup; see note)

To get the rich, earthy flavor of dried chilies without having to toast, soak and puree whole dried chilies, we use ancho chili powder, which is pure ancho chilies pulverized to a fine consistency. If you can't find ancho chili powder, increase the regular chili powder (which is a blend of ground chilies and other spices and herbs) to ⅓ cup. We thicken our chili with crushed tortilla chips. The easiest way to crush them is to place them in a zip-close bag, seal the bag and roll with a rolling pin until the chips are finely crushed. Serve the chili with shredded cheddar cheese, pickled jalapeños, sour cream, chopped cilantro and hot sauce, if desired.

Don't be shy about trimming the beef. Chuck is a fat-rich cut, so removing as much fat as possible before cooking helps prevent the chili from becoming greasy. Also, don't drain the tomatoes before use; their liquid is needed for proper cooking.

START: In a large bowl, stir together both chili powders, the sugar, cumin, oregano and 2 teaspoons salt. Add the beef and toss until evenly coated; set aside. On a 6-quart Instant Pot, select **More/High Sauté**. Add the oil and heat until shimmering. Add the onion and cook, stirring occasionally, until lightly browned, about 5 minutes. Add the garlic and cook, stirring, until fragrant, about 30 seconds. Stir in the tomato paste and cook, stirring, until the tomato paste is well browned, about 3 minutes. Stir in the tomatoes with their juice, the chipotle chilies and adobo sauce and 1 cup water, scraping up any browned bits. Add the beef; stir to combine, then distribute in an even layer.

FAST

Press **Cancel**, lock the lid in place and move the pressure valve to **Sealing**. Select **Pressure Cook** or **Manual**; make sure the pressure level is set to **High**. Set the cooking time for 50 minutes. When pressure cooking is complete, let the pressure reduce naturally for 15 minutes, then release the remaining steam by moving the pressure valve to **Venting**. Press **Cancel**, then carefully open the pot.

SLOW

With the pot still on **More/High Sauté**, bring the mixture to a boil. Press **Cancel**, lock the lid in place and move the pressure valve to **Venting**. Select **Slow Cook** and set the temperature to **More/High**. Set the cooking time for 8 to 9 hours; the chili is done when a skewer inserted into a piece of beef meets no resistance. Press **Cancel**, then carefully open the pot.

FINISH: Using a large spoon, skim off and discard the fat from the surface of the cooking liquid. Stir the crushed tortilla chips into the chili. Select **More/High Sauté** and cook, stirring occasionally, until the chili is lightly thickened, about 5 minutes. Press **Cancel** to turn off the pot. Let stand for 10 minutes, then taste and season with salt.

INDONESIAN COCONUT-CURRY BEEF

Active time: 30 minutes

Fast start to finish:
1½ hours

Slow start to finish:
7½ to 8½ hours

Servings: 4

½ cup unsweetened shredded coconut

3 Fresno or serrano chilies, stemmed, seeded and roughly chopped, plus 1 chili, stemmed and thinly sliced

3 medium garlic cloves, smashed and peeled

1 lemon grass stalk, tough outer layers removed, trimmed to lower 6 inches and thinly sliced

1-inch piece fresh ginger, peeled and roughly chopped

1 medium shallot, roughly chopped

½ teaspoon ground turmeric

⅛ teaspoon ground cinnamon

1 star anise pod

1 tablespoon grated lime zest, plus 1 tablespoon juice

Kosher salt and ground black pepper

¾ cup coconut milk

2½ to 3 pounds boneless beef chuck roast, trimmed and cut into 1½- to 2-inch chunks

Fresh cilantro, to serve

This is a simplified version of beef rendang, a dry-style curry that usually involves a long, slow simmer in coconut milk spiked with an aromatic spice paste. The fall-apart tender beef is left coated with a thick, rich and intensely flavorful sauce. Toasted coconut is a key flavoring in the dish; we use the Instant Pot's sauté function to toast it as the first step, then turn off the pot by pressing **Cancel**; the residual heat is ideal for gently cooking the aromatics and spices. Serve the curry with plenty of steamed rice.

Don't use sweetened shredded coconut. Its sugariness will cause the coconut to scorch during toasting and will throw off the flavor balance in the dish.

START: To a 6-quart Instant Pot, add the shredded coconut, then select **Normal/Medium Sauté**. Cook, stirring frequently, until the coconut is golden brown, about 5 minutes. Press **Cancel**, then add the chopped chilies, garlic, lemon grass, ginger, shallot, turmeric, cinnamon, star anise, lime zest and 1½ teaspoons each salt and pepper. Using the pot's residual heat, cook the mixture, stirring, until fragrant, about 1 minute. Stir in the coconut milk and beef, scraping up any bits stuck to the bottom, then distribute in an even layer.

FAST

Lock the lid in place and move the pressure valve to **Sealing**. Press **Pressure Cook** or **Manual**; make sure the pressure level is set to **High**. Set the cooking time for 25 minutes. When pressure cooking is complete, let the pressure reduce naturally for 15 minutes, then release the remaining steam by moving the pressure valve to **Venting**. Press **Cancel**, then carefully open the pot.

SLOW

Select **More/High Sauté** and cook until vigorously sizzling. Press **Cancel**, lock the lid in place and move the pressure valve to **Venting**. Select **Slow Cook** and set the temperature to **More/High**. Set the cooking time for 7 to 8 hours; the beef is done when a skewer inserted into a piece meets no resistance. Press **Cancel**, then carefully open the pot.

FINISH: Using tongs, transfer the meat to a small bowl and set aside. Pour the cooking liquid into a fine mesh strainer set over a bowl. Add the solids in the strainer to a blender, then pour in ¼ cup of the strained liquid; discard the remaining liquid or reserve for another use. Blend on high until very smooth, 1 to 2 minutes, scraping the sides as needed. Pour the puree back into the pot, then stir in the beef and lime juice. Select **Normal/Medium Sauté** and cook, stirring often, until the sauce clinging to the bottom of the pot is golden brown, 3 to 5 minutes. Press **Cancel** to turn off the pot. Taste and season with salt and pepper. Serve garnished with sliced chilies and cilantro.

KOREAN BRAISED SHORT RIBS

Active time: 45 minutes

Fast start to finish:
2 hours 10 minutes

Slow start to finish:
7¾ to 8¾ hours

Servings: 6

2½ to 3 pounds bone-in beef short ribs

½ cup soy sauce

½ cup sake

8 medium garlic cloves, peeled

4-inch piece fresh ginger (about 3 ounces), peeled and roughly chopped

3 tablespoons packed light brown sugar

2 tablespoons sesame seeds, toasted, plus more to serve

1 ripe pear (about 8 ounces), cored and roughly chopped

10 dried shiitake mushrooms (about 1 ounce), broken in half

1 medium carrot, peeled and cut into 1-inch chunks

1 small daikon radish (about 8 ounces), peeled and cut into 1-inch chunks

6 scallions, thinly sliced on the diagonal

Salty, sweet and nutty with toasted sesame seeds, these braised short ribs are an Instant Pot version of Korean galbi jjim. Traditional versions often are sweetened with Asian pear, but we found any firm, ripe pear works perfectly well. Some markets may offer two different short rib cuts; chunky, single-bone English-style and thinner flanked ribs that are cut across several bones. The former is the type to use here. Soaking the ribs in cold water helps remove impurities so the braising liquid becomes shiny and glossy; use this time to prepare the other ingredients. Serve with steamed rice and, if you like, toasted sesame oil for drizzling. Spicy, tangy kimchi is a great accompaniment, too.

Don't use raw sesame seeds. Toasted seeds have a rich nuttiness that adds complexity to the dish. Already toasted (or roasted) sesame seeds are sold in large plastic shaker bottles, usually in the Asian aisle of supermarkets. Or, to toast your own, stir them on Normal/Medium Sauté in the Instant Pot until lightly golden and fragrant, about 5 minutes.

START: In a large bowl, cover the short ribs with cool water. Set aside at room temperature for at least 10 minutes or up to 1 hour. In a blender, combine the soy sauce, sake, garlic, ginger, sugar, sesame seeds and pear, then puree until smooth, scraping down the sides as needed, about 1 minute. Pour the mixture into a 6-quart Instant Pot. Drain the short ribs and briefly rinse under running water, then arrange them in an even layer in the pot and add the mushrooms.

FAST

Lock the lid in place and move the pressure valve to **Sealing**. Select **Pressure Cook** or **Manual**; make sure the pressure level is set to **High**. Set the cooking time for 55 minutes. When pressure cooking is complete, let the pressure reduce naturally for 15 minutes, then release the remaining steam by moving the pressure valve to **Venting**. Press **Cancel**, then carefully open the pot.

SLOW

Select **More/High Sauté** and bring the mixture to a boil. Press **Cancel**, lock the lid in place and move the pressure valve to **Venting**. Select **Slow Cook** and set the temperature to **More/High**. Set the cooking time for 7 to 8 hours; the ribs are done when a skewer inserted into the meat meets no resistance. Carefully open the pot.

FINISH: Using a large spoon, skim off and discard the fat from the surface of the cooking liquid. Select **Normal/Medium Sauté**, then add the carrot and daikon. Cook, stirring occasionally, until the vegetables are tender and the cooking liquid thickens to a light glaze, about 15 minutes. Press **Cancel** to turn off the pot. Remove and discard the beef bones, then stir in half of the scallions. Serve sprinkled with the remaining scallions and additional sesame seeds.

MEXICAN SHREDDED BRISKET SALAD

Active time: 30 minutes

Fast start to finish: 2 hours 10 minutes, plus cooling

Servings: 4

6 tablespoons extra-virgin olive oil, divided

1 medium yellow onion, halved and thinly sliced

5 medium garlic cloves, smashed and peeled

Kosher salt and ground black pepper

3 bay leaves

2 teaspoons dried oregano, divided

2 pounds beef brisket, trimmed and cut into 2- to 2½-inch pieces

½ cup lime juice, plus lime wedges to serve

½ cup pitted green olives, chopped

1 medium head romaine lettuce, roughly chopped (6 to 7 cups)

6 radishes, halved and thinly sliced

1 cup lightly packed fresh cilantro, roughly chopped

1 ripe avocado, halved, pitted, peeled and diced

This classic Mexican dish—known as salpicón de res—combines a shredded beef salad with a tangy lime dressing. Beef brisket, normally a slow-cooking cut, becomes fork-tender in a fraction of the time when pressure-cooked. To be efficient, while the beef cooks, prepare the other ingredients, except for the avocado (which will discolor), and keep them chilled until ready to use. For an appealing crunch and toasty corn flavor, serve on tostadas (corn tortillas that are fried flat).

Don't allow the brisket to cool completely in the pot. Shredding and dressing the beef while still warm helps it more readily absorb the dressing. Also, don't discard the remaining cooking liquid. It's rich and meaty and, once strained, can be used in place of beef broth or stock in soups and stews.

START: On a 6-quart Instant Pot, select **Normal/Medium Sauté**. Add 1 tablespoon oil and heat until shimmering, then add the onion and cook, stirring occasionally, until softened, about 5 minutes. Add the garlic and cook, stirring often, until the onion is golden brown, another 2 to 3 minutes. Stir in 1½ teaspoons salt, 1 teaspoon pepper, the bay, 1 teaspoon oregano and 1 cup water, scraping up any browned bits. Add the beef in an even layer, slightly overlapping the pieces if needed.

FAST

Press **Cancel**, lock the lid in place and move the pressure valve to **Sealing**. Select **Pressure Cook** or **Manual**; make sure the pressure level is set to **High**. Set the cooking time for 45 minutes. When pressure cooking is complete, allow the pressure to reduce naturally for 15 minutes, then release the remaining steam by moving the pressure valve to **Venting**. Press **Cancel**, carefully open the pot and let the contents cool for 5 to 10 minutes.

FINISH: While the beef is cooking, in a large bowl whisk together the lime juice, the remaining 5 tablespoons oil, the remaining 1 teaspoon dried oregano and 1 teaspoon each salt and pepper. Set aside. Once the meat is done, use a slotted spoon to transfer the meat and onion to a medium bowl; do not discard the liquid remaining in the pot. With two forks, shred the beef into bite-size pieces. Whisk the dressing to recombine. Add ½ cup of the dressing, the olives and ¼ cup of the reserved cooking liquid to the shredded meat, then toss to coat. Let cool to room temperature. Whisk the remaining dressing once again. Add the lettuce, radishes and cilantro to it, then toss to coat. Transfer to a platter and top with the beef and the avocado. Serve with lime wedges.

BRAISED BEEF WITH PANCETTA, MUSHROOMS AND RED WINE

Active time: 40 minutes

Fast start to finish:
2 hours 40 minutes

Slow start to finish:
10¾ to 11¾ hours

Servings: 4 to 6

4½- to 5-pound boneless beef chuck roast, pulled apart at the natural seams into 3 pieces, trimmed, each piece tied with twine at 1-inch intervals

1 teaspoon grated nutmeg

Kosher salt and ground black pepper

1 teaspoon extra-virgin olive oil

6 ounces pancetta, chopped

8 ounces cremini mushrooms, trimmed and quartered

3 medium garlic cloves, thinly sliced

2 tablespoons tomato paste

¼ cup dry red wine

3 tablespoons all-purpose flour

1 cup roughly chopped fresh flat-leaf parsley

¼ cup chopped fresh tarragon

This recipe is a pot roast spin on classic French boeuf bourguignon, brightened with a generous handful of fresh herbs. For faster cooking, we divide a chuck roast into three pieces by pulling the roast apart at its natural seams, then trim away the excess fat. Tying each piece with kitchen twine compacts the shapes so all the pieces fit in the pot and cook evenly. The parsley and tarragon aren't needed until the end, so to save time and ensure that their flavors and color stay fresh, prep them during the natural pressure release. Chunks of warm, crusty bread or buttery mashed potatoes are the perfect accompaniment for this hearty braise.

Don't discard the fat left in the pot after cooking the pancetta. Using it to brown the tomato paste creates a meaty, flavorful base for the braise.

START: In a small bowl, mix together the nutmeg, 2 teaspoons salt and 1 teaspoon pepper. Use to season the beef on all sides. On a 6-quart Instant Pot, select **Normal/Medium Sauté**. Add the oil and pancetta, then cook, stirring occasionally, until the pancetta has rendered its fat but is not yet crisp, 3 to 5 minutes. Stir in the mushrooms and ½ teaspoon each salt and pepper. Cook, stirring occasionally, until the liquid released by the mushrooms has evaporated and the mushrooms begin to brown, 6 to 8 minutes. Add the garlic and cook, stirring, until fragrant, 1 to 2 minutes. Using a slotted spoon, transfer the mixture to a bowl and set aside. To the fat remaining in the pot, add the tomato paste and cook, stirring occasionally, until browned, 1 to 2 minutes. Add the wine and ¼ cup water, scraping up any browned bits. Nestle the beef in the pot.

FAST

Press **Cancel**, lock the lid in place and move the pressure valve to **Sealing**. Select **Pressure Cook** or **Manual**; make sure the pressure level is set to **High**. Set the cooking time for 1 hour. When pressure cooking is complete, let the pressure reduce naturally for 25 minutes, then release the remaining steam by moving the pressure valve to **Venting**. Press **Cancel**, then carefully open the pot.

SLOW

Select **More/High Sauté** and bring the mixture to a boil. Press **Cancel**, lock the lid in place and move the pressure valve to **Venting**. Select **Slow Cook** and set the temperature to **More/High**. Set the cooking time for 10 to 11 hours; the beef is done when a skewer inserted into the largest piece meets no resistance. Press **Cancel**, then carefully open the pot.

FINISH: Transfer the beef to a cutting board and tent with foil. Using a large spoon, skim off and discard the fat from the surface of the cooking liquid. In a small bowl, whisk the flour with about ¼ cup of the cooking liquid until smooth, then stir into the pot along with the mushroom mixture. Select **Normal/Medium Sauté**. Bring the mixture to a simmer and cook, stirring often, until lightly thickened, 3 to 5 minutes. Press **Cancel** to turn off the pot.

Stir in the parsley and tarragon, then taste and season with salt and pepper. Cut the beef into ½-inch slices against the grain, removing the twine as you go. Arrange the slices on a platter, then pour the sauce over the top.

SHORT RIB RAGU WITH PAPPARDELLE

Active time: 40 minutes

Fast start to finish: 1¾ hours

Slow start to finish: 8¾ to 9¾ hours

Servings: 4

1 tablespoon extra-virgin olive oil

1 large yellow onion, finely chopped

1 large fennel bulb, trimmed, halved, cored and roughly chopped, divided

Kosher salt and ground black pepper

8 medium garlic cloves, smashed and peeled

2 tablespoons tomato paste

1 cup dry red wine

28-ounce can whole peeled tomatoes, crushed by hand

2-inch piece Parmesan cheese rind (optional), plus finely grated Parmesan, to serve

2½ pounds boneless beef short ribs, trimmed and cut into ¾-inch chunks

3 medium carrots, peeled and finely chopped

½ cup heavy cream

3 tablespoons finely chopped fresh flat-leaf parsley

12 ounces dried pappardelle pasta (see note), cooked until al dente and drained

An Instant Pot makes it possible to put a rich, hearty beef ragu on the table fast and with minimal effort. We use meaty boneless short ribs cut into small chunks. After cooking, simply mash the beef directly in the pot to break it into shreds. If you happen to have a piece of Parmesan rind, add it to the pot along with the meat; it will lend the ragu an added layer of depth and savoriness. We think long, wide strands of pappardelle pair especially well with this sauce, but any pasta shape works nicely, even short, stubby ziti and penne.

Don't drain the tomatoes; their juice is important for proper pressure cooking. And don't cook the pasta in advance, as it should be just-drained and steaming-hot when it is sauced.

START: On a 6-quart Instant Pot, select **More/High Sauté**. Add the oil and heat until shimmering, then add the onion, half of the fennel and ½ teaspoon salt. Cook, stirring occasionally, until softened, about 5 minutes. Stir in the garlic and tomato paste and cook until fragrant, about 30 seconds. Add the wine and cook, stirring occasionally, until the liquid has almost fully evaporated, about 4 minutes. Stir in the tomatoes with their juice, add the Parmesan rind (if using) and the beef, then distribute in an even layer.

FAST

Press **Cancel**, lock the lid in place and move the pressure valve to **Sealing**. Select **Pressure Cook** or **Manual**; make sure the pressure level is set to **High**. Set the cooking time for 30 minutes. When pressure cooking is complete, quick-release the steam by moving the pressure valve to **Venting**. Press **Cancel**, then carefully open the pot.

SLOW

With the pot still on **More/High Sauté**, bring the mixture to a boil. Press **Cancel**, lock the lid in place and move the pressure valve to **Venting**. Select **Slow Cook** and set the temperature to **More/High**. Set the cooking time for 8 to 9 hours; the beef is done when a skewer inserted into a piece meets no resistance. Press **Cancel**, then carefully open the pot.

FINISH: Remove and discard the Parmesan rind (if used). Using a potato masher, mash the beef until shredded. Stir in the carrots, the remaining fennel and the cream. Select **Normal/Medium Sauté** and cook, stirring occasionally, until the sauce thickens slightly and the carrots are tender, 10 to 15 minutes. Stir in the parsley, then taste and season with salt and pepper. In a large warmed bowl or the pot used to cook the pasta, toss the pasta with about 5 cups of the ragu. Serve sprinkled with Parmesan and pass the remaining sauce at the table.

ROPA VIEJA

Active time: 40 minutes

Fast start to finish:
1¾ hours

Slow start to finish:
10 to 11 hours

Servings: 6 to 8

2 tablespoons extra-virgin olive oil

2 medium white onions, halved and thinly sliced

2 medium red bell peppers, stemmed, seeded and sliced ¼-inch thick

2 jalapeño chilies, stemmed and sliced into thin rounds

10 medium garlic cloves, smashed and peeled

Kosher salt and ground black pepper

2½ tablespoons ground cumin

2½ tablespoons ground coriander

28-ounce can whole peeled tomatoes, drained, ¼ cup juices reserved, tomatoes crushed by hand

3 pounds flank steak, halved lengthwise with the grain, then cut across the grain into 1½-inch-wide strips

1 cup pimiento-stuffed green olives, roughly chopped

3 tablespoons lime juice, plus lime wedges to serve

Ropa vieja is a Cuban dish of shredded beef with tomatoes, onions and bell peppers, often accented with briny olives. The name translates as "old clothes," a reference to the tattered look of the slow-simmered and shredded meat. We preferred flank steak for its rich, meaty flavor, and for the way its fibers shred easily after braising. Look for an extra-large flank steak, which should weigh about 3 pounds, or use multiple steaks. This recipe makes a generous amount, but leftovers reheat well. Ropa vieja traditionally is served with rice and beans; we also like a simple cabbage slaw alongside to add crunch and bright flavor.

Don't forget to reserve ¼ cup of the tomato juices when draining the can; adding the reserved liquid to the pot along with the tomatoes will prevent the "burn" error message from appearing on the display. Before shredding the beef, make sure to discard the accumulated liquid in the bowl; if poured back into the pot, the liquid will water down the dish.

START: On a 6-quart Instant Pot, select **More/High Sauté**. Add the oil and heat until shimmering. Add the onions, bell peppers, jalapeños, garlic and 2 teaspoons salt, then cook, stirring occasionally, until the vegetables are softened and beginning to brown, about 10 minutes. Stir in the cumin and coriander, then cook until fragrant, about 30 seconds. Add the tomatoes and reserved juices, scraping up any browned bits. Add the meat and stir to combine, then distribute in an even layer.

FAST

Press **Cancel**, lock the lid in place and move the pressure valve to **Sealing**. Select **Pressure Cook** or **Manual**; make sure the pressure level is set to **High**. Set the cooking time for 20 minutes. When pressure cooking is complete, let the pressure reduce naturally for 25 minutes, then release the remaining steam by moving the pressure valve to **Venting**. Press **Cancel**, then carefully open the pot.

SLOW

With the pot still on **More/High Sauté**, bring the mixture to a boil. Press **Cancel**, lock the lid in place and move the pressure valve to **Venting**. Select **Slow Cook** and set the temperature to **More/High**. Set the cooking time for 9 to 10 hours; the meat is done when a skewer inserted into a piece meets no resistance. Press **Cancel**, then carefully open the pot.

FINISH: Using a slotted spoon, transfer the beef and peppers to a large bowl (it's fine if some pieces of pepper remain in the pot). Select **Normal/Medium Sauté**. Bring the cooking liquid to a simmer and cook, stirring often, until reduced and slightly thickened, about 15 minutes. Press **Cancel** to turn off the pot. Pour off and discard any accumulated liquid in the bowl with the beef. Using 2 forks or your fingers, shred the meat. Stir the meat, olives and lime juice into the reduced cooking liquid in the pot. Taste and season with salt and pepper. Serve with lime wedges.

AUSTRIAN POT-ROASTED BEEF WITH ROOT VEGETABLES

Active time: 45 minutes

**Fast start to finish:
1 hour 40 minutes**

Slow start to finish:
11 to 12 hours

Servings: 4 to 6

2 tablespoons grapeseed
or other neutral oil

1 large yellow onion, cut
into 6 wedges

6 medium carrots, peeled
and cut into 3-inch lengths,
thicker pieces halved
lengthwise

6 medium parsnips, peeled
and cut into 6-inch lengths,
thicker pieces halved
lengthwise

4½- to 5-pound boneless
beef chuck roast, pulled
apart at the natural seams
into 3 pieces, trimmed, each
piece tied at 1-inch intervals

3 cups low-sodium
beef broth

5 bay leaves

2 tablespoons caraway
seeds

2 tablespoons allspice
berries

2 thyme sprigs

Kosher salt and ground
black pepper

2 pounds red potatoes
(about 2 inches in diameter),
halved

3 dill sprigs, plus ¼ cup
chopped fresh dill

Prepared horseradish and/
or Dijon mustard, to serve

For this wintry one-pot meal, inspired by Austrian Tafelspitz, or boiled beef and vegetables with horseradish sauce, we use some of the carrots and parsnips to build flavor in the broth that later is served with the beef. The remaining carrots and parsnips are then pressure cooked with potatoes for serving alongside the meat. This two-step process allows the vegetables to be cooked to perfection; if cooked with the meat, they would be soft and overdone. Prepared horseradish or Dijon mustard offers a spicy, punchy kick.

Don't worry if the vegetables aren't fully tender after pressure cooking (you should be able to easily insert a skewer or the tip of a paring knife). If needed, select **More/High Sauté** and simmer them for a few more minutes until done, then press **Cancel** to turn off the pot.

START: On a 6-quart Instant Pot, select **More/High Sauté**. Add the oil and heat until shimmering, then stir in the onion and cook, stirring, until softened and golden brown at the edges, 5 to 7 minutes. Add 4 pieces each of carrot and parsnip, then nestle in the beef. Add the broth, bay, caraway, allspice, thyme and 1 tablespoon pepper.

FAST

Lock the lid in place and move the pressure valve to **Sealing**. Press **Cancel**, then press **Pressure Cook** or **Manual**; make sure the pressure level is set to **High**. Set the cooking time for 1 hour. When pressure cooking is complete, allow the pressure to reduce naturally for 25 minutes, then release the remaining steam by moving the pressure valve to **Venting**. Press **Cancel**, then carefully open the pot.

SLOW

With the pot still on **More/High Sauté**, bring the mixture to a boil. Press **Cancel**, lock the lid in place and move the pressure valve to **Venting**. Select **Slow Cook** and set the temperature to **More/High**. Set the cooking time for 10 to 11 hours; the beef is done when a skewer inserted into the largest piece meets no resistance. Press **Cancel**, then carefully open the pot.

FINISH: Transfer the beef to a cutting board and tent with foil. Using potholders, carefully remove the insert from the housing and pour the broth into a fine mesh strainer set over a medium bowl; discard the solids in the strainer. Use a wide spoon to skim off and discard the fat from the surface of the cooking liquid, then return the liquid to the pot. Add the remaining carrots, the remaining parsnips and the potatoes, distributing them evenly.

Lock the lid in place and move the pressure valve to **Sealing**. Select **Pressure Cook** or **Manual**; make sure the pressure level is set to **High**. Set the cooking time for 7 minutes. When pressure cooking is complete, quick-release the steam by moving the pressure valve to **Venting**. Press **Cancel**, then carefully open the pot. Using a slotted spoon, transfer the vegetables to a large platter and tent with foil. Add the dill sprigs to the cooking liquid. Cut the meat against the grain into ½-inch slices, removing the twine as you go. Place the slices on the platter with the vegetables.

Taste the broth and season with salt and pepper. Remove and discard the dill sprigs, then ladle about 1 cup of the broth over the meat and sprinkle with the chopped dill. Serve with the remaining broth on the side and with horseradish and/or mustard.

COLOMBIAN SAVORY-SWEET BRAISED BEEF WITH QUICK PICO DE GALLO

Active time: 45 minutes

Fast start to finish:
2¼ hours

Slow start to finish:
10¾ to 11¾ hours

Servings: 4 to 6

4½- to 5-pound boneless beef chuck roast, pulled apart at the natural seams into 3 pieces, trimmed, each piece tied at 1-inch intervals

Kosher salt and ground black pepper

2 tablespoons grapeseed or other neutral oil

1 large yellow onion, chopped

10 medium garlic cloves, smashed and peeled

2 tablespoons tomato paste

½ cup packed dark brown sugar

2 cinnamon sticks

1 tablespoon allspice berries

1 cup dry red wine

¼ cup Worcestershire sauce

1 cup pitted prunes, roughly chopped

1½ tablespoons cornstarch

3 to 4 tablespoons red wine vinegar

Colombian posta negra is made by braising beef in a flavorful liquid seasoned with panela (raw cane sugar) and spices. We use a beef chuck roast, divide it into three pieces along its natural seams, trim it well (it's a fat-rich cut), then tie each piece with kitchen twine. This ensures the meat cooks evenly and as quickly as possible. In Colombia, the dish might be served with fried plantains, yucca fritters and a simple salad; we liked it with an easy pico de gallo and/or mashed potatoes.

Don't forget to scrape the underside of the strainer after pressing on the solids with a spatula. The thick pulp tends to cling to the mesh; scraping ensures you collect as much of it as possible so the sauce has the correct consistency and flavor.

START: Season the beef on all sides with salt and pepper. In a 6-quart Instant Pot, select **More/High Sauté**. Add the oil and heat until shimmering. Add the onion and ½ teaspoon salt, then cook, stirring occasionally, until the onion is well browned, about 9 minutes. Add the garlic and cook, stirring, until fragrant, about 30 seconds. Add the tomato paste and cook, stirring constantly, until it begins to brown, about 1 minute. Stir in the sugar, cinnamon, allspice and 1 teaspoon pepper, then add the wine, scraping up any browned bits. Bring to a simmer and cook, stirring occasionally, until thick and syrupy, 3 to 5 minutes. Stir in the Worcestershire sauce, prunes and 1 cup water. Nestle the beef in the pot.

FAST

Press **Cancel**, lock the lid in place and move the pressure valve to **Sealing**. Select **Pressure Cook** or **Manual**; make sure the pressure level is set to **High**. Set the cooking time for 1 hour. When pressure cooking is complete, let the pressure release naturally for 25 minutes, then release the remaining steam by moving the pressure valve to **Venting**. Press **Cancel**, then carefully open the pot.

SLOW

Select **More/High Sauté** and bring the mixture to a boil. Press **Cancel**, lock the lid in place and move the pressure valve to **Venting**. Select **Slow Cook** and set the temperature to **More/High**. Set the cooking time for 10 to 11 hours; the beef is done when a skewer inserted into the largest piece meets no resistance. Press **Cancel**, then carefully open the pot.

FINISH: Transfer the beef to a cutting board and tent with foil. Set a fine mesh strainer over a medium bowl. Using potholders, carefully remove the insert from the housing and pour the contents of the pot into the strainer. Press on the solids with a silicone spatula to extract as much liquid and pulp as possible; scrape the underside of the strainer to collect the pulp. Discard the solids. Let the liquid and pulp settle for about 5 minutes, then use a large spoon to skim off and discard the fat on the surface; you should have about 3 cups defatted liquid.

Return the liquid to the pot. Select **Normal/Medium Sauté**. Bring to a simmer and cook, stirring occasionally, until slightly reduced, about 10 minutes. In a small bowl, stir together the cornstarch and 3 tablespoons water. Whisk into the simmering liquid and cook, stirring constantly, until lightly thickened, about 2 minutes. Press **Cancel** to turn off the pot. Stir in the vinegar, then taste and season with salt and pepper.

Cut the beef into ½-inch slices against the grain, removing the twine as you go. Arrange the slices on a platter, then pour about 1 cup of the sauce over the top. Serve with the remaining sauce on the side.

QUICK PICO DE GALLO

Start to finish: 40 minutes (10 minutes active)
Makes about 1 cup

3 medium plum tomatoes, cored, seeded and finely chopped

1 jalapeño chili, stemmed, seeded and sliced into thin half rings

¾ teaspoon kosher salt

3 tablespoons red wine vinegar

2 tablespoons finely chopped fresh cilantro

In a small bowl, stir together all ingredients. Cover and let stand, stirring a few times, for at least 30 minutes or up to 2 hours.

INDEX

in green mole, 154–55

Indian stew with, 143, 152–53

Korean braised, 172–73

lemony orzo with, 114–15

miso and bourbon smothered, 156–57

paprikash, 143, 158–59

pulled, 143, 180–81

rogan josh, 160–61

Senegalese braised, 143, 168–69

Sichuan steamed, 143, 182–83

soup with bok choy, ginger, and, 148–49

soup with chickpeas, yogurt, and, 146–47

spicy braised, 164–65

tagine with squash and spinach, 162–63

vermouth-braised, 170–71

Vietnamese-style soup with, 144–45

chickpeas, 69, 74

bulgur pilaf with, 48–49

couscous with, 138–39

cucumbers and, 76

curried, 69, 100–101

hummus with, 88–89

mashed, 77

Moroccan beef or lamb soup with, 228–29

salad with pita chips and, 75, 77

soup with chicken, yogurt, and, 146–47

stew with beef and, 248–49

tagine with, 3, 20–21

Tunisian braised, 86–87

chilies

arroz con pollo with jalapeño, 57

black beans with chipotle, 69, 105

braised chicken with habanero, 165

chicken mole with green, 154

chili con carne with chipotle, 258–59

collard greens with habanero, 17

corn chowder with green, 10–11

Filipino pork adobo with serrano, 207

Indian chicken stew with jalapeño, 153

Indonesian coconut-curry beef with, 260–61

mojo shredded pork with chipotle, 217

Peruvian quinoa stew with habanero, 43

pico de gall with jalapeño, 275

pinto bean and pork stew with habanero, 99

pulled chicken with chipotle, 143, 180–81

ropa vieja with jalapeño, 270–71

Senegalese braised chicken with habanero, 169

South African beef stew with, 242–43

split pea soup with, 85

sweet potatoes with jalapeño, 3, 27

turkey meatballs with chipotle, 188–89

See also gochujang; harissa

chili-garlic sauce, 201

chili powder

black beans with, 71, 73

chili con carne with, 223, 258–59

Vietnamese-style beef soup with, 225

chives

cider-braised lentils with, 69, 82–83

risotto with, 60–61

cilantro

arroz con pollo with, 57

beef and chickpea stew with, 248–49

carrot soup with, 8

chicken mole with, 154–55

chicken soup with, 148–49

curried chickpeas with, 100–101

Georgian-style chicken stew with, 143, 150–51

Indian stew with, 152–53

Mexican brisket salad with, 264–65

mojo shredded pork with, 216–17

Persian barley-lentil soup with, 45

Persian stew with, 230–31

pico de gallo with, 275

pork and hominy stew with, 196–97

Portuguese pork and clams with, 204–5

potato and pea curry with, 22

sweet potatoes with, 3, 26–27

Vietnamese-style soup with, 144–45

cinnamon

beef noodle soup with, 226–27

chicken rogan josh with, 160–61

Greek beef stew with, 253

baby back ribs with, 193, 214

Korean braised chicken with, 173

grains, 35

See also barley; bulgur; farro; oats; quinoa; rice

grapes

agrodolce pork loin with, 208–9

hummus with, 89

H

harissa (spiced chili paste)

cauliflower with, 28, 31

lentil and bulgur soup with, 94

vegetable tagine with, 21

hazelnuts, agrodolce pork loin with, 208–9

hoisin sauce

baby back ribs glazed with, 214–15

dan dan noodles with, 201

hominy

arroz con pollo with, 56–57

chowder with, 10–11

stew with pork and, 196–97

honey

agrodolce pork loin with, 209

baby back ribs with, 214

cauliflower with, 3, 29, 31

Filipino pork adobo with, 207

polenta with, 41

hummus, 88–89

I

Instant Pot, viii–xiii

beans in, 69

beef in, 223

chicken in, 143

cooking modes for, ix

grains in, 35

pasta in, 111

pointers for, xi–xiii

pork in, 193

vegetables in, 3

J

Jaffrey, Madhur, 100

K

Khan, Yasmin, 147

L

lamb, 223

French stew with, 250–51

Moroccan soup with, 228–29

Persian stew with, 230–31

Lee, Edward, 157, 165

leeks

cider-braised lentils with, 69, 82–83

soup with potato and, 6–7

lemon

coriander-braised pork with, 213

hummus with, 89

mashed chickpeas with, 77

orzo with, 114–15

Pakistani-style beef stew with, 239

lentils, 69

bulgur and, 69, 102–3

cider-braised, 69, 82–83

Moroccan beef or lamb soup with, 228–29

pasta sauce with tomato and, 111, 126–27

Persian soup with, 44–45

soup with red, 94–95

lettuce, Mexican brisket salad with romaine, 264–65

lime

beef and sweet potato stew with, 235

curried chickpeas with, 100

Mexican brisket salad with, 264

mojo shredded pork with, 217

Persian barley-lentil soup with, 45

Persian stew with, 230–31

pinto bean and pork stew with, 99

pork and hominy stew with, 196–97

Senegalese braised chicken with, 168–69

M

meatballs

beef, 223, 254–55

turkey, 143, 188–89

mint

cauliflower with, 28, 31

chicken mole with, 154–55

chickpea and pita salad with, 75, 77

FAST AND SLOW

ACKNOWLEDGMENTS

Milk Street is a real place with, oddly enough, real people. It's a small crew, but I want to thank everyone who has made this book a reality. In particular, I want to acknowledge J.M. Hirsch, our tireless editorial director, Matthew Card, food editor, Michelle Locke, books editor, and Dawn Yanagihara, recipe editor, for leading the charge on conceiving, developing and editing all of this. Jennifer Baldino Cox, our art director, and the entire design team who deftly captured the look and feel of Milk Street, including Brianna Coleman, Connie Miller, Christine Tobin, Gary Tooth and Ben Schaefer. Our team of production cooks and recipe developers kept the bar high, throwing out recipes that did not make the cut and improving those that did. Our team includes Diane Unger, Wes Martin, Courtney Hill, Julia Rackow, Phoebe Maglathlin, Rose Hattabaugh and Angie Marvin. Also, Dana Beninati, David Domedion, Alison Ladman, Bianca Borges and Laura Russell. Deborah Broide, Milk Street director of media relations, has done a spectacular job of introducing Milk Street to the world.

We also have a couple of folks to thank who work outside of 177 Milk Street. Michael Szczerban, editor, and everyone at Little, Brown and Company have been superb and inspired partners in this project. Yes, top-notch book editors still exist! And my long-standing book agent, David Black, has been instrumental in bringing this project to life both with his knowledge of publishing and bourbon. Thank you, David!

Finally, a sincere thank you to my business partner and wife, Melissa, who manages our media department, from television to radio. Melissa has nurtured the Milk Street brand from the beginning so that we ended up where we thought we were going in the first place! Thanks.

And, last but not least, to all of you who have supported the Milk Street project. Everyone has a seat at the Milk Street table, so pull up a chair and dig in!

Christopher Kimball

FAST AND SLOW

ABOUT THE AUTHOR

Christopher Kimball is founder of *Christopher Kimball's Milk Street*, a food media company dedicated to learning and sharing bold, easy cooking from around the world. It produces the bimonthly *Christopher Kimball's Milk Street Magazine*, as well as *Christopher Kimball's Milk Street Radio*, a weekly public radio show and podcast heard on more than 220 stations nationwide. Kimball is host of *Christopher Kimball's Milk Street Television*, which airs on public television. He founded *Cook's Magazine* in 1980 and served as publisher and editorial director through 1989. He re-launched it as *Cook's Illustrated* in 1993 and founded *Cook's Country* magazine in 2004. Through 2016, Kimball was host and executive producer of *America's Test Kitchen* and *Cook's Country*, the two highest-rated cooking shows on television. He also hosted *America's Test Kitchen* radio on public radio. Kimball is the author of several books including, most recently, *Fannie's Last Supper.*

Christopher Kimball's Milk Street is located at 177 Milk Street in downtown Boston and is home to our editorial offices and cooking school. It also is where we record *Christopher Kimball's Milk Street television* and radio shows. *Christopher Kimball's Milk Street* is changing how we cook by searching the world for bold, simple recipes and techniques. Adapted and tested for home cooks everywhere, these lessons are the backbone of what we call the new home cooking. For more information, go to www.177milkstreet.com